LINCOLNOMICS

LINCOLNOMICS

How President Lincoln Constructed
the Great American Economy

JOHN F. WASIK

DIVERSION
BOOKS

For more information, email info@diversionbooks.com

Diversion Books

A division of Diversion Publishing Corp.

www.diversionbooks.com

First Diversion Books edition, April 2021

Hardcover ISBN: 978-1-63576-693-6

eBook ISBN: 978-1-63576-687-5

Printed in The United States of America

1 3 5 7 9 10 8 6 4 2

Library of Congress cataloging-in-publication data is available on file

To Kathleen Rose, Sarah Virginia, and Julia Theresa

CONTENTS

CONTENTS

The Once and Future President

I write this amid the coronavirus pandemic and on the anniversary of the start of the Civil War. When I began my research several years ago for *Lincolnomics*, I was motivated to address the outdated infrastructure in my state of Illinois and across the world, and Lincoln's views on the subject during his time. But these needs—pernicious as they are—nearly became an afterthought when the global health crisis of a generation came to bear in early 2020. COVID-19 shut down commerce, triggered massive unemployment and a recession, and claimed the lives of more than 400,000 Americans and more than 1.5 million worldwide (at the time this book went to press). More Americans have died from the virus than the combined US combat fatalities of World War I, Korea, and Vietnam.

While sheltering in place during the pandemic, my persistent thought was: "What would Lincoln do?" Can Lincoln, our foremost moral architect of economic and social opportunity, still guide us? How do we reinvigorate his ideas in our times, when people storm our streets demanding change? There's little doubt that were Lincoln alive today, he would see the necessity of creating a strong safety net in health, physical, and social infrastructure, and indeed act on it. It is clear, though, that Americans need more than what Lincoln called "internal improvements" to fix its broken healthcare, environmental management, infrastructure, and social justice systems.

Most Americans are familiar with the Lincolnian highlights: his Gettysburg Address, Emancipation Proclamation, and assassination by John Wilkes Booth. Little did we know that Lincoln's other work, words, and ideas would become stunningly relevant in a twenty-first-century global health crisis and movement against systemic racism.

As I wrote this book during one of the most turbulent times in recent history, other extraordinary events impacted the conclusions of *Lincolnomics*. Widespread protests spread to nearly every major American city in the aftermath of a policeman's murder of George Floyd on May 25, 2020 (and several prior and subsequent murders of Black people by police). Wildfires, hurricanes, and floods ravaged the country (and other nations). From Beijing to Washington, citizens experienced failures of health and emergency infrastructure, excessive police actions, and politicized pandemic government aid and response (or lack thereof). Many—myself included—masked up and took to the streets to oppose police brutality and killings of Black Americans, and hundreds of years of racial injustice.

A number of these crises were uniquely tackled, indirectly and directly, by Lincoln and his successors. To be sure, recent history shines a new light on Lincoln's progressive policies. Yet many, if not most, of these issues have vexed our country since before it was a nation. Discrimination and suppression of individual freedom, in tandem with the unbridled imperialistic aspiration that led to the United States' economic dominance, became a hydra in Lincoln's time—and is no less present now.

Raised in Illinois, I've always felt a spiritual tether to Honest Abe. I was born in Chicago Heights on the Lincoln Highway where it intersected Dixie Highway, locally anointed as the "Crossroads of America." Lincoln was an inescapable presence: an oracle, tragic icon, and immortal prophet of how to live free and prosper. His name and likeness were ubiquitous. His image is just about everywhere in the Prairie State, including on its license plates.

Growing up, I visited Lincoln's home, his tomb, his law office, and walked by the site of his 1860 presidential nomination hundreds of times. At my favorite museum, a vending machine melted plastic into busts of Lincoln. The railroad he shepherded as a legislator and defended as a lawyer—the Illinois Central—ran through my town, Matteson. I rode it to college at the University of Illinois-Chicago and later to work in the Windy City. It rumbled every day I lived there: a constant reassurance that life and commerce continued along this iron ribbon of time and space—at least from Chicago to New Orleans.

Yet nearly all things Lincoln that I knew as a child and well into my adulthood concerned the *iconic* Lincoln: martyred Civil War president, brilliant author of the Gettysburg Address and inaugural speeches. Virtuous rail-splitter. Issuer of the Emancipation Proclamation. I remember seeing his epic burial edifice in Springfield—heralded with an obelisk—for the first time on a school field trip; those unfamiliar with Lincoln might think a pharaoh was buried in his resting place. Nevertheless, to Prairie Staters who have endured decades of corrupt politicians and incarcerated governors, Abe was our Moses.

For me, researching and writing *Lincolnomics* illuminated a spiritual and political tablet for a fundamental direction forward through loss, grief, political combustion, ecological catastrophes, and social upheaval. We are always seeking the better angels of our nature. Lincoln's celestial guidance is still essential. On how to move ahead, Lincoln's philosophies and actions could not be more instructive.

====INTRODUCTION====

Why Lincoln Was Our Greatest Builder, But Doesn't Get the Credit

As a moral policy leviathan, Lincoln reshaped the world. His role of Civil War commander-in-chief, and as author of the Emancipation Proclamation and Gettysburg Address, still ignites our aspirations for a more perfect union. He also was a proactive and progressive genius when it came to economic policy. Universal access to personal economic progress—to Lincoln, an inalienable right—was at the core of his mission.

Yet Lincoln was more than his great speeches and status as victor of a defining war. He was a global influencer of labor recognition, capital investment, and nation building. Long before he became president, Lincoln believed that American egalitarianism *should* be the model for the rest of the world—and his work toward this ideal had a global impact. Few know the extent to which Lincoln embraced innovation; he is the only president who patented his own invention. He personally sought to understand the relationship between labor and capital.

The core of *Lincolnomics* is the sixteenth president's belief that building infrastructure, and promoting technology, economic opportunity, and education, were the keys to America's future. This vision was so profound, comprehensive, and enduring that it helped engender the maturation of the most powerful nation and economic colossus on earth—a vision we desperately need to revive. Historian Jan Morris points out that Lincoln's proclivity for championing internal improvements at every level, even at the height of the Civil War, made him unique among American presidents:

> With his lifelong interest in rivers, canals, and railroads, he studied the techniques of military communications. He concerned himself with weaponry, both naval and military: He tried out new guns, inspected new ships, he eagerly interviewed inventors who brought their new ideas to the White House.

In the light of economic progress, Lincoln was much more than the Great Emancipator. As a man who cherished the kind of education he never received, he helped revolutionize college education, research, development, and infrastructure. Emerging from the wilderness shaped his thinking on how to equitably link a growing nation with the needs of commerce and industry. Not only did Lincoln view economic progress through a pragmatic lens of what would get Illinois grain, hogs, lumber, and industrial goods to Eastern—and later global—markets, he used the Declaration of Independence as its basis. Slavery, of course, was the leaden impediment to this view.

Lincolnomics looks at Lincoln in a new light: Spiritual Economics married to the Culture of Innovation. Not only was he one of our greatest presidents on the questions of equality and fairness, he was a pragmatic progressive, seeking fresh economic solutions to level the playing field for laboring Americans. His philosophy expanded over time to embrace a radical idea for developing democracies: In order to build a more equitable future for everyone, you had to plan, invest, and build it.

ENTER LINCOLNOMICS

Lincoln's economic philosophy, which I call "Lincolnomics," was aspirational and practical. In the nineteenth century—before the Industrial Revolution—land was a primary source of wealth. In order to create a better non-Hobbesian state for all, Lincoln believed that one could ascend the broken economic ladder only if one shared, donated, and utilized both land and intellectual capital to create wealth and commerce. Lincoln the Innovator evolved over decades, learning from incremental failures, a story in progress. The result is the evolution of an agricultural-industrial-information economy that is globally connected and unsurpassed in history.

What is Lincolnomics in practice? His tenets, rooted in the Whig "American System," are based on these principles and ideas—in twenty-first-century terms:

Aspirational Economic Progress. If you can own and work land free and clear, you can benefit directly from your own labor and build a life for yourself. But economic progress should be as evenly distributed as possible; every individual should enjoy the fruits of their labor and be able to participate in democracy. These ideas were the core of Lincoln's philosophy, inspiring the Thirteenth, Fourteenth, and Fifteenth Amendments and countless labor laws in the twentieth century. His economic theory is not a rigid free-market ideology, however. It's spiritual in nature, based on yearning, intellectual adventure, and personal progress.

Educational Progress Is Essential. A knowledge base is necessary for better agricultural and industrial technology and innovation. This is the keystone for a broad foundation of public college education and research, fueled by state support.

A Culture of Innovation. Lincoln intimately understood the importance of invention and innovation. He worked to institutionalize new systems of knowledge and technology to meet the expanding nation's needs. This evolving culture seeded a transcontinental transportation system.

Commercial Expansion Funded by Public-Private Partnerships. When capital is scarce, the land grant can propagate transportation, education, and industry. Through such grants and policies, government plays a vital role as a global source of capital and public works' financing.

Strong Institutions, United Government, and Laws Seed Progress. Lincoln believed in a robust federal government and laws that protected free labor and intellectual property. He often cited the Declaration of Independence as a founding document. Rule of law protects everything from patents to land to voting rights; free agency is a fundamental part of freedom. Robust government institutions are essential to building knowledge, aiding commerce and agriculture, and cultivating innovation and public works.

Lincoln did not originate all of these principles, yet he endorsed them in the course of his political awakening and implemented them during the Civil War. What emerged was a system of prosperity built on these tenets. Although America and other countries globally still struggle with economic equality, these tenets remain powerful precepts for a better society.

Indeed, a better society is what the president ultimately strove for with his Lincolnomics principles. Like many of his contemporaries, Lincoln saw slavery as a moral wrong. Over time, however, he came to understand how difficult it was to dislodge this evil—rooted in American soil since 1619, when enslaved Africans were first kidnapped to Virginia. The economy of the slave states—and throughout the Northeast—was firmly entrenched in the profits that came from slavery. This system was a leviathan of cruel dollars reaped by landowners, merchants, and other capitalists. It would not be displaced without violence.

To be sure, the Civil War was a moral battle undergirded by economic conflicts. Most of related scholarship on the president focuses on Lincoln's struggles to win the Civil War and end slavery. But there's another component relevant to Lincolnomics: the underlying economic tension pitting slaveholding land barons against the industrial capitalism and free labor of the North and far West, where workers were realizing they needed rights, better opportunities, and vastly improved working conditions. "In a sense, the war over slavery was also a war over the future of the economy and the essentiality of value," notes Mehrsa Baradaran in the 1619 Project. Those tensions still roil American society today.

Backdropping the nation's greatest conflict was a growing culture of finance. A national fiat currency and income tax emerged during Lincoln's first presidential term to pay for government operations and to finance the war. Funds were appropriated and lands granted to build railroads, universities, and homesteads. Agriculture, manufacturing, and education were forever altered. Markets developed for commodities, stocks, and bonds. Specialized labor, research and development, and technology were vastly encouraged on institutional and industrial scales. The country was eventually connected coast-to-coast; an economic miracle was unfolding—at great cost. Lincoln had a hand in all these developments.

By placing a priority on economic and technological innovation, Lincoln transformed the American project in a profoundly immutable way. He rejected millennia of forced labor wherein people were tied to the land and the gentry, instead creating a new model of self-made prosperity built on opportunity, industry, and personal liberty.

Lincoln built upon the bricks of liberal democracy laid by the writings of Enlightenment philosophers. In what economic historian Deirdre McCloskey calls the "Great Enrichment," which she says began in 1800, the societal transformation of Lincoln's time "is explained by a proliferation of bettering ideas springing from a new liberalism." Lincoln embodied the idea that anyone could improve their economic and intellectual standing. Where one was born or who one was born to was not an impediment; class could be transcended. The old order could not keep innovation, commerce, and free labor from exerting itself. McCloskey notes:

> What led to our automobiles and our voting rights, our plumbing and our primary schools, were the fresh ideas that flowed from liberalism, that is, a new system of encouraging betterment and a partial erosion of hierarchy.

Lincoln's "new birth of freedom" gave a voice and intention to this enlightened and evolving view of the future of the United States. Indeed, some of his most enduring policies came to him long before the Civil War.

Decades before the first shot was fired at Fort Sumter, Lincoln dreamed of how to link states and territories from ocean to ocean. Infrastructure initiatives were his way of creating democracy through economic progress and freedom. He wanted to open the vast prairie from the Western Great Lakes to the Pacific to the global economy— no longer would a small town rely on what was grown and made within a few miles. Ending economic isolation mattered: Chicago and other cities became major global transportation and commercial hubs through infrastructure initiatives Lincoln seeded and supported. All of his many cherished internal improvements, fostered by a culture of innovation that he encouraged, made America one of the most advanced economies in the world in the nineteenth and twentieth centuries—a model that has been copied all over the globe.

There is an urgency to revisiting Lincoln's views on internal improvements. It's clear that nearly *every* county in the nation is sorely in need of repairs to roads, water mains, sewers, and infrastructure that is more than fifty years old, in many places (see chapters ten and eleven). And with climate change exacting damage on edifices from residential areas to waterways, upgrading infrastructure is a top public priority, globally.

It's past time to explore and revisit the deeper, innovative, structural ideas Lincoln left us: national and personal economic progress; robust higher education; public works; and a sustainable culture of innovation. Infrastructure, to Lincoln, was more than championing canals and railroads. He wanted to fulfill aspirations and create a foundation for the future. Lincoln imbued deeply spiritual economics in his policies: The dignity of work, equality, education, and innovation should guide global advancement for generations to come.

Lincolnomics centers the president as a long-term spiritual and pragmatic economic thinker: an early, devoted infrastructure advocate and a fervent developer-builder who saw canals, roads, bridges, railroads, free land, and public education as the backbone of democracy. These brick-and-mortar advances were more than building blocks; they were essential elements of what every nation could become, lifting souls above poverty and their oppressive origins.

I

BEFORE LINCOLN
Negotiating the Wilderness

"These banded powers, pushing into the wilderness their indomitable soldiers and devoted priests, unveiled the secrets of the barbarous continents, pierced the forests, traced and mapped out the streams, planted their emblems, built their forts, and claimed all as their own."

—Francis Parkman, *France and England in North America*

I first came to know the Land of Lincoln through maps of topography that could only be imagined. One cannot fully see the ancient glacial moraines that formed long, graceful ridges in the long-ago drained Lake Chicago, grandmother of Lake Michigan. Nor can one experience "Blue" or "Stony" Islands, tiny land masses (now towns) once surrounded by water. Yet there is something mystical about this land and its cloaked shapes, laced with ancient indigenous trails—at one time in harmony with the landscape's undulations—that had long been subsumed into roads, highways, and interstates. It takes a poet's imagination to see how some people connected with the earth, how others thought they could conquer it.

The true bones of the topography were buried under canals, railroad lines, factories, and cities. The "Old Northwest" was magnificent and ever-shifting on massive plates of rock and ice, creating great lakes, rivers, and streams—sculpting the landscape over millions of years. The ancient continents shifted from Pangaea to separate land masses and islands; the atmosphere cooled and massive rivers of ice moved down from the north, sculpting the earth. Glaciers retreated and left behind thousands of the most pristine freshwater lakes, along with some of the most fertile soil on the planet. When the glacial basins drained through gaps in the moraine—sediment displaced by the rivers of ice—torrents of glacial melt created great rivers like the Mississippi, Ohio, and Missouri.

The land from the Great Lakes to the mountains of the West was bountiful. Eagles flew above while deer, bobcats, muskrats, and beaver found plenty to sup on. Fish teemed in the lakes, rivers, and streams. Flora mushroomed in the wide, flat wetlands and prairies that undulated with amber grasses and efflorescent forbs. The earth pulsed with life above and below the surface.

But when first viewed by Europeans, the land beyond the great oceans presented stark conflicts and fear, largely borne of ignorance. West of the Great Lakes to the Rockies were treeless expanses, falsely signaling to the French and other Europeans that the land was infertile. The opposite was true, since the glaciated soil was rich in nutrients and constantly replenished by the grassland biome. It was not an unpopulated, "barbarous" wasteland, either. It had been home to Native Americans for thousands of years.

Three tribes among many thrived along the Great Lakes, building trading, food, and transportation networks that complemented the area's natural topography: the Potawatomi, Ojibwe, and Odawa Nations, organized as the "Three Fires Confederacy." The Ojibwe (also known as the Chippewa) were said to be the "Keepers of Tradition." The Potawatomi came down from Lakes Huron and Superior to the shores of the *Mitchigami,* or "Great Lake" (Lake Michigan), and called themselves *Neshnabek*, meaning the "original" or "true" people.

Tragically, Europe's economic and cultural chauvinism overwhelmed the indigenous tribes. Its monarchs and corporations weren't interested in synergy or harmony; they built their empires on domination, hegemony, and greed, colonizing everything they could. At first, only a handful of aristocrats reaped a fortune, relying upon Native American suppliers and a complex network of Euro-American traders, agents, storekeepers, and other middlemen. The population of Indigenous Americans was vastly massacred by the time the second major wave of Europeans arrived in the seventeenth century; up to 90 percent of the Native population had succumbed to smallpox. Their immune systems simply had no defense against the virus.

Ultimately, Euro-Americans had little interest in sharing wealth—or land—with the native people, who were expelled by force over time. Under President Andrew Jackson, the US Congress would pass the 1830 Indian Removal Act and force Native Americans west of the Mississippi River, opening their land to commerce and Euro-American settlement. Forced resettlement was a genocide of thousands of Indigenous people in the Potawatomi Trail of Death and more broadly the Trail of Tears, among other atrocities.

At first, the European view was built on encroaching imperialism and entrepreneurialism. What the French first saw in the land west of Lake Michigan was a garden or *praerie*—a vast complex of tallgrass prairies, wetlands, and riverine systems. It wasn't until well into the 1830s that European settlers discovered what Native Americans had known and lived by for tens of thousands of years: The land beyond the Great Lakes was fertile and biodiverse beyond comprehension, teeming with game such as bison, deer, beaver, and muskrats. While Western plains, mountains, and deserts would never provide an easy water passage to China or India, a portion of it would become the breadbasket of the North American continent. Yet for most Europeans, the land offered endless commercial opportunities and a chance for economic mobility absent in the feudal monarchies of their homelands.

NATURAL CAPITAL ABOUNDED IN THE NORTHWEST

Enormous biological wealth was buried deep in the prairie soil, infused with essential minerals and elements such as carbon, nitrogen, and phosphorous. The ecology of the prairie, with its perennial, giant grasses such as big and little bluestem, literally renewed itself—taking carbon, nitrogen, and oxygen from the air and building deep layers of fertile topsoil through its sub-terranean biomass. Such grasses became the genetic foundation for grains like corn, a Native American staple, and later wheat, oats, and barley. Rice could be grown in the abundant wetlands. Limestone, the fossilized remains of creatures from an ancient tropical sea, would become the bedrock of more than a million miles of road and a key ingredient of steel.

That the word "prairie" was not synonymous with "paradise" might be explained by the vicious extremes in weather and environment. Unless you were traveling along existing Native American trails, which usually followed river basins or morainal ridges, traversing the prairie was a brutal enterprise. What roads existed were clotted with mud, ice, and snow in the wet season, and buffeted by sub-arctic winds and unforgiving blizzards in the winter. People, horses, and oxen were virtually swallowed by the quagmire. Summer wasn't much more accommodating to travelers: Epic thunderstorms, tornadoes, wildfires, swarming insects, and grasses taller than a horse's haunches made overland routes a cruel test of survival and persistence.

The reservoir of natural capital that resided in the soil, waterways, and wetlands was long apparent to Northern American native tribes. Where they praised and thanked animals and the land for providing sustenance, Europeans—first the French in the sixteenth century— saw opportunities for trade and enrichment of their noble patrons. Beaver pelts became luxurious hats for European gentlemen. Resplendent birds like whooping cranes, whose haunting calls echoed in the prairie wetlands, were shot—their exotic plumage decorating ladies' hats. The French learned native customs, languages, and trade routes.

The forested "emptiness" that English settlers first saw in Eastern North America—where thousands of Native Americans had already perished from European diseases—was not what the French found in the mid-seventeenth century, when they came to the surly mouth of a lazy river at the southwest coast of Lake Michigan. The land was occupied, hunted, and cultivated by the Odawa, Ojibwe, Pottawatomi—and also the Ho-Chunk, Meskwaki, Fox, and Sac Nations, among others.

Native Americans came and went in the region, depending upon the time of year, establishing villages near rivers and creeks in the dry season. Their adaptations to oft-dramatic shifts in weather and environmental conditions ensured their survival. The area called *Chicagou*, roughly "place of wild onions" (native plants that thrived in the local wetlands), was home to indigenous settlements that "formed a network not only *across* the land but *within* the land—a network that bound the land together with human beings, animals, plants, water, and other animate entities into a sustaining and sustained systems," observes Professor John Low, a member of the Pokagon Band of the Potawatomi. Indigenous nations had their own discrete transportation networks that formed trails along geographic features, such as morainal ridges and waterways that eventually flowed into the "Great River" (the Mississippi).

Settlers morphed the Native American trail system into a primitive network of roads, "used to travel between fur trading posts and places used by the Europeans as seats of governments or military garrisons," according to historian Frances Hagemann. Indeed, the expeditions of

French explorers Louis Jolliet and René-Robert Cavelier, Sieur de La Salle established forts throughout the Illinois River and Mississippi valleys in the late seventeenth century.

Yet the French realized that their fur trading empire would not be entirely navigable without a decent way of passing from the Chicago River to the unreliable Des Plaines and onto the Illinois and Mississippi Rivers. The infamous Chicago-Des Plaines Mud Lake *portage* became a leech-infested quagmire during drier periods. Father Jacques Marquette suggested that a canal could be built to link the sluggish, shallow Chicago with the Illinois River to the southwest. It would not only parallel an established trail into the Illinois valley, but facilitate commerce as far as New Orleans, later claimed by the French in the name of King Louis XIV.

THE FRENCH CEDE THE NORTHWEST TO THE BRITISH

After the French lost the French and Indian War in 1763, *Anglo*-American colonization took off like a wildfire, spreading east to west in what became known as the Northwest Territory. After the American Revolution, the Northwest Ordinance of 1787, written largely by Thomas Jefferson, subdivided the region into grid-like sections—that is, turned Native lands into parcels that could be organized and sold. It ordained that states eventually created by Congress within the region would be free from slavery. But it was draconian for Native Americans, as Low recounts:

> In the United States and elsewhere across the globe, settler colonialism was a project to seize land from the Indigenous people who inhabited and sustained it, and to transfer that land to the colonial state. In the U.S., this seizure was accomplished by the conjoined

program of coerced treaties between the U.S. government and Indigenous people and frontier violence, both state-sponsored and state-encouraged.

The Anglo-American ethos was one of mercantilism, where land and resources were acquired, exploited, and sold for the purposes of personal, corporate, and state enrichment. The monstrous project of colonialism mushroomed to near-total seizure of Native lands for commerce.

A series of treaties ceded lands to the British and later the Americans. The Potawatomi alone signed six treaties between 1803 and 1809 in Northwestern Illinois, and moved out of the area completely by the mid-1830s. The city of Chicago was incorporated in 1837, although the grid platting out discrete parcels began in 1830. The tribes who had sustained their lives at *Chicagou* for generations left with great sadness and a deep reserve of resentment. They later sued the US government (and lost), claiming they did not legally cede territory along Chicago's lakefront, which was expanded through extensive landfilling.

In the "old" Northwest—territory comprising the present states of Michigan, Minnesota, Illinois, and Wisconsin—there had been Native American settlements, trading posts, and forts built by the French in the seventeenth and eighteenth centuries, later taken over strategically by the British. After the American Revolution, the United States won most of the land south of Canada, and Congress acquired the formerly Franco-Anglo outposts. Captain John Wheeler built Fort Dearborn at the mouth of the Chicago River in 1803, where the Creole settler Jean Baptiste Point du Sable had built a home in 1779. The fort was one of many in a network that connected other trading centers through the Northwest, anchoring connections to the Mississippi and Missouri River basins after the Louisiana Purchase that year. The land that would be the state of "Illinois" (so named for a Francophone pronunciation of the tribe that lived there) became a territory in 1809, the year Abraham Lincoln was born in Kentucky, on February 12.

THE NEW REPUBLIC EXPANDS

As heirs of the Enlightenment, Congress and presidents of the new republic wanted to imprint their sense of rational organization on the Northwest. That meant mapping it out in grid-centric order; creating blocks of well-defined real estate out of formerly borderless tribal homelands. President John Quincy Adams backed the General Survey Act of 1824, which directed the Army Corps of Engineers to map the new territory with an eye toward creating ports and navigable waterways.

At first, the Act focused on "surveys to be made for routes requiring roads and canals, for a military or commercial point of view," although the new nation was also laying down feasible routes for delivering the mail. Congress and chief executives had been horrified at the lack of infrastructure in the War of 1812, during which the British gained access to Washington and burned down the first White House. The contemporary Army Corps of Engineers—loosely formed in 1775 during the Revolutionary War—would gain a key role in water transportation through the 1824 Navigation Act and the 1826 Rivers and Harbors Act, a position it still holds today.

TRAILS BECOME ROADS

In their unwritten cultural cartography, indigenous tribes had created a brilliantly complex system of trails that followed the landscape. A set of trails went southwest from Chicago, through a glacial valley to the Des

Plaines and Illinois Rivers. Another essential route called the "Portage" trail connected Lake Michigan to a fickle, vexing wetland called Mud Lake, which flooded briefly during the wet season to allow canoe travel from the South Branch of the Chicago River to the Des Plaines, Illinois, and Mississippi Rivers. The "Sauk" trail was a major East-West route that connected Detroit with Chicago (later the rough route of the "Lincoln" Highway). One trail, called the Vincennes or Hubbard Trail, later "Old Chicago Road," linked the Wabash/Ohio Valley to the south to Chicago.

Named after the fur trader Gurdon Hubbard (later a father of Chicago and Illinois, and Michigan Canal commissioner with Lincoln), Hubbard Trail linked present-day Danville, Illinois, with the murky swamp-port at the mouth of the Chicago River. Trails in those days tortured all but the hardiest travelers. Hubbard was a rare enduring soul who traversed hundreds of miles relatively swiftly, bringing pelts to market. A shareholder in John Jacob Astor's American Fur Company by 1827, Hubbard traded extensively with Native Americans and the few Euro-Americans in the region. A year later, the entrepreneur had bought out all of Astor's interests in Illinois.

The extant trails were grossly inadequate for the growing demands of a global economy, used to ship pelts from the wetlands of the Midwest to the haberdashers of Paris and London. Simply getting across the Chicago Portage (Mud Lake) to the Mississippi River system was a time-consuming ordeal. Having first met fellow Chicago city cofounders John H. and Juliette Kinzie when he arrived in 1818, Gurdon Hubbard would come to know the portage well, thoroughly convinced that a canal would be a better way of getting to the Illinois River. The journey was brutalizing, even though it was less than a dozen miles from Lake Michigan. He writes of the passage through Mud Lake in his autobiography:

> Those who waded through the mud frequently sank to their waist, and at times were forced to cling to the side of the boat to prevent

going over their heads; after reaching the end and camping for the night came the task of ridding themselves from the blood suckers [leeches] . . . Having rid ourselves of the blood suckers, we were assailed by myriads of mosquitoes, that rendered sleep hopeless . . . Those who had waded the lake suffered great agony, their limbs becoming swollen and inflamed, and their sufferings were not ended for two or three days . . . It took us three consecutive days of such toil to pass all of our boats through this miserable lake.

Hubbard's experience was common for travelers in the days before transportation infrastructure. Before the times of railroads and later modern interstate highways, which didn't emerge until the middle of the twentieth century, the miserable experience of travel in the West was the norm. John H. Kinzie, appointed Indian agent in 1829, built a home in Chicago and later became its first mayor. The Kinzie family, along with William Ogden and John Wentworth, owned key parcels in what would become a bustling port area—later downtown Chicago. (Like Hubbard, Kinzie would also become a friend of Abraham Lincoln, who appointed him an army paymaster in 1861.) The Kinzies, like most early Euro-Americans, arrived in Chicago via water routes or overland routes connected to them.

While Euro-Americans were rapaciously seizing land for settlement and commerce, it was violently clear that Natives would not be invited to live under evolving Western concepts of enlightenment: equality and prospect for economic progress. This massive abrogation of dignity and human rights—a term that didn't exist at that time—would be extended to captured and enslaved Africans, shipped to the American continent to labor and die on settler plantations.

HOW SLAVERY CAME TO THE AMERICAS

It was the Portuguese who led Europe in establishing the slave trade as a global commercial enterprise around 1430, more than a half-century before Columbus landed in the Caribbean. Benefitting from Arabian advances in navigation, the Portuguese—and later the Spanish—also exploited advances in sailing technology. Wooden ships became larger, faster, and more durable. Eventually they were seaworthy enough to cross the Atlantic with the aid of skilled navigators who employed instruments like compasses and astrolabes. Adding cannons and bigger, more specialized crews, the slave ship evolved to be a floating fortress, torture chamber, and transport vehicle. Historian Marcus Rediker describes these vessels of terror and domination:

> The wide-ranging, well-armed slave ship was a powerful sailing machine, and yet it was something more, something *sui generis* ... it was also a factory and a prison, and in this combination lay its genius and horror. The word "factory" came into use in the late [sixteenth] century as global trade expanded. Its root word was "factor," a synonym at the time for "merchant." A factory was therefore "an establishment for traders carrying on business in a foreign country." It was a merchant's trading station.

By no means was slavery Portugal's exclusive domain; it had existed for millennia in various forms, such as child labor, indentured servitude, debt slavery, and the practice of pawning people as collateral for debt. But the capitalistic zeal with which Europeans enslaved people in vast regions of West Africa (such as Guinea, Cameroon, Benin, and the Niger River Delta) was a savage economic underpinning for the growth of the North and South American economies—and the countries and corporations that colonized these continents. The

Portuguese and other European powers saw slavery as a commercial activity; conquered lands in West Africa were leased to "prominent entrepreneurs for fixed payments." It was a Portuguese slave ship that arrived in Virginia in 1619 and introduced the economics of enslaved labor to the English colony.

Enslaved humans became faceless economic goods in a global accounting system that valued them based on a number of factors. Seen as *tangible assets*, they could be collateral for an entire system of credit. The debts incurred in buying slaves were securitized into bonds, a system that expanded as more merchants and global banks from New York to London participated in "the market," centered in New Orleans until 1863. European investors purchased some $2.5 million in "slave-based" bonds in 1828, a market that would grow by a factor of 10 over the next thirty years in Louisiana alone. There were cruel accounting methods behind this growth:

> The value of a slave can be interpreted as the discounted sum of expected lifetime earnings net of consumption and as such was heavily dependent on skills, life expectancy, and interest rates . . . Slaves who had just arrived from Africa tended to have lower values than those who were born in the Americas or had lived there for several years . . . Slaves born in the Americas lived longer than their migrant counterparts, but it is worth making a further distinction in the latter group between those who were sold from the slave vessel and those who, though born in Africa, had survived what eighteenth-century observers termed the 'seasoning' process.

Profit drove the Euro-American slave trade for nearly 400 years. Enslaved people transported as human cargo were worth as much as $2 million *per ship* in today's dollars, Marcus Rediker estimates. Profits continuously flowed back to ship captains and their investors, and the inhuman Transatlantic Slave Trade continued unabated until the early nineteenth century, when Great Britain and the US abolished the slave trade in 1807 (although American plantations continued using enslaved labor for another half-century). When triangular slave trade collapsed, the human toll was horrific: Some nine million people had been abducted to the Americas. More than half a million died on their way to the ships; five million died in Africa; and some quarter million died in the first year of labor from 1700 to 1808. Yet the grim totals alone don't reflect the full impact of how enslaved labor fed the commercial machines of four continents before abolition. Observes Rediker:

> In 1807 alone, Britain imported for domestic consumption 297.9 million pounds of sugar and 3.77 million pounds of rum, all of it slave-produced, as well as 16.4 million pounds of tobacco and 72.74 million pounds of cotton, almost all of it slave produced. In 1810, the enslaved population of the U.S. produced 93 million pounds of cotton and most of 84 million pounds of tobacco; they were themselves, as property, worth $316 million.

This was the extensive reach and economic basis of slavery in Euro-American capitalism around the time of Lincoln's birth. It was more than an institution. It was a global system of cruel capitalistic enterprise, based on horrific, racist laws that protected this unspeakable commercial model. Enslaved individuals who rebelled or refused to eat were whipped, lashed, or cut. Women were raped. On slave ships, they died of disease and slept in excrement and vomit. When they arrived at the slave ports, they were inventoried and sold as merchandise. Countless Africans never made it to North America, having perished in the journey or been thrown overboard for insurance payouts.

The slavery-based economy anchored the country's top export prior to the Civil War: cotton. Although at first most cotton produced in the Southern US was exported to British textile mills, domestic growth led to American industrialization. By 1800, enslaved individuals were producing 1.4 million pounds of cotton. Euro-American plantation owners enforced higher picking quotas—using whippings and other hideously barbaric methods of torture—and put more land into tillage, upping production to more than one *billion* pounds by 1860. Measured in cold economic terms, productivity rose 40 percent during that period. By the time Lincoln ran for president, the widespread Southern use of the cotton gin and New England textile factories added cloth and clothing production to the country's growing industrial portfolio.

THE ILLINOIS PATHWAY
THAT LINCOLN HELPED OPEN

While the early nineteenth century was bleak and genocidal for Native Americans and enslaved Africans, it promised a better life for Euro-American white men. Lincoln and his family were making their way out of Kentucky into Indiana at a time when Euro-Americans were longing for land they could pasture, till, and own. But in order to settle the land and cultivate it, they had to buy it or seize it by force from Native Americans. This was a conflicted and tortuous venture. The Eastern US was blanketed with mostly deciduous forests; in the days before steam power and hydraulics, the land could only be cultivated with extensive hard labor, something Lincoln experienced deep in his sinews.

Life was unforgiving of those who worked the backwoods in the early nineteenth century. Lincoln's first seven years in Hardin County, Kentucky, saw his father struggling to hold onto a small plot due to legal challenges to his title. His mother would later die in 1818 and sister in 1828 in Indiana. He lived in a small county of Kentucky in which 1,000 enslaved people resided; his parents and pastor professed anti-slavery views. He later said that his family moved from Kentucky to Indiana in 1816 "partly on account of slavery." Struggling to survive with little money and no education, his father thought little of educating young Abe and worked him every chance he could. Thomas Lincoln's ever-curious young son, though unusually strong, tall, and healthy, resented his father's punitive attitude on book reading and education in general. His father's harsh treatment shaped Abe's worldview.

"As a youth, Lincoln was like a slave to his father," writes biographer Michael Burlingame, "who insisted that his son not only labor on the family farm, but also that he work for neighbors, turning over every penny that he had earned." This was common in most early nineteenth-century households, notes historian James Cornelius, although Thomas "did pay for Abe and his sister to attend school for parts of four or five years, which was not universal." In his later work as an attorney, Lincoln's deep sense that "he had been abused as a child" translated into an intimate identification with clients of all identities who had been in similar positions of abuse and disenfranchisement. "During his political career after 1854," Burlingame notes, "he became, in effect, an attorney for all slaves." Of course, Lincoln advocated for others, as well, in his legal career; he took cases for anyone who asked, from widows to patent holders.

Those moving West alongside the Lincolns had a powerful motivation in common: the pursuit of their own destiny, finding their own path. The Illinois territory opened up possibilities. There was plenty of fresh water and land to cultivate. It was bordered by Lake Michigan and the Wabash on the east, by the Mississippi on the west, and by the Ohio River to the south. New Orleans' bustling port was easier reached from southern Illinois than Ohio and Pennsylvania.

Yet that path wasn't a congruent one before the Lincolns arrived in Illinois. Generations of Native Americans lived on or near the most important routes linking the Great Lakes to the Mississippi River system. Such a fluid connection would be established in the form of a major internal improvement: a canal that would link Lake Michigan and the turgid Chicago River to the Illinois River, a tributary that led to the Mississippi just north of present-day St. Louis. The water route revolutionized transit between the Atlantic and Gulf Coast; those few overland routes that did exist were treacherous before the creation of major roads and railroads, nearly two centuries away at the time of the French colonization.

But in the days when the French, British, and early Americans traded guns and silver with the Native Americans for beaver pelts fashioned into European top hats, no technology other than brute-force labor could build such a canal. Nevertheless, the promise persisted like a prairie fire, growing larger in scope each passing year, eventually transforming a swampy trading post at the mouth of the Chicago River into a colossus. Rivers were the highways then, flowing with promise—and commercial dreams.

II

LINCOLN AND THE WHIGS' AMERICAN SYSTEM

"In democracies, nothing is more great or more brilliant than commerce: It attracts the attention of the public, and fills the imagination of the multitude; all energetic passions are directed towards it."

—Alexis de Tocqueville, *Democracy in America*, 1835

The Sugar Coast was a siren beckoning to nineteen-year-old Abraham Lincoln as he grew into a man, divorcing himself from rural Kentucky and Little Pigeon Creek, Indiana. He wanted to see the world and make some money on his own. Deeply resentful of his father, who rented him out for physical labor, Abe was exhilarated in 1828 to copilot a flatboat to New Orleans from the Ohio River in Southern Indiana. For the then-princely sum of $8 a month, the rangy, somewhat melancholic teenager served as a "bow hand" on a crudely constructed timber boat well-suited for shifting river currents and hidden shoals.

The journey from Southern Indiana to New Orleans, however, was full of perils. He would have to first navigate his cargo west to the confluence of the Ohio and Mississippi Rivers near Cairo, Illinois, then head south and downriver into plantation country—trading, and hopefully avoiding trouble, along the way. Although his biographers say little of this odyssey, Lincoln was likely hauling surplus from local farms—salt pork, ginseng, corn, and other commodities. New Orleans was the ideal marketplace for this cargo because it was one of the country's largest port cities, serving as a distribution point for the South and its many plantations.

Sugar and cotton dominated the Deep South during the time Lincoln was voyaging. The crops did well in the hot, humid climate south of Memphis, Tennessee, and could be shipped easily out of New Orleans to ports across the world. New Orleans and Memphis hosted Cotton Exchanges alongside slave markets; enslaved labor was part of the brutal economic formula that kept the price of these commodities competitive in world markets. Decades after Lincoln made his river trips, Mark Twain recalled similar riverscapes in his *Life on the Mississippi*: "From Baton Rouge to New Orleans, the great sugar plantations border both sides of the river all the way." In almost journalistic prose, former Missouri-born steamboat pilot Twain extols the mighty extent of the Mississippi system, which likely awed Lincoln, an early stand-in for a Huck Finn-like hero:

> The area of its drainage basin is as great as the combined area of England, Wales, Scotland, Ireland, France, Spain, Portugal, Germany, Austria, Italy and Turkey; and almost all this whole region is fertile; the Mississippi Valley proper, is exceptionally so.

As steamboats were just beginning to ply major waterways, the contemporary river system was the cheapest, most expedient way to travel from North to South before the advent of railroads, although it was hardly quick due to the multiple eccentricities of a river that daily changed in subtle ways. With his boatmate Allen Gentry, Lincoln first experienced closely a thrilling and unforgiving world. Enslaved individuals in New Orleans were openly bought, sold, and scourged. Upon witnessing people traded in commerce, Lincoln was outraged, exclaiming to Gentry: "That's a disgrace." After that trip—and a similar sojourn with his cousin John Hanks in 1831 from New Salem, Illinois—Lincoln's views of slavery solidified. As his own economic progress advanced, the moral repugnance of the peculiar institution festered in his mind's eye.

The adventure to and from New Orleans wasn't without incident. Lincoln and his crewmate repelled a vicious attack by robbers, most likely on the lower Mississippi. Buoyed by his tenacity, he survived to make it back to Indiana via steamboat—a 2,400-mile round trip—invigorated by the promise of his own free labor (although he likely handed over his earnings on his first trip to his father). Still, grief enveloped him like a dense fog. In addition to losing his mother, he lost a baby brother, sister, aunt, and uncle in his early years. Michael Burlingame highlights a letter that Lincoln would later empathetically write to a young girl who lost her father in the Civil War: "In this sad world of ours, sorrow comes to us all; and, to the young, it comes with the bitterest agony, because it takes them unawares."

The Lincolns made their way to Illinois after living a few years in southern Indiana, his father Thomas ever searching for fertile land that wouldn't poison his family. Until he was free of his father's mostly involuntary servitude, Abraham Lincoln could not experience his own intellectual or economic freedom. After a childhood that saw the loss of his mother to "milk sickness" (due to cows eating poisonous plants) and a family move to southern Indiana, near the Ohio River, he valiantly tried to educate himself. Sarah Bush Lincoln, his stepmother, did her best to encourage him to read, offering up such books as *Pilgrim's Progress, Aesop's Fables,* and *Lessons in Elocution.*

Reading was an instrument of Abe's liberation from a life of backwoods laboring. His formative years (1816 to 1830) in Little Pigeon Creek, Indiana, saw him absorb the printed word in every way he could. Although his near-illiterate father thought book learning was useless, young Abe persisted. And flatboat voyages did more than open his mind to the possibilities of escaping meager wage labor; they showed him how the world operated beyond his rural upbringing. What he saw along the Ohio River and in New Orleans exposed him to a national and global economy that was rarely fair to working people and never fair to the enslaved. These experiences developed the intellect that transformed Lincoln into a powerful and relevant political thinker who envisioned entire systems benefiting an ever-larger swath of society.

Abe turned twenty-one in 1830, although he would stay with his family another year after the "Winter of the Great Snow." Though Lincoln occasionally sent money to his father, he left with entrenched bitterness (when Thomas died in 1851, Abe never bought a marker for his grave). Lincoln had mixed luck in the growing town of New Salem—a small, frontier community nestled on the Sangamon River just north of Springfield—where he settled after leaving his family. He tried his hand at running the local store, reading and telling stories every chance he got. New Salemites liked the earnest young man, but they didn't quite know what to make of him, as his nose was constantly in a book when he wasn't helping customers. Some thought him lazy.

After *two* general stores failed—one of his partners drank away the profits—leaving Lincoln in debt, he tried his hand at being a postmaster and surveyor, which forced him to learn advanced math. Following his stint as a soldier in the Black Hawk War (he never encountered the recalcitrant chief, justly aggrieved over treaties), he turned to politics, then the law.

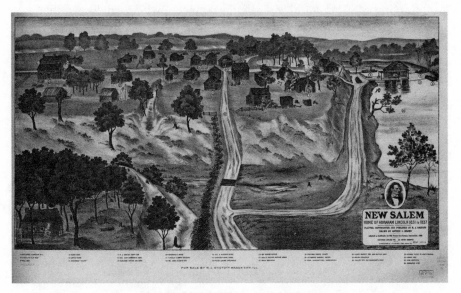

New Salem, a tiny village where he got his start in politics, was where Lincoln landed after leaving Indiana. (Library of Congress)

CHICAGO BEFORE LINCOLN

As Lincoln's relationships with rivers, transportation, and his nascent pre-political ideas grew, commerce was slow to develop in the upper Midwest where there was unreliable direct access to the Mississippi River system, the Atlantic Ocean, and continental markets. This changed rapidly after Lincoln's first river journey. Following the 1825 completion of the Erie Canal, political and commercial interest turned its glaring gaze west. Speculators, merchants, and settlers knew that the route to the Mississippi River and New Orleans would become a virtual highway to untold riches—but first a canal needed to be dug from the Chicago to the Illinois River to bypass the unrelenting misery of Mud Lake. Lincoln wanted a canal for his neck of the woods, particularly one to link the churlish Sangamon River to the wider Illinois to the north and west (and on to the Mississippi). His evolving political worldview saw the connection between local public works and advancement on a global scale. Historian Gabor Boritt illuminates his wider inspiration:

> His political activity was inspired, beyond the hope of personal or party gain, by a vision of endless material progress, the heritage of Western Civilization. This vision, it is often said, came true swiftly enough only in the New World, where both the individual and society could advance and where it was proclaimed that 'all men are created equal.' It thus became the American Dream.

A VILLAGE EMERGES

The federal government began aggressive campaigns forcing Native Americans off their land through treaties from 1795 to 1816, focusing on acquiring narrow strips of waterway corridors from Ohio to Chicago, southwest to the Illinois River Valley. By 1827, the US "owned" the land it needed to build a canal into Chicago. Maps were made, lots were eventually put on paper, and the frenzied land rush began—first as a modest trickle, then surging like a river after the Potawatomis signed the Treaty of Chicago in 1833.

The nucleus of what would become the unique, Euro-American city of Chicago formed in a sustained chain reaction sometime after 1830, roughly as Lincoln was settling in New Salem. At the time, Chicago was a small, diverse, multilingual mixture of Creole, Potawatomi, English, and French residents who traded with Native Americans and lived alongside them, learning their languages and customs. Yet it was a town tormented by perpetual conflict. Euro-Americans from east of the Appalachians had been engaged in a series of battles and forced treaties to expel Indigenous people off their land for more than 100 years. "Indian" boundaries were constantly drawn and redrawn. On one side of these artificial lines were platted grids of Euro-American rectangles, discrete demarcations of land entirely foreign to the tribes who lived there.

Some families, like the Kinzies and the Wolcotts, lived among the Native Americans and respected their ways, though often white settlers came from the east to "civilize" the Northwest. Juliette and John Kinzie were slightly older contemporaries—and later friends—of Abraham Lincoln. Juliette's husband and her uncle Alexander Wolcott worked in Chicago as Indian agents, appointed federal officers who controlled annuity payments to tribes after treaties were signed. More importantly, these agents controlled post-treaty access to former tribal lands that became US property; they were the early gatekeepers.

Fort Dearborn, the US government's army outpost at the mouth of the Chicago, provided a sentinel for Euro-Americans coming into Chicago from Lake Michigan or the East, downriver to the Mississippi River basin. The unassuming fort was destroyed by Native Americans allied with the British in 1812, rebuilt in 1816, occupied by troops until 1823, and reoccupied in 1823. Troops were again withdrawn in 1831, returning in 1832; it was twice more vacated and reoccupied. It was finally abandoned at the end of 1836.

Undaunted by the spotty military presence in Chicago, the government saw the land as a valuable asset and surveyed within several miles of the Chicago River's mouth in 1830. The Kinzies—along with a group of families who had real estate interests in the village, such as the Wentworths and Ogdens—purchased soon-to-be valuable property north of the river, built a home, and transitioned from residents of "Indian Country" to a commercial *entrepot* that grew exponentially while the city went up around them. Lots were priced from $10 to $60 apiece in 1830, although much of it was swampland. Juliette, with pride, notes that her husband's family observed, "the geographical position of this place, and the vast fertility of the surrounding country, had always foretold its eventual prosperity and importance."

Juliette kept a house a few blocks from Fort Dearborn in the "Kinzie addition" on the North Side of the Chicago River: "It was a long, low building, with a piazza extending along its front, a range of four or five rooms. A broad green space was enclosed between it and the river, shaded by a row of Lombardy poplars." The Kinzie home was nothing less than a mansion in the early days of the city, which lacked the functional geography for a working port. The lakeshore constantly shifted and eroded, taking down homes built too closely to the shoreline. A sandbar blocked the river's opening. In 1833, after cutting a channel to provide direct access to the river, the Army Corps began a series of improvements that would transform Chicago into a major port.

Many more engineering upgrades were still needed to make the harbor and river viable for commerce. The water level rose and fell or was blocked by ice depending upon the time of the year. Since most everything drained into it—and, eventually, the lake—the river became an open sewer. Downstream, it diminished at times to a trickle, as would the nearby Des Plaines—which, with the Kankakee, formed the Illinois River, meandering southwest into the Mississippi just above St. Louis. Traveling anywhere, except north and east on the Great Lakes (to the Erie Canal and New York City), was a typically dreadful, slow trek. Juliette Kinzie recounts:

> The land was a low, wet prairie, scarcely affording good walking in the driest summer weather, while at other seasons it was absolutely impassable . . . we were often compelled, as we rode, to break away the projecting branches of the shrubs which impeded our path.

Juliette's hospitality was legendary as the town advanced building by building, and as her cadre transitioned from trading post and Indian agency officials to founding families of a great city. Gurdon

Hubbard, whom her family befriended, would build a large warehouse a few blocks from the Kinzies only to see it burn down in 1868. He would also champion the building of the Illinois & Michigan Canal in the state legislature; later yet Hubbard became a canal commissioner, working alongside the promising young lawyer Abraham Lincoln.

In 1840, John Kinzie had campaigned for William Henry Harrison, the short-lived Whig president. Years later, when Lincoln was headed to the White House, Juliette sat on a settee with the new president and opined: "Well, now you are the father of the country and I'm the grandmother of Chicago." Kinzie, Hubbard, and many of their neighbors became friends of Lincoln and benefitted greatly from his support of the Illinois & Michigan Canal and the Illinois Central.

LINCOLN THE LOCAL HERO
ENTERS POLITICS

The man who would become a successful lawyer, congressman, and president was rough-hewn and eager to please. Despite his uneven start as a prominent New Salem citizen, Lincoln almost always made a good impression. His steely frame, reedy voice, and ample storytelling endeared him to his neighbors. He was also a bit of an adventurer.

Local mill owner Vincent Bogue secured investors to bring the steamboat *Talisman* up the river to Springfield, where it docked in 1832. A gallant celebration ensued, as townspeople believed the steamboat— and access to New Orleans markets—was a vanguard of commerce coming to town. But the crooked, churlish Sangamon was not nearly wide enough for such a vessel, even with local strongmen like Lincoln heroically piloting, hacking away at tree limbs that crowded the river. And in low-water season (most of the year), the lack of depth only provided for canoes or small flatboats. When the oversized boat hit a mill dam at New Salem, it got stuck, so Lincoln rammed *Talisman* full steam ahead—much to the aggravation of the mill owners. The voyage was a financial bust, and the charterer of the excursion fled town, leaving a pile of bills in his wake. New Salem and Springfield would never be the recipients of regular steamship service, although Lincoln earned a much-needed $40 for his troubles.

That hardly chastened Lincoln's Whig "American System" improvements rhetoric and political views, which he held steadfast when he took his seat in the legislature two years later. The *Talisman* affair lifted his political fortunes, elevating him to the heroic status of an emerging leader who deserved attention. Lincoln didn't waste this bounteous political capital: He shook hands and gave speeches; all of Sangamon County would eventually know him. Lincoln's calling card became internal improvements that would connect his county to the national economy. During his short-lived position as surveyor, Lincoln also proposed a new road linking the county to New Salem, preparing a petition for the county commission. When he ran again for the legislature in 1834, his public works agenda was clear:

Time and experience have verified to a demonstration, the public utility of internal improvements. That the poorest and most thinly populated countries would be greatly benefitted by the opening of good roads, and in the clearing of navigable streams within their limits, is what no person will deny.

Lincoln customized the Whig platform for the needs of his county, virtually landlocked due to inadequate roads and river routes. He signaled that these kinds of projects were for everyone regardless of their economic status and believed that public works should foster development in an egalitarian way, embodying the Whig ethos to "triumph over the physical environment" through better infrastructure.

LINCOLN'S FACTIONAL WORLD

In the struggling democracy into which Lincoln was born, there was always conflict between "factions," so-called by James Madison. America's early presidents, leaders, and authors of the founding documents were mostly white, Protestant landowners. Many of them profited from slavery, which the 1787 Constitution ignores with a nod and a wink. *Their* faction was based on preserving their own economic security through land ownership—and forcing people to work on it. Women and people of color had no rights and no voice. But even for impoverished, poor white men, landowning was challenging. Lincoln's father was forced to uproot his family over dubious ownership of the marginal backwoods properties he settled. Without land that could be cultivated or pastured, poverty was a constant burden; Lincoln gleaned this early in his life. If you worked the land with fettered labor, as did the founding Virginians, prosperity would not extend into the fields and shacks of laborers—even those who could cultivate land for subsistence. Economic freedom was elusive, denied to those who toiled.

Even George Washington, the putative "Father" of a country founded on individual freedom, had 124 enslaved workers. (As per his will, all of his slaves were freed when his wife Martha died.) While his contributions in winning the Revolutionary War are beyond dispute, Washington's wealth in land holdings was epic. He was an avid land speculator, building a fortune by holding some 52,000 acres, including about 7,000 on his Mt. Vernon estate. That would have placed him in a ranking of the 100 richest

Americans of all time, amounting to more than $26 billion in inflation-adjusted dollars.

Even though Enlightenment geniuses like Madison recognized the horrible legacy of bondage, economic inequality that permitted slavery was embedded in the Constitution. The ascension of would-be Platonic "philosopher kings" like Jefferson did not undo this cruel flaw, as vested as they were in their own fiscal interests. Madison noted this pitfall in the following prescient phrase about factional economic interests in his *Federalist 10* paper:

> But the most common and durable source of factions has been the various and unequal distributions of property . . . A landed interest, a manufacturing interest, a mercantile interest, a moneyed interest, with many lesser interests, grow up of necessity in civilized nations, and divide them into different classes, actuated by different sentiments and views. The regulation of these varying and interfering interests forms the principal and modern legislation and involves the spirit of party and faction in the necessary and ordinary operations of government.

Madison foresaw the regulation of interstate commerce, the growth of manufacturing, and evolution of government's role. He was not optimistic that even an "enlightened statesman" such as himself, *Federalist* coauthor Alexander Hamilton, or other early founders could "adjust these clashing interests and render them all subservient to the common good."

Long after the founding fathers died, the perverse stain on the American template survived in the form of Jefferson's Democrat-Republican party, later shortened to the (old) Democratic Party, the organ of Jacksonian and Southern interests—a power base that existed until the 1960s.

Yet how could the government of a republic claim "all men were created equal" when more than half the population had no voice, virtually no land, and little hope of economic progress? Were the federal government to take a dominant role in *regulating* these factions, it would mean diminishing the power of the old, feudal order of landowners, who had unlimited power to use—and abuse—the land and the people shackled to it. Could greed be reined in?

Indeed, the lust for property never abated; plantation owners planted ever more tobacco and cotton. The original Southern colonies had extended their borders all the way to the Mississippi before the Revolution. Virginia, for one, laid claim to Illinois in 1755.

In the 1800s, one way to balance the interests of the landed and un-landed was to connect farmers and merchants to markets far from home. Lincoln experienced this shuttling to boats on the Ohio River near his home in Indiana, and later on the Mississippi. Canals were instruments of economic equalization: A poor boy from Central Illinois could sell goods in the thriving markets of New Orleans. Impoverished Irish became landowners in Northern Illinois. German and Scandinavian farmers from Minnesota or Wisconsin sold their hogs or grain in New York City, after the Erie Canal was completed in 1825.

The question wasn't so much *where* to build this needed infrastructure, but how to pay for it. Would growing states and territories foot the bill, or the federal government, diminishing local and state control? From the time of the Republic's founding and the Civil War, there was an epic tension between the two factions. Lincoln always seemed to be in the middle of the argument.

LINCOLN CHAMPIONS
THE AMERICAN SYSTEM

It was difficult for the nation to advance from an agrarian republic of Jefferson's "gentleman farmers" to a Hamiltonian state of industry and manufacturing. Merchants, farmers, and factory owners moved goods across ever greater distances as the country expanded to the Pacific. There was certainly no easy or direct overland route or waterway that led to the Pacific. No canal cut the distance, and the railroad was more than six decades in the future. Those favoring internal improvements were frustrated by the Constitution's silence on federal funding for improvements. Until Lincoln's Republican years, the prevailing wisdom was that it was *unconstitutional*, leaving decisions about public works initiatives—and who would pay for them—up to the states. It was no surprise that James Monroe made this declaration in his Annual Message of 1817—the written equivalent to Congress of the State of the Union—on Congress's ability to finance improvements on a national level:

> Disregarding early impressions I have bestowed on the subject all the deliberation which its great importance and a just sense of my duty required, and the result is a settled conviction in my mind that Congress does not possess the right. It is not contained in any of the specified powers granted to Congress, nor can I consider it incidental to or a necessary means, viewed on the most liberal scale, for carrying into effect any of the powers which are specifically granted.

As settlers streamed through the Cumberland Gap to claim land west of the Appalachians, the conflict between the national need for infrastructure and the Constitution's vague answer to that need inspired Whig legislators like Henry Clay to create an entire political platform around it. Broad-based and multi-regional, Whig infrastructure would grant market access to small yeoman farmers and merchants from the Mississippi to the Atlantic. The rousing success of the Erie Canal, which further bolstered New York City as America's fastest-growing port, created an impetus. Why couldn't towns with access to the Ohio River and other Mississippi tributaries have the same benefits? Whigs argued this point as a means to expand the West.

Henry Clay animated Lincoln's early political life as a "beau ideal" philosophical and would-be mentor, although they met long after Clay's ideas first permeated Lincoln's mind in the 1830s. "Master of compromise" Clay was a Kentucky-born lawyer, statesman, and legislator, the toast of Lexington who once hosted a precocious Mary Todd. As a Whig, Clay firmly believed in progress rooted in internal improvements. Clay's ideas reached Lincoln around 1829 as he was just emerging from his father's servitude, exploring the possibilities of commerce on his flatboat trips. Chastened by the War of 1812 (in which the British laid waste to Washington, DC, and shut down American shipping for a time), Clay extolled an "American System," advocating punitive tariffs on imported goods and merchandise shipped mostly from England. Tariff income would become a major source of revenue for the fledgling republic in the early years of the nineteenth century. Promoting domestic industry was the prime aim of the tariffs, which filled state and federal treasuries in the days before income taxes.

But the major moving part of Clay's American System—in addition to a nascent national banking system—was internal improvements. Without dynamic access to markets, farmers would have great difficulty getting goods to market; the young country would struggle to become an exporting nation, stifling economic opportunity. How did Clay and his contemporaries foresee connecting producers with merchants and consumers?

Canals would bypass shallow rivers and chokepoints like the Chicago River and Niagara Falls. Railroads would then replace canals as the major mode of transportation, linking North to South and East to West across the continent. What was more, internal improvements meant a system creating more infrastructure in its broadest sense: digging ports, dredging channels. It was a holistic view merging transportation with commerce and migration. Steamships had revolutionized transportation in the first decades of the nineteenth century, but they required reliable channels, docks, and facilities. Historian Mark Neely, analyzing the development theme of the American System, writes that the tariffs and national banking also were meant to bolster the weak economy of the nation in the first third of the nineteenth century:

> Clay, emphasizing what modern economists would call 'comparative advantage,' foresaw a great nation in the New World united by harmoniously complementary regional economic specialization . . . Clay supported the establishment of a Bank of the United States to provide a sound national currency to facilitate commercial transactions.

Although Clay's ideas were reviled by many Southerners, including Andrew Jackson, they made eminent sense to Lincoln—who would adopt several modes of the concept during the Civil War. A strong national banking system eliminated dependence on state-chartered banks, which issued their own currencies and were often poorly capitalized. With financial transactions kept largely within states' borders, interstate commerce was difficult. Nevertheless, Clay's system laid the groundwork for a modern global economy, striving to diminish crony capitalism wherein local merchants and politically connected party hacks reap the "spoils," jobs and loans. But Clay's program was a hard sell in a time when Whigs were usually in the minority in state Houses and Congress, where Southern Democrats often ruled. Running relentlessly on his platform, Clay failed to win the presidency not once but three times.

The American System further sought to diversify the American economy. Iron and steel could be produced closer to transportation corridors, instead of imported from England. Miners could one day ship coal from Appalachia to any point on the continent. And cotton and sugar could more easily reach Northern mills and markets. Clay, a slaveholder who condemned the practice publicly, like Jefferson, had initial support from President Monroe, the founding father who weathered the near-ruinous War of 1812.

In the "Era of Good Feelings," 1817 to 1825, the first push for internal improvements began. The ambitiously titled "National Road" sliced through the Appalachians and would extend from Maryland to Vandalia, where Illinois situated its second state capital and Lincoln served his terms in the state General Assembly. Contrary to its grandiose title, the National Road was nothing like a modern interstate. The roadbed was rough and muddy. It was not an efficient way to get from East to West.

Serving as a congressman and senator from the Bluegrass State, Henry Clay also held the positions of Speaker of the House and Secretary of State. A silky orator, he was adept at selling legislation and cobbling together coalitions; along with Daniel Webster, Andrew Jackson, and James Polk, Clay was one of the dominant political figures of the early nineteenth century. Though his American System became a template for infrastructure in later years, it consistently angered Southern legislators like John C. Calhoun, who grew to despise it for how he believed it threatened Southern interests. Calhoun and fellow Southerners argued vociferously against the American System, trumpeting a doctrine they called *nullification*, or the supreme ability of states to ignore or discard federal laws. After all, wasn't the United States a *confederation* of states that had dominion within their borders? Clay worked earnestly against this mounting tension and is often credited for holding together the fragile union.

Indeed, as the North grew more populous and industrialized through free labor in the decades prior to the Civil War, Southern "states' rights" advocates rightly feared that such an expansion would give Northerners an unfair economic advantage if such a program was nationalized. The Constitution allocated more seats to states in the House of Representatives as their populations increased, giving another edge to the North. Anxieties escalated as the admission of new states (such as California) under the aegis of free labor threatened to put Southern slaveholders in the political minority. Euro-American settlers kept pushing to the Pacific—repartitioning the "old Northwest" as "Midwest" and changing the political dynamic of the country with the expansion of each new state.

In the Midwest, championing a system of internal improvements was a natural fit for Lincoln. He could see how creating a kind of equality between producers and sellers mattered on a visceral level. Transportation brought rural folks like him to places that allowed for gains in economic independence. Having traveled a good portion of the Mississippi River highways, Lincoln knew that a man building his own inexpensive flatboat with local materials (which were not subject to import tariffs) could make a decent living by trading cargo from the diverse, agricultural North to the limited sugar-cotton economy of the South—although it took an absurd amount of time getting goods to market. There was a direct, lived relationship between the Sangamon River and New Orleans. New Salem and Springfield could access world markets! All you needed was a decent canal to get boats to the Illinois River and you were on your way.

LINCOLN ADOPTS THE AMERICAN SYSTEM

In 1832, Lincoln embraced Clay's American System when he first ran for the Illinois legislature, but the run was thwarted by his enlistment in the Black Hawk War. Owing to poor transportation—it took him weeks to return from northwestern Illinois—he finished eighth in a field of thirteen, largely because he was unable to campaign due to his service. Although he didn't see any action, his fifty-one days as a militiaman earned him the respect of his fellow soldiers, who elected him captain—an honor, he later told confidantes, that gave him "more pleasure than I have had since."

Lincoln ran again in 1834, securing a seat that represented Sangamon County. In his first political address to his neighbors on March 9, 1832, he presented themes that he would wrap into his economic platform for the rest of his career. Clearing the shallow, virtually unnavigable Sangamon River was at the top of his list, followed by canal and railroad building, which he thought was too expensive a proposition at the time.

"How far I shall succeed in this gratifying this ambition is yet to be developed," Lincoln said, "[as] I was born, have ever remained, in the most humble walks of life."

In this time of great regional and national optimism, local leaders and merchants felt their community was opening to a larger world. In addition to internal improvements, Lincoln favored two other major points: control of interest rates (capping usury), and "a system of education." Lincoln deeply felt his lack of formal schooling, barely two years. He continued his studies with a local teacher (Mentor Graham), reading every chance he had while working as a store clerk, postmaster, and surveyor. The law also interested Lincoln—mostly as an opportunity to transcend his humble station. He befriended Whig John Stuart, who encouraged him in his legal pursuits and shared a room with him in Vandalia. Stuart later became his first law partner.

Naturally, Lincoln and Stuart backed Illinois Governor Joseph Duncan's call for an internal improvements package, an ambitious plan that first stumbled out of the gate after a Duncan veto. At the time, states had to finance infrastructure legislation without any direct capital from the federal government, a major impediment to improvements. States had to float bonds and find investors, who were mostly in the East or England, as local capital was scarce. State revenue was also dear: State receipts totaled $147,000 in 1834, a fraction of what the improvements plan would cost—tens of millions, often poorly subscribed by investors. One local project Lincoln backed would have built a canal from Beardstown on the Illinois River to bypass the Sangamon River. Shares in the enterprise were sold and bought, including by Lincoln, but the canal was never built.

When Governor Duncan vetoed a $10 million package of improvements in 1837, Lincoln and the legislature overrode it. Springfield went wild at the legislature's actions, lighting bonfires to celebrate the progress, but the elation was short-lived: In 1837, a financial panic that triggered a recession swept the country. Thousands of businesses failed. Men walked the streets empty-handed. The downturn lasted through 1842, snuffing most states' internal improvement projects. Nine states defaulted on related debts; four states repudiated debts of some $14 million.

Illinois was particularly hard hit. The bonds that it had floated to pay for the Illinois & Michigan Canal—completed in 1848—would not be paid off until 1882. The state struggled with fiscal solvency. By the time the recession ended, so did much debate on which infrastructure improvements were needed. Railroads had replaced canals and waterways as the dominant mode of transportation.

LINCOLN AND DOUGLAS: ROUND ONE

In his quest to build internal improvements, one of the most compelling lawmakers Lincoln met was a pit bull of a man with a tussock of dark hair and a baritone voice: Stephen Arthur Douglas, a lawyer from Jacksonville. Douglas was a force to be reckoned with in the Democrat-dominated legislature, procuring advantages any chance he could. In the nineteenth-century sense, he was a political powerbroker on the make, occupying the same space as Lincoln—but lacking Lincoln's casual air and moral compass. Douglas worked for Douglas; he was the boss of the political apparatus that would control land deals, railroad rights of way, and expansion of commercial corridors in the Prairie State.

Having arrived in Illinois from Vermont, Douglas (originally spelled "Douglass") was relentlessly desirous for power and wealth. The "Little Giant" proved to be a one-man lobbying machine for his personal interests; in one instance, he rewrote a state law that allowed him to be Morgan County State's Attorney—*and* State Representative—simultaneously, thus broadening his power base and income. He later assumed the position of Registrar of the Land Office in Springfield, which not only gave him a first look at promising real estate, but opportunities to gain influence in the state's Democrat party. Douglas near-fully controlled the state party by the time he became US Senator in 1847 at the age of thirty-three. Lincoln came to know his politics well in their legendary "Great Debates" for the Illinois Senate seat in 1858.

Years prior to those face-offs, in their legislative terms in the mid-to-late 1830s in Vandalia, Lincoln and Douglas formed a curious initial alliance. Both wanted the state to finance railroads and provide lands for their construction. They agreed that Illinois should put its modest financial muscle behind a canal connecting the then-obscure village of Chicago (at the time, there were more people in Central Illinois) to the Mississippi River through the Illinois River at LaSalle. Their resulting improvements package called for the creation of the Illinois Central Railroad, which, despite being a superior mode of transportation, would come into being well *after* the canal's construction.

Lincoln and Douglas emerged on parallel paths at a time when the American population and its need for public works was burgeoning. During the Revolution, the country's population was around four million, about one-tenth the size of France. From the first settlements in Virginia, historian Daniel Immerwahr observed that "the frontier advanced by only two miles a year in the 150 years following Jamestown's [1607] establishment." Whereas after the Revolution, when England ceded land that reached the Mississippi, Euro-Americans poured over the Appalachian Mountains at a rate of forty miles a year—an unprecedented expansion in human history. By 1900, when westward expansion was mostly completed, the US population had surged to more than 76 million: "[a] violently expansive empire of settlers, feeding on land and displacing everything in its path."

Immerwahr also writes of how the industrialization that Lincoln favored contributed mightily to the population boom:

> You could see it in the cities the settlers built. Cincinnati, a village in 1810 [the year after Lincoln was born], had a nine-story, steam-powered mill by 1815 and a fleet of 150 steamboats by 1830. Chicago grew from a settlement of fewer than a hundred people (and 14 taxpayers) in 1830 to a towering megalopolis with the world's first dense cluster of skyscrapers and more than a million residents in 1890—despite being burned to the ground in 1871.

Cheap labor and coal, wood, steam, and later petroleum—abundant commodities in North America—powered such growth. It also was facilitated by the reach of a robust rail network, connecting cities hundreds—and then thousands—of miles away.

The Illinois Central, which Lincoln advocated for in the decades before the Civil War, became the country's largest land-grant railroad (before the Transcontinental Railroad), one of its largest corporations, and the longest such line. At 700 miles in total length and initially costing $25 million, it traversed the state from northwestern lead mines in Galena to the Ohio River at Cairo in the south. Such spectacular growth was facilitated when the state of Illinois gave the railroad corporation 2.6 million acres of federal land along the forked right of way, which would link Chicago to St. Louis (through Alton, Illinois). It would run right through Vandalia, which lost the state capital in 1839 to Springfield—a move engineered in no small part by Lincoln and his country's "Long Nine" legislators (assemblymen of tall stature like himself). For his part, Douglas had a large say in the railroad's route, which cut into the center of land he purchased in Chicago and was the site of his future city estate.

Yet the iron highway's core, in-state network would not be complete until 1856 (it expanded after the Civil War). It would have to wait while the state began work on the Illinois & Michigan Canal, a seminal new transportation route that seeded a city of global importance.

III

ABE'S GREAT DEPRESSION

How Lincoln Recovered from the Failure of His First Infrastructure Push

"If a channel were cut through this ridge, one could sail from Lake Illinois [Lake Michigan] to the Sea of Florida [Gulf of Mexico]."

—Pere Jacques Marquette, 1673

The scrappy teenage mule driver tussled with the bullies, throwing them into the turgid canal. He may have been just a barge hauler, but he wasn't going to put up with surly bastards insulting his sense of propriety. Besides, they were abusing some hapless mules unable to defend themselves.

James Butler yearned to be anywhere but towing barges with flea-bitten half-horses on the Illinois & Michigan (I&M) Canal. Thinking his combatants had drowned, he fled his home of Troy Grove, Illinois, to find his fortune out West. He had little to lose: Butler was one of many raw laborers on the lowest rung of the nation's growing transportation network. Like young Abe Lincoln, he sought a future away from the filthy waterway. Although he was barely a man, he was man enough to have an innate sense of justice—and was willing to fight for something beyond his degraded station.

Life on the towpath of the I&M Canal attracted brazen, leather-hided characters able to endure the long, boring hours spent guiding mules as they towed barges across stagnant, diseased waters. Most of them were teenage boys who earned their reputations for drinking, swearing, and stealing—gaining such ill repute that the Sunday School Union renounced their wild lifestyles. Parents were advised to keep their sons away from such rowdy work ("Mommas, don't let ya babies grow up to be mule drivers!"). In the words of local newspaperman William Grinton, the typical canal driver "was not a man, but a by-product of the canal, recruited from time to time from the rowdy gang and averaged from 14 to 18 years of age." These child laborers had to be hardier than the mules they managed, given how often they were abused and shorted of their wages by barge captains. It was little wonder their "chief vices were profanity and pilfering."

Once he abandoned canal work forever, James Butler "Wild Bill" Hickok's self-imposed exile out West led to legendary adventures as a soldier, drover, lawman, gunfighter, gambler, bear wrestler, Union spy, and unsuccessful actor. Like a supernova on the horizon, the West called to him—as it did to millions of Americans wanting to cross the perilous geographical divide from endless menial labor to a life tending one's own land. Such a journey often commenced with the epic canal—and later, railroad—building that began a short distance from where Lincoln was developing his political and professional infrastructure.

Wild Bill's meteoric life ended with violence: He was shot in the back of the head by an aggrieved rival while gambling, "holding the dead man's hand." Several hundred men who had worked on the Illinois & Michigan Canal would also perish, although in much more mundane ways. Yet they all sought a better life, devoting endless grueling labor to find it.

LIFE ON THE CANAL

To Lincoln and his contemporaries, the allure of a canal was like a golden cable undergirding an ocean of possibilities. You could voyage without having to traverse some of the continent's most treacherous roads—if you could even call them that. Native Americans had created an ingenious system of trails and villages that later *became* roads, but they were not suitable for carriages and year-round horse and buggy travel—a mere change in weather (a constant peril) could turn an established Indian Trail into a mucky, miserable sojourn.

In this transition from trails to canals, the Native "Old" Northwest indigenous territories were virtually eradicated by documents— among them the 1795 Treaty of Greenville, and a series of agreements between twenty-three tribal leaders and the US government— pushing Indigenous people further West. "While the treaty itself is evidence of the intent of the settlers of European descent to wrest the lands away from the first peoples of the region," John Low writes, "the document also reflects the cosmopolitan nature of Indigenous life and community in the number of tribes and signatories involved and their desire for peaceful coexistence." A complex civilization that had interacted with the land for thousands of years would be forcibly relocated, clinched by the Indian Removal Act of 1830.

"Cosmopolitan" is not a word often used to describe Native American trails and villages in the early nineteenth century, although it's stunningly applicable to pre-urban maps of the Chicago area. Settlements were situated at key river junctions along prominent geographical features such as morainal ridges, "islands," or streams. According to a 1919 (based on an 1804 settlement) map by Albert Scharf, southwest of Chicago there was a trail running from the mouth of the Chicago River to its portage with the Des Plaines River. Creeks and streams could be canoed or forded at strategic points. Native habitation patterns followed natural contours of the land where glacial till was left behind, and the massive, ancient Lake Chicago drained through carved channels into the Des Plaines and Illinois Rivers. This waterway became the route for the I&M Canal.

HOW THE CANAL WAS BUILT

In a historical sense, there was nothing unprecedented about the I&M Canal. Romans built their aqueducts thousands of years earlier. In the seventeenth century, the French erected the *Canal du Midi*, which ran 149 miles in Southern France and could have inspired Marquette's vision of a channel cutting from Lake Michigan to the Gulf of Mexico. All of Europe had canals; now, in the early nineteenth century, America was catching up. The I&M Canal would stretch ninety-six miles along across the mostly flat expanse from the Chicago River's mouth to the Illinois River, near (present-day) LaSalle, named after the French explorer who established a network of forts on his way to the Mississippi River's mouth in the late seventeenth century.

Yet the I&M Canal had distinct possibilities reverberating from Washington to the Western frontier. It could create a modern-day ancient Corinth, the influential Greek city that stood at the crossroads of the Greco-Roman world at the edge of the Peloponnese peninsula. The four-mile Corinth Canal would not be dug until the 1890s, although it had been planned during Julius Caesar's time. The Prairie State, contrastingly, moved at a rapid clip: After a national financial and state hiccup—Illinois was nearly bankrupt in 1840—the I&M Canal was underway.

Like nearly all of the young state's public works projects, the I&M Canal experienced a number of delays from its Euro-American conception in the seventeenth century to its first excavation in 1836. While the Erie Canal was underway in 1810, Peter Porter offered the idea of the I&M Canal to Congress. Federal land granted by the first canal commission (later dissolved) laid out towns along the route as early as 1829. By 1836, 375 Chicago lots offered near the canal route were sold—netting more than $1.3 million.

Ground was broken at Canalport, the Chicago River terminus of the canal, later renamed Bridgeport. Chief Engineer William B. Gooding—who had worked on the Erie Canal—shoveled the first dirt along with Colonel William B. Archer, a contractor who owned property along the I&M. Commissioner Gurdon Hubbard, who walked and canoed the portage that would finally be retired, was also on hand. As a canal commissioner, Hubbard was not only a landowner, but had unique powers as a land agent and town planner. What took him three weeks to travel would take a single day after the canal was built.

The canal project triggered a massive transfer of land from the federal government—about 284,000 acres—to the state of Illinois, which then sold some acreage to finance the project. The transaction led to the founding and eventual incorporation of several "canal" towns: Chicago, Ottawa, Lockport, LaSalle, and Morris.

Thousands of Irishmen were attracted to the prospect of work and land in America, arriving in the 1830s and 1840s to work for contractors. Though recruited for their raw labor, Celtic laborers were hardly welcome; escaping famine and political oppression, the Irish were subjected to regular abuse in America. Their Catholicism threatened the Protestant ruling class; as "papists," they were regarded as a dangerous, unruly minority. And their detractors saw any hint of dissent as yet another sign of their "uncivilized nature." Indeed, they rioted during the opening of the canal, pelting dignitaries with rocks. They were treated badly before, during, and after the project—subject to awful living conditions, miserable food rations, and the cruelty of Midwestern weather.

"The Irish were not merely ignorant and poor," wrote journalist James Buckingham, "but they are drunken, dirty, indolent and riotous, so as to be the objects of dislike a fear to all in whose neighborhood they congregate in large numbers." Undaunted by universally abysmal treatment, most of the Irish—and other poor European emigrants—put down roots, establishing themselves socially and politically in the area, building churches like the handsome limestone "St. James of the Sag" near the canal's summit. They founded Chicago political dynasties whose power would become legendary in the years to come.

Canal work proceeded smoothly when it officially began on July 4, 1836. Colonel Archer built a supply road from Chicago to Joliet that would later be named after him. In the days before modern hydraulics, most of the work had to be done by hand—requiring grunt pick-and-shovel labor by gangs of workers. The sparsely populated city didn't have the manpower, drawing more workers from Europe. Not only did the canal burrow into solid limestone, it dropped 140 feet from its highest "summit" point to the Des Plaines River; locks, and eventually hydraulic basins and feeder channels, would be required to keep the canal watered. Contractors were awarded 197 distinct sections to dig and build along with fifteen locks and four aqueducts. It did not continue to go smoothly, by any means: The 1837 Panic dried up investment capital and construction lulled until 1841.

None of the canal building was high technology, but it demanded ingenuity: using aqueducts, the tiny, wooden channels would cross sub-tributaries of the Illinois River such as the Fox and DuPage. The I&M essentially crossed a subcontinental divide separating the Great Lakes and Mississippi River watersheds, so it required creative engineering to keep water flowing down the channel from the shallow Chicago River to the Illinois. The lack of a current and reliable supply was filled by the creation of a steam-operated pumping station at Bridgeport in the early 1840s. This innovation kept the water moving to the highest point of the canal, and to several feeder channels from existing rivers and streams.

Relative to its younger cousin—the Sanitary & Ship Canal, completed in 1900—the I&M Canal was a humble affair. Its channel would be only six feet deep and sixty feet wide, just large enough to handle the small barges, or "packet boats," of the time. Though miniscule compared to today's massive river barges traversing the Illinois, Mississippi, and Ohio Rivers, the boats triggered a commercial revolution. Freight rates plummeted across the country; goods could be shipped from St. Louis to New York in twelve days, versus up to forty days along the Ohio River and adjoining canals. Tolls along the route also helped pay the canal's expenses. Freight boats were charged 3.5 cents per mile, although passengers could bring aboard sixty pounds of baggage for free. Commercial transportation ranged from three to twenty-five cents per thousand pounds.

THE ECONOMIC EXPLOSION
THAT THE I&M CANAL BEGOT

Lincoln, no doubt, took pride in Clay's American System morphing from an aspirational theory to an economic reality in the time he ascended from rural laborer to country lawyer. Local commercial development, directly fueled by local improvements, mattered to him personally and politically. The I&M Canal was a case in point that Lincoln would eventually operate as a commissioner and president who championed internal improvements on a continental scale.

Commodities such as sugar, salt, and molasses traveled from markets to consumers down the canal. Chicago's role as a terminus of the canal pushed it to the top tier of ports: By 1869, it was the busiest in the nation. From 1848 to 1860, the city's population quintupled from a few thousand to more than 112,000. More people meant larger, more robust markets for everything from meat to timber, retail and wholesale demand that mushroomed in Chicago from 1830 to 1860.

The canal completed a transportation network linking New York City's harbor to the Gulf of Mexico, giving everyone along it access to shipping goods. Early versions of the pig iron (and later, steel) bladed plow crossed the Illinois Valley from the 1830s on—empowering farmers from the East Coast to the High Plains to break hard soil, particularly the dense prairie earth. Country-wide agricultural production grew exponentially as farming became widely mechanized.

Towns along the canal route developed specialized industries well-positioned to take advantage of indigenous minerals. "Athens Marble"—a local limestone that was the bedrock of Illinois and plentiful in the Des Plaines River Valley—was quarried at several points. Used to build canal locks and erect buildings, some of which still adorn graceful canal towns like Lockport and Lemont, limestone also became a major component of roadbuilding and steel production. Its abundance fueled the growth of the building and steel industry in Joliet and South Chicago. Coal, sand, and gravel could also be mined within a few miles of the canal. An essential fuel of the steam age, mined coal—plentiful underneath the soil of the Prairie State— grew metalworking industries, such as zinc smelting, centered near Lemont. Common building materials such as hydraulic cement, glass, and bricks (key commodities in building towns and cities) were also manufactured in the area. Hydraulic cement, a heated limestone masonry mortar made in a kiln, proved invaluable in constructing locks because of its durability in water. Widespread deposits of sandstone, silica, and clay were also used extensively in construction.

Trade was a two-way enterprise: when commodities like limestone and coal were exported from the area, other goods could be imported. As tiny towns like Lockport exported grain and limestone, they imported "lumber, agricultural products, machinery, hide, tobacco—150 different items in all," as per Lockport historian, executive, and native Gerald Adelmann. Lockport, the headquarters for the canal commission, became "Queen of the Canal" with its elegant downtown and business districts.

Many technologies were perfected along the canal route, such as "elevator" grain storage. These giant facilities dominated the Chicago ports (and now tower like skyscrapers in many farming communities). One Lockport elevator stored up to 50,000 bushels of corn, an epic volume at the time. The canal and the railroads that followed its route heightened proximity to raw commodities and agricultural goods, fostering an increasing level of manufacturing in the Illinois Valley and Chicago metropolitan area where everything from clocks to furniture was made. The exponential growth of shipping, manufacturing, and population centers gave the upper Illinois Valley "an enviable head start in regional development," writes historian Michael Conzen—a momentum propelling the nation, which was replicated in areas where internal improvements were made well into the twentieth century. The available transportation and access to raw materials created a nexus for a variety of manufacturers in the Illinois River Valley, ranging from electronics parts to its most well-known global manufacturer, Caterpillar, which is based in Peoria.

HORRID WORKING CONDITIONS
BEDEVILED CANAL WORKERS

Contrary to the canal's positive impact on national commercial progress, the labor in and around the I&M Canal was enmeshed in unforgiving misery. Canal construction hours were wretched, wooly, frost-bitten, ice-bound, and often deadly. Irish, Norwegian, and German canal workers emigrated to escape desperate, landless poverty, and famine. In Illinois, they shivered in winter blizzards and sub-zero cold, and endured mosquitoes, mud, and disease in the warmer months. Irish-Catholic laborers, especially, were derided, underpaid, underfed, and ill-housed.

Malaria from mosquito swarms killed and disabled laborers in the hot and humid months. Typhus and cholera from the filthy water ravaged the overcrowded camps. Leeches plagued those working in the muck. Blasts through the dense dolomite limestone on the canal's Eastern end likely killed even more workers. Although the canal commission kept copious records of contracts, land sales, litigation, and transactions, it does not account for how many perished in construction. In a study cited by local historian Ronald Vasile, "in 1838 alone, between 700 and 1,000 canal workers died on the line." It's likely that private contractors refused to tally the grim mortality figures to the commission—so as not to scare off present or future laborers. It was a dreadful, high-mortality occupation.

Nevertheless, Lincoln's joint legislative project certainly provided better transportation to the Mississippi from the Great Lakes, although it was generations before meaningful labor laws. Fixed hours and pay, benefits, safe working conditions, and overtime did not exist. The men digging the canal, constructing locks and aqueducts by hand, worked for independent contractors who acquired the work by bidding low on discrete sections of the canal. Salaried employment with fixed hours and health care was nearly a century away.

Like countless immigrants fleeing oppressive servitude, canal diggers were discriminated against and barred from better employment. They fought and rioted over miserable working conditions and poor representation, as seen in this *Joliet Courier* letter from April 6, 1840:

> To Irishmen—Fellow countrymen; Do you remember the Victoria meeting got up last August at the Court House? I was present and heard WILSON the canal candidate for representative, deal out up on us, the most unmeasured abuse. He said we were *worse* than savages, and more, he declared that we were more *disgusting, and filthy* than the *hogs* upon the public street, and a great deal more of the same kind of stuff.　　　　　　　　—An Irishman.

ABE'S PSYCHOLOGY

To understand where Lincoln was headed, one must revisit where he came from. As a young man virtually enslaved to his father, an illiterate hardscrabble farmer, he didn't have much freedom. If wood needed to be chopped or a stump dug out, Abe was the only able body around in the backwoods of Indiana and Kentucky who could do it. There were no tree services to call, no handymen available. It was Lincoln who performed every form of labor with his incredible endurance and strength—though his mind was engaged elsewhere. If he had not yet been a legislator drawn to politics, the law, and upward mobility, he may well have become a laborer building the I&M Canal. As it stood, the canal reflected his personal aspirations. He was developing along with the country around him.

Thomas Lincoln reportedly saw little need for Abe to rise above his humble beginnings, to do anything but hard farm labor. His son was his indentured servant. Young Abe probably hated him for that. When he was twenty-one, Abe was legally entitled to make his own choices, but Thomas surmised that labor would be his destiny. Although his intelligence was extraordinary by any measure—and his stepmother Sarah Bush encouraged his book learning—Thomas had no patience for literacy. Abe was whipped if caught reading in the field.

Lincoln had many other talents, though, that transcended the backwoods he was born into. Curiosity drove him the way an oxen team could plow a field, but *his* field went beyond his father's farm. Lincoln's field encompassed rivers and roads, rails and superhighways. Although we know little of Abe's internal mindset in the first decades of the nineteenth century, it was clear that he had a quantum idea of himself; somehow, he knew he could project his intelligence and character far beyond his father's subsistence misery. His ambitions would propel him out of the wilderness. Education mattered. So did internal improvements, including those that would build his agile mind.

LINCOLN THE URBAN PLANNER
AND RIVERBOATMAN

Lincoln's short stint as a surveyor in New Salem before he became a lawyer gives us insight into his expansive mind. He had to pick up math and surveying techniques as he learned the craft from scratch, ever eager to master a new trade, earn some money, and expand his employability.

In May 1836, Lincoln was asked to survey a town near Springfield called "Huron." It would grow in importance as a terminal between Springfield and the Illinois River near present-day Havana. Huron was to be built because a canal (one that Lincoln had advocated for) would bypass the torpid Sangamon River, giving Springfield a reliable water route to the Mississippi River system. Canal towns sprung up from the Mohawk Valley and moved West at a rapid clip during the first three decades of the nineteenth century. Where they were built, commerce and civic life followed, and people generally prospered from the corollary community activities. Such was the case for putting Huron on the map.

Huron was roughly seven blocks long with neatly delineated square lots, according to Lincoln historian Christian McWhirter (who found a map of the town in the archives of the Lincoln Presidential Library in Springfield). "According to contemporary accounts," McWhirter discovered, "he [Lincoln] became pretty good at it and this cleanly-drawn map testifies to that."

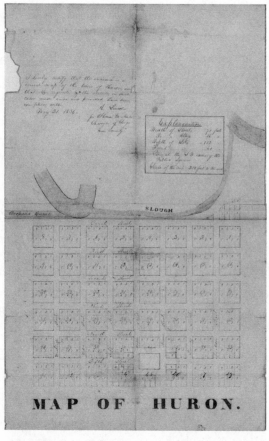

Lincoln's one stab at urban planning, based on his platform for "internal improvements." (Papers of Abraham Lincoln Digital Library)

Although Lincoln left New Salem the following year to practice law in Springfield, his map provides a snapshot of how he envisioned evolving communities: logically organized and with access to a transportation link. State representative at the time but aspiring to become a successful lawyer, Lincoln echoed the template of a country that was burgeoning to become a commercial and industrial behemoth. It was not yet seen through to fruition, though: His Huron town survey and the Sangamon Canal were dead ends, never built.

But the Industrial Revolution could not be stopped, with the steam age coming to Central Illinois and the Northwest. When England began using steam engines to operate iron mills, rail lines, and drain coal mines, the upper Midwest of America was still a changing frontier. Illinois did not become a state until 1818; Chicago, until fully connected to the Mississippi River system in the mid-1850s, was not solidly established. Like most of his contemporaries, Lincoln became keenly aware of the potential of linking the Atlantic to the Gulf of Mexico. But before American rail lines went up, Westerners nearly one thousand miles from saltwater were held hostage by navigable freshwater routes.

The massive Louisiana Purchase, consummated only six years before Lincoln's birth in 1809, blossomed possibilities in his mind as he learned his nation's history. How could one get from the frigid waters of the Great Lakes to the balmy port of New Orleans? When Lincoln settled in New Salem, there were no reliable roads leading to the mouth of the Mississippi. Railroads mostly served East Coast cities.

Before his New Salem days, a commercially minded nineteen-year-old Lincoln saw the need to get goods to market in 1828, so he took a flatboat from Indiana to New Orleans. Three years later, he accompanied a three-man crew north up the Sangamon to the Illinois River, where he headed downriver to its confluence with the Mississippi. A flatboat was the contemporary equivalent to an

18-wheeler in those days, though it looked more like a shanty on a barge. Flatboats held a fair amount of cargo to be sold or traded, then would be reloaded with goods for the return trip.

These voyages shaped Lincoln's ideas on the importance of interstate commerce; they also galvanized his views on slavery, as New Orleans was one of the South's most established slave markets. The river journey stimulated an internal conflict: While commerce elevated most white people above their station, was there a moral component being ignored? How could slavery exist within an ethical Enlightenment framework? Slavery certainly did not elevate *everyone* to a place of economic prosperity. How could you argue that *all* men were created equal?

During a second 1829 trip, Lincoln took a job transporting hogs and produce to the Crescent City—and gained another painful insight into the difficulty of a circuitous, 2,400-mile round trip. He was attacked along the way by a gang of seven men intending to rob him of his cargo. Although Lincoln fended off the assault, it toughened him for future endeavors.

Lincoln's last river trip in 1831 nearly ended in disaster as he navigated a stretch of the shallow, fickle Sangamon River, which connected the city of New Salem to the wider Illinois River. Loaded with hogs, corn, and pork, his flatboat got stuck on a mill dam and started taking on water. Lincoln offloaded some cargo and drilled a hole in the boat. Most of the town watched the young man in action as he managed to start towing again, marveling at his ingenuity and persistence. Seizing the moment, a town leader crowed to the crowd that one day Lincoln would captain a steamboat up the river, connecting his hamlet to the world. Indeed, he would later succeed in making such a connection, yet innovation came to him as a pragmatic matter. In this early part of Lincoln's life, his love of improvisation bloomed.

Newly founded New Salem was not destined to become a capital of commerce, a truth Lincoln refused to believe when he first embraced the Whig internal improvements agenda. As the Sangamon was only navigable in the spring with shallow-draft flatboats or canoes, the best place for a port was at Beardstown on the Illinois River—but there were no decent roads, rails, or canals to get there from New Salem. That did not stop Lincoln from envisioning a better way. He saw rivers as fluid interstates: whoever mastered their mercurial nature would gain commercial and political currency. The Mississippi was a conduit of commerce intertwined with misery. It offered a drink of freedom to some poor white folks, and cruelty to all Black folks.

Historian Michael Burlingame gives this account of Lincoln's impression of the peculiar institution during his second river trip:

> When they reached New Orleans in May, Lincoln was appalled, as he had been two years earlier, at the sight of slavery. John Hanks [his cousin] alleged that he and Lincoln 'Saw Negroes chained—maltreated—whipt and scourged.' Lincoln's 'heart bled,' though he 'said nothing much' and 'was silent from feeling—was sad—looked bad—felt bad—was thoughtful and abstracted.' Hanks maintained that 'it was on this trip that he formed his opinions of Slavery; it ran its iron in him then and there—May, 1831. I have heard him say—often and often.'

Lincoln's intellect was also animated by the prospect of liberating the economies of remote towns, which then had little or no access to navigable waterways (or rails). He imagined a tanner or craftsman in even the tiniest hamlets gaining access to markets a thousand miles away. No longer would merchants rely upon local sales to earn a meager living.

Lincoln knew from experience that water routes were salvation highways: before he came to Illinois, he earned his first dollar rowing customers out to steamers buoyed in the Ohio River. Working the rivers was a novel source of income, as his father didn't pay Abe an allowance and often burned the books he bought. Carl Sandburg writes:

> The Mississippi River was vividly real to him all his life . . . He had seen that river as a flatboatman, as a Black Hawk war soldier, as a lawyer trying cases in cities overlooking it; he had traveled to an island of that river to fight a duel; he had tried a law case involving the right of railroads to build bridges over it.

The river loomed large in Lincoln's psyche: It was aspiration and incarceration, transportation and desperation. Its fluid grace and savagery profoundly shaped his worldview.

COMMERCE CAME FIRST

With a passion girded by a belief that his community could be opened to interstate commerce, Lincoln ran for the state legislature in 1832. Though he did not run on slaves' emancipation, it directly related his Whig Party ideals to the *economic* emancipation of his community and those across the nation. In a political announcement entitled "Communication to the People of Sangamo [now Sangamon] County," Lincoln outlined his ambition:

> Time and experience have verified to a demonstration, the public utility of internal improvements. That the poorest and most thinly populated countries would be greatly benefitted by the opening of good roads, and in the clearing of navigable streams within their limits, is what no person will deny.

His Kentucky hero Henry Clay had long been a champion of such ideals, but Lincoln went a step further in marrying "public utility" with "internal improvements." He applied these principles to American progress and a political agenda that he would promote for the rest of his life.

At the time of Lincoln's political emergence, internal improvements were all the rage in taverns, parlors, state houses, and places of worship. Rural Americans east of the Alleghenies were more concerned with how they could conduct business with the rest of their region, and the East and Gulf Coasts, than with what was going on in Washington or London. They yearned to be global citizens—to sell their commodities and materials outside of their towns. Their desire was met by Lincoln's idea to bypass the unreliable Sangamon with a canal to the Illinois River, earning him a legislature seat. Even his great rival-to-be, Stephen Douglas, espoused internal improvements as a ticket to the future.

LINCOLN HITS THE SKIDS, THEN REBOUNDS

Failure vexed Lincoln's early aspirations in political policy. Initially financed with $5 million in state-issued bonds, the I&M Canal project sputtered to a halt after the 1837 Panic and following recession.

Lincoln had voted with the majority on the state internal improvements bill in the General Assembly, setting his eyes on other projects. Contemporary critics chastised Lincoln and his allies for plunging the state into financial ruin, but the truth was that the state couldn't raise enough capital for the canal by itself—not even by hiring independent contractors to save money. Then the national economy took a dive. Investors from Europe and the East Coast eventually came to the rescue; in the interim, the canal commission issued scrip to workers and contractors, which they later cashed in to buy land along the corridor. Work halted for several years while the state economy recovered, then the canal commission brought in new funding.

Yet the narrative line for internal improvements and Lincoln's life were not smooth progressions, but as jagged and singed as a lightning bolt. His emotional state veered from a perennial mania for internal improvements to a depressive state over romantic pursuits. During the first year of his 1835 state legislature term, Lincoln fell into deep melancholy when his first love, Ann Rutledge, died that August (he likely had three or four other relationships before Mary Todd). By year's end Lincoln rebounded to help the legislature pass a local canal project, one of his signature vows to Springfield voters. Despite the promise of riches and prestige, most statewide political attention shifted north to Chicago and the canal. Lincoln continued advocating for a canal to bypass the problematic Sangamon River, but it was never dug.

What did come to be deeply entrenched was a popular obsession: the notion that public improvements inflated land prices. Speculation was rampant, and fortunes were made in and around the I&M corridor. Any parcel considered for a canal, port, town, or railroad depot was snapped up by those with cash and political influence. Land was one of the most valuable assets to be had in the nineteenth century (and well into the twentieth), before financial markets had fully developed, although self-dealing was an accepted practice. Public land transactions were constantly tainted with irregularities and corruption. The government often gave away or cheaply sold land once occupied by Native Americans, a practice advocated by Lincoln and many of his contemporaries.

Lincoln saw the public sentiment targeting land acquisition and the growing reach of railroads as two harbingers of a country that could—and would—stretch into one commercial and political entity from the Atlantic to the Pacific, from the Great Lakes to the Gulf Coast. He couldn't help but be enraptured by the fervor of the times in which he lived, when canals meant freedom and railroads were iron-clad promises for a better life. But there was a major stumbling block: access to capital. State banks had little, and Congress had no overarching plan for internal improvements. It was usually a state or local initiative that got things done.

When Lincoln got back to business after his first depression, he served diligently on the state legislature's internal improvements committee. He knew that his state's rich soil, access to two water systems, and Midwestern geography positioned it ideally for growth. One of the legislature's first major rail allocations was a meager $3.5 million to build the Illinois Central from Galena—sitting near the Mississippi and lead mines—to Cairo, at the confluence of the Ohio River. When Lincoln saw other states spending millions on similar projects, he dreamed of a system of canals and rail lines within the state and outside of it.

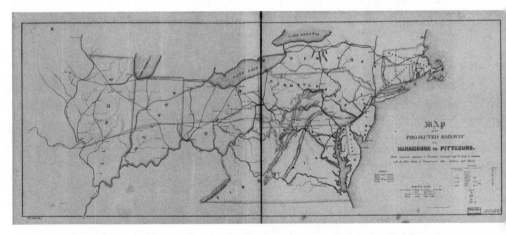

How rail expanded in Illinois, creating the longest rail network of its day. (Library of Congress)

Lincoln still advocated for public infrastructure as a private citizen, but his professional attention turned to building a legal practice. Being a legislator paid little, and he was beyond his days of postmastering and surveying. Lincoln began studying the law during his legislative terms and was admitted to the Illinois Bar in 1837, around the time of the Panic. Although he elevated his status and economic potential by becoming an attorney, Lincoln's love life was in turmoil: Grieving over Ann Rutledge, his later courtship of Mary Owens never took off. His courtship of Lexington belle Mary Todd was even rockier. Where Mary was lively, tempestuous, and highly engaged in local and national politics—particularly the platform of the Whigs and Lincoln's idol Henry Clay, a neighbor in her native Lexington, Kentucky—Lincoln was tongue-tied among women and uncomfortable in society. Her in-laws, the prominent Edwards family, likely thought him a rube.

Mary Todd had heard of Lincoln through her cousin, lawyer and legislator John Todd, as early as 1837. She may have heard Lincoln speak on national politics or improvements in early Whig orations. They would not have been a natural match in nineteenth-century eyes: Lincoln was tall and ungainly, prone to storytelling in back-woods vernacular. For a family accustomed to eloquence and polished Southern manners, Lincoln was likely doomed to status as a hopeless country outsider. Mary, owing to her fine schooling and middle/upper class Lexington pedigree, knew French and was well read. She could converse on a number of topics, although she said of herself she was short and a "ruddy pine knot."

As a highly eligible woman in Springfield's power circle—her brother-in-law Ninian Edwards's father had been governor—Mary attracted other suitors, including the ambitious, short-statured Stephen Douglas. His politics derailed the romance: Mary was a confirmed Whig. Douglas was a Democrat.

Mary reportedly spoke in confidence years later about the Douglas courtship: "I shall become *Mrs.* President, or I am the victim of false prophets, but it will not be as *Mrs.* Douglas."

Lincoln came to court Mary in earnest in 1840, though he may have been uncertain about his ability to support a wife and family. He was doing fairly well: His income from legal work, which fluctuated, was up to $2,000 a year in addition to $300 a year from the legislature. But a middle-class man was expected to be the sole breadwinner, his wife exclusively managing home and family. Lincoln was older, thirty-one, and wary about his future as a country lawyer riding a vast circuit in the cold-weather months. The couple vehemently argued and parted on January 1, 1841. Frustrated and angered by Lincoln's erratic social behavior, Mary reportedly told him: "Go, and never come back."

Lincoln spiraled into another inconsolable funk, getting involved in a duel challenge that was thwarted. William "Billy" Herndon, who later became his law partner, noted that his break-up with Mary "made him as crazy as a loon." Lincoln's friend Joshua Speed took away his razor as a precautionary measure. "To remain as I am is impossible," Lincoln wrote at the time. "I must die or be better, it appears to me."

What broke the emotional logjam and reunited Mary and Abraham, history does not fully reveal. Perhaps it was time's healing balm, or that they could not be without each other when both were meant to indelibly reshape history. Despite opposition from Mary's sister and brother-in-law, they were married by Reverend Charles Dresser in a simple Episcopalian ceremony on November 4, 1842. The reverend also sold the Lincolns the only house they ever owned, on 8th Street in Springfield, after they first lived at the Globe Tavern and in a rented cottage. Their elegant Springfield home, bought for $1,500 (about $50,000 in today's dollars, and a handsome sum at the time), would be their abode for the subsequent seventeen years. They later added a second story in 1856. Of their four sons, only Robert Todd, their firstborn (August 1, 1843), survived into adulthood and old age.

While their marriage was riven with grief and other troubles, what held the couple together may have been the undaunted political ambition that infused their partnership. Mary saw in Lincoln something intangible and inchoate, something few others had seen. Had she intuited his unrealized potential? Was she captivated by one of the century's best writers? Billy Herndon and others later heaped doubt on their ultimate compatibility and whether Lincoln loved Mary, who intensely disliked Herndon, but it seems like idle gossip from an outsider to the relationship. It was like looking through a darkened glass upon something complex, symbiotic—this union of two highly intelligent and passionate people. But the stark images of their tumultuous age were just becoming clearer.

LINCOLN RETURNS TO POLITICS

As Lincoln prospered in his new marriage, enjoying domestic life—he spoiled his boys—and expanding his law practice, his vision of internal improvements became more luminous as he took on cases for the growing railroad industry. The idea of a national transportation system haunted him, even as he tried the murder cases that built his reputation as an adroit lawyer who constructed irresistible arguments even the most uneducated juries could understand. By 1847, he was back in the political fray, having been elected to the US House of Representatives.

Lincoln in his sole term in Congress. (Library of Congress)

As the only Illinois Whig in Congress, Lincoln swam against the tide of "popular sovereignty" Democrats like Stephen Douglas, who endorsed the so-called "right" of emerging states to adopt slavery. Lincoln's commitment was to a national plan of internal improvements. Early in his political and personal life, he believed that slavery would die of attrition. His June 20, 1848, speech in the House argued that although the Constitution did not reference the funding of infrastructure—or how to even raise the money—Congress needed to find a "stern, unbending basis of facts" for financing such projects in order to avoid local favoritism. The speech is one of the first, highly prescient indications of a need for an unbiased, *evidence-based* approach to federal public works financed by Congress; and it's among the least-quoted of his seminal speeches while he was briefly in Congress.

For a speaker later known for crystalline brevity and eloquence, Lincoln's lengthy 1848 improvements speech is overshadowed by his more well-known oratories. Yet it deserves attention as the US and the world struggle with building and financing twenty-first-century infrastructure, accommodating more than 7 billion people, and mitigating climate change.

Although his term in the House would be short, and he would fail a decade later to win a Senate seat—against Douglas, no less—this would hardly be Lincoln's last word on internal improvements. He was warming up his intellectual maul to split the conservative opposition against spending the necessary capital to build a great nation.

IV

LINCOLNOMICS HITS THE RAILS

Attorney Lincoln and the Illinois Central

"The President stood before us as a man of the people. He was thoroughly American, had never crossed the sea, had never been spoiled by English insularity or French dissipation; a quite native, aboriginal man, as an acorn from the oak; no aping of foreigners, no frivolous accomplishments, Kentuckian born, working on a farm, a flatboatman, a captain in the Black Hawk War, a country lawyer, a representative in the rural legislature of Illinois;—on such modest foundations the broad structure of his fame was laid."

—Ralph Waldo Emerson

The riverboat *Effie Afton* was surging her way upriver on the Mississippi near Davenport, Iowa, when her captain suddenly steered clear of something no steamboat pilot of the time had ever seen: a *bridge* spanning the great river. Night was looming and the currents were perilous. The bridge, which carried the "mighty fine" Rock Island Railroad line cross-river from Illinois into Iowa, was only fifteen days old. At the sight of the steamer, the bridge tender actuated a device that moved the span on the main channel to one side to allow the boat to pass through. But something went tragically—or intentionally—wrong.

Effie's captain sounded her shrill whistle as she moved through the slowly opening draw. Two hundred feet after she cleared the opening, she heeled hard to the right. Mysteriously, her starboard engine stopped, and the engine on the ship's other side powered up—violently forcing her into the span next to the opened draw. *Effie* was smashed, the span catastrophically damaged. With *Effie* out of control in the middle of the river, the situation went from bad went to worse: A cabin stove fell over and fire quickly consumed the boat, spreading to the timber bridge. All crew and passengers were rescued. But the *Effie* was incinerated within five minutes, and the livestock aboard perished in the river. "By the following day, the rest of the bridge caught fire and was completely destroyed. Steamboats up and down the river celebrated, blowing whistles and ringing bells," according to local accounts.

Steamboat pilots and owners had been aggrieved at the bridge's presence, the first and only one to span the river at that time. Paddle-wheelers despised any competition on the water highways to which they felt entitled, having ruled them for decades; they saw the railroads as the end of their way of life. The bridge was not only an affront to their masculine domination of the river, it was a symbol of progress that they were not willing to accept.

When the steamship *Effie Afton* careened into the bridge on May 6, 1856, it was more than a symbolic equivalent of Luddites breaking looms. An avatar of an older era was attacking progress, inflaming the passions of railroad advocates who would dominate the growing nation as it lunged for the Pacific, mere years away from a more efficient means of transport there. *Effie's* owner, Captain Jacob Hurd, and fellow investors sued the Rock Island Bridge Company in Chicago federal court, claiming $930,000 in damages. Although the well-equipped ship was only worth $50,000, and usually steamed the Ohio River rather than the Mississippi, Hurd claimed the bridge was a navigation hazard: Had it not been there (despite the dubious engine problems), the *Effie* would have drifted downstream without incident. The ship was only insured for $15,000, providing an economic impetus for the suit.

The bridge company hired a top team of trial attorneys—joined by Lincoln, who had deep experience in railroad cases by then. Lincoln prepared carefully, visiting the site and talking to locals who had witnessed the "accident." Rumors circulated that Captain Hurd deliberately rammed the bridge, but Lincoln sought the truth, studying everything from river currents to piloting. He studied the Mississippi's eddies and water flow, and even calculated the speed of the current at the time of the collision with the son of one of the bridge's engineers; as a former boat pilot, Lincoln understood the complex nature of river navigation. His evidence-based argument focused on defeating the plaintiff's claim that the bridge itself caused dangerous disruptions in river flow.

A variety of experts—river pilots, engineers, and bridgemen—testified and were cross-examined in the Chicago trial, which lasted fourteen days. In his summary, Lincoln let the facts rest to argue a larger issue: If such bridges were banned, it would interrupt the economic progress of the *entire country*. Rail commerce and passenger travel would be perversely prevented from crossing rivers. Western expansion would slow to a crawl, as there was no water route to the Pacific and a canal was out of the question.

Lincoln's summation lasted two days, concluding that the volume of east-to-west traffic "is growing larger and larger, building up new countries with a rapidity never before seen in the history of the world." Lincoln's argument conceptualized that the bridge was essential as a public amenity fostering economic development and migration into the West. Not only was one era ending and another one beginning, the imminent possibility of traversing the continent in days instead of weeks was a profound challenge to the status quo. Lincoln articulated this strange brew of fear, promise, and catapulting progress.

The idea of a transcontinental railroad—a simmering undercurrent of the *Afton* trial—was popular, although the politics of *where* to build its main route aggravated growing tensions between the North and South. The South already had access to the Gulf of Mexico and Southeastern ports. The increasingly industrial North did not. A clear rail route to the Pacific would confer enormous economic advantage to the states directly linked by rail across the plains, mountains, and deserts leading to California.

Mississippian Jefferson Davis, an army engineer and Secretary of War under President Franklin Pierce from 1853 to 1857, was one of the early gatekeepers for the route across the Mississippi River. Davis himself had surveyed Rock Island—a strategic, narrowing point in the river where the army located Ft. Armstrong—for a rail crossing. If a bridge was to be built, Davis—being a fervent son of Dixie—of course favored a Southern rail route that would cross the river well below St. Louis. Although he didn't openly object when the Rock Island bridge was considered, he knew that Northerners, particularly those against establishing slavery in new Western states, would likely flow West over it in greater numbers than his regional compatriots.

After the bridge was built and Stephen Douglas successfully championed the "Kansas-Nebraska Act," green-lighting slavery in states where "popular sovereignty" allowed it, politics shifted. Davis made his intentions known:

On April 19, 1854, Davis reasserted the War Department's jurisdiction [over Rock Island] and declared that he opposed the [bridge] company's use of the island. According to contemporary newspaper accounts, Davis did not want to permit a [N]*orthern* railroad route to get a head start over a [S]outhern railroad route, thereby allowing the [N]orth to take the lead in settling Nebraska and Kansas. In a letter to the contractors, John Warner and Company, he ordered construction on the bridge halted. The order was ignored.

Davis promptly sued in Chicago federal court, claiming the army still had a right to the land, so construction should halt. He lost: Judge John McLean of the US Supreme Court ruled that "because Rock Island had been abandoned by the War Department, it could not be considered a military preserve," and further, "the bridge would be an *improvement* in the interest of the general public." Such use of public lands promoted population growth and increased land values. McLean maintained, "a State has the power to construct a public road through public lands."

Judge McLean's ruling came before the *Effie Afton* trial—presaging Lincoln's contention that an improvement was squarely in the national public interest and should not be impeded. The precedent was critical: Lincoln didn't get a verdict in the *Effie* trial due to a hung jury, but later declared a victory in principle. Several subsequent court actions kept the rebuilt bridge in place. Many more bridges followed, including engineering marvels such as the Eads Bridge in St. Louis and the Stone Arch Bridge in Minneapolis. Although Lincoln didn't win the railroad bridge case, the nonverdict was one of his biggest legal victories of national significance.

Some historians cite the *Effie* case as Lincoln's most important legal case. Although it wasn't a clear legal victory, it opened up the West in an unprecedented way: The great river was no longer a political and geographic barrier, and receded into history as its primary North-South thoroughfare after the Civil War. The National Archives account concludes of the landmark case:

The issue of the right to cross navigable streams was decided for all time. It also found Jefferson Davis and Abraham Lincoln on opposite sides of a case with wider ramifications, involving issues that would soon bring the country to civil war.

Davis, ironically, was eventually correct in his view that Mississippi bridges would give the North an edge in the westward push beyond the Plains and Rockies. Railroad bridges crossing the Ohio River south of its mouth were slow to be built. The first such span was erected in Memphis in 1892, another one in Vicksburg in 1930, and finally in New Orleans—the South's most vibrant port—in 1935, notes lawyer-historian Brian McGinty.

LINCOLN'S BOUNTIFUL RAILROAD CASELOAD

Railroad expansion created a heavy caseload for country lawyers like Lincoln. As the nation's fastest growing and most powerful corporations, they were in constant legal disputes with landowners and local governments.

When the Illinois Central was chartered in 1851, it became a powerful economic entity. Nearly 3 million acres of federal and state land were ceded to the railroad's right of way, creating towns and depots along its route. The land grant alone was roughly twice the size of Delaware. Largely British and Dutch financiers made an initial investment of $27 million. The terms for the creation of the railroad were generous: Other than acquiring the land for next to nothing, it would pay a "7% annual tax to the state, in lieu of all taxes, forever."

But having such a deal enshrined in state law did not deter other taxing bodies from suing the deep-pocketed railroad, which became one of the continent's largest corporations. Rail was undisputedly a manically growing industry—akin to technology companies in the 1990s and today. During the 1850s alone, the Illinois rail network expanded from 111 miles to 2,790. The Illinois Central, running 705 miles from the state's northern to southern borders in 1856, was the longest railroad in the world prior to the Civil War. Where the rails were laid, people followed: The state's population doubled from 800,000 in 1850 to 1.7 million by 1860. The rail also cut travel times dramatically— by a factor of four. A trip that once took four days by stagecoach and canal took a day by rail.

Lincoln took on a number of cases defending and suing railroads. Other than the *Effie Afton* case, Lincoln represented railroads like the Illinois Central in several other suits. His first retainer from the IC was $250 in 1853. In one hallmark case—*Illinois Central Railroad v. County of McLean*— the county (whose seat was Bloomington) claimed it could assess property tax against the railroad. Seeing the cash-rich railroad pass through its towns without paying a cent of real estate tax, the county of McLean wanted its fair share.

Facing his former law partners John Stuart and Stephen Logan (representing McLean), Lincoln argued that the state could not exempt the railroad from county taxes because the corporation's charter "applied to state taxes only." Lincoln's argument was relatively simple: Counties couldn't levy property taxes because the original state railroad charter didn't allow for additional taxation. That simple statement of statute enhanced the railroad's bottom line in perpetuity. The railroad could be exempted from *county* taxes: The state law was constitutional, the ruling stated. Lincoln stuck to the facts—the Illinois Constitution had granted the corporation a special exemption on property taxes. He won, saving the railroad millions.

A win for the county could have bankrupted the railroad by granting *every* Illinois county the railroad crossed the right to tax the corporation. Its executives, which included future general George McClellan, were less than generous and stiffed Lincoln on his fee. Lincoln took *them* to court to collect on what the railroad itself stated "was the most important case handled by Lincoln because of its far-reaching effects." A jury awarded Lincoln a $4,800 fee in 1857—a pittance relative to the money he saved the railroad in potential tax liability. When it refused to pay the judgment, only a sheriff's writ to seize railroad property forced the corporation to cut Lincoln a check.

LINCOLN FRUSTRATED IN CONGRESS

While Lincoln proved adept at handling cases for the railroad and others—arguing alternately as plaintiff or defendant and winning, for the most part—he was markedly less successful in his earlier sole term as a congressman.

Opposed to President Polk's aggressive expansion of the Mexican War, Lincoln was incensed at the president's veto of an 1846 improvements bill that would have granted major infrastructure upgrades throughout the Midwest (including Chicago). The I&M Canal, nearly finished when Lincoln served in Congress, could not handle the explosion in shipping volume from the Great Lakes to the Gulf Coast. If Great Lakes commerce from New York State to

St. Louis was to grow, more improvements—and on a much larger scale—were needed. The modest canals of the nineteenth century's first four decades would not support the economic growth of the epoch's second half.

Anchored by the boosterism of marquee newspapermen Horace Greeley and Thurlow Weed, a Chicago convention was planned to coordinate a counterstrategy to the Polk veto, made because such a grand improvement plan was "unconstitutional." Behind the stroke of the veto pen was ire for those who would benefit from the improvements: Northern industrial states. South Carolina's John C. Calhoun became one of the most powerful detractors of Clay's American System, as he knew that connecting Northern industrial centers further neglected and sidelined the mostly agricultural South.

The 1847 Chicago River and Harbor Convention was one of many events held in Northern states to bolster the cause of internal improvements. Harbors needed to be dug, rivers made navigable by dredging. Northeastern shippers and merchants wanted easier access to the Midwest. On July 5–7 of that year, some 10,000 boosters gathered in Chicago to press their case.

Lincoln was one of the least-heralded members of the assembly, headlined by luminaries from New York, Boston, and throughout the East Coast. It was an epic event on the sweltering, mud-laden streets of Chicago, occupied by 16,000 residents at the time—just a decade into its existence as an incorporated town. The convention doubled as a celebration featuring floats, processions, and military bands, largely organized by pro-development Whigs. Boisterous attacks of Polk stressed the hazards of lake travel; letters from absent improvements supporters like Henry Clay and Martin Van Buren were presented. Rail expansion was mentioned, but the subject was largely confined to the sidelines. This convocation focused on ports and rivers.

Regional jealousies escalated into political bulwarks against local improvements, trumpeted by Democrats and Southerners. How could deepening the port at Buffalo help Louisville? How could Kentucky and Tennessee benefit, or would the spoils go exclusively to the Great Lakes and Northeastern states? Or, better yet, how could inland waterways increase ocean-going commerce? Lincoln's short convention speech argued that *all* local improvements aided the greater nation: The I&M Canal might have been solely within Illinois state boundaries, but it connected markets from New York City to New Orleans. Southern sugar flowed north and Midwestern corn moved south.

In the House of Representatives on June 20, 1848, Lincoln made essentially the same argument. It was one of his longest speeches, again spotlighting his economic argument for improvements:

> Take, for instance, the Illinois and Michigan canal. Considered apart from its effects, it is perfectly local. . . . In a very few days we were all gratified to learn, among other things, that sugar had been carried from New-Orleans through this canal to Buffalo in New-York. This sugar took this route, doubtless because it was cheaper than the old route. Supposing the benefit of the reduction in the cost of carriage to be shared between seller and buyer, the result is, that the New Orleans merchant sold his sugar a little dearer; and the people of Buffalo sweetened their coffee a little cheaper, than before—a benefit resulting from the canal, not to Illinois where the canal is, but to Louisiana and New York, where it is not. In other transactions Illinois will, of course, have her share, and perhaps the larger share too, in the benefits of the canal; but the instance of the sugar clearly shows that the benefits of an improvement, are by no means confined to the particular locality of the improvement itself.

After the convention and his sole congressional term, Lincoln's political capital appreciated. His passionate defense of improvements endeared him to Northeast powerbrokers such as Horace Greeley, who put him on the national radar as an advocate for economic development. It was not a stretch to say that improvements were reducing the cost of commerce, but it was a leap to claim they could somehow unite the country in a new shared purpose of moving all its people up the economic ladder. That was the Whig ideal, but Lincoln nurtured the concept, fusing the political and economic realities of the changing country. Mentor Williams wrote of what he saw firsthand at the convention:

> While no outstanding Whig presidential timber was discovered at the convention, many who would soon figure in politics in a lesser capacity were given the chance to make themselves known to West and East alike. Such men were Edward Bates of Missouri and Abraham Lincoln of Illinois.

Having challenged the national political friction derailing local improvements, Lincoln would demonstrate the economic power of public works later in his career. In due course, Congress acquiesced—principally through land grants, the favored way of conducting large-scale finance between 1790 and 1860 (according to research by Stephen Minucci). Of the $77 million Congress dedicated to improvements during that period, nearly $49 million was in the form of land grants.

Still, Lincoln had to overcome the South's political resistance: Some twenty-one of the fifty-one presidential vetoes prior to the Civil War "were specifically related to improvements," Minucci found. Vetoes had been the tool of legislative rejection for presidents from Monroe through Polk. White House opposition to improvements abated somewhat while Whig Zachary Taylor was president during the 32nd Congress (1851–53). Taylor, a general during the Mexican War, didn't live out his term: Serving from March 1849 to July 1850, he died after only sixteen months in office, succeeded by his undistinguished vice president, Millard Fillmore. Nevertheless, during Taylor's short tenure, some 100 improvements projects were funded, totaling more than $2 million.

LINCOLN'S SOLE INVENTION

Congressman and lawyer Lincoln did more than champion national internal improvements—he came up with one of his own: an invention designed and patented between congressional duties. Recalling his troubles in the shallow Sangamon River—and later, returning by boat from Washington—he wanted to devise a way of buoying a ship in shallow water.

Lincoln's experience of being grounded on a sandbar in Lake Erie was the final impetus to innovate a solution. The captain of the lake excursion ordered all hands "to force barrels under the side of the ship below the water line." Lincoln observed this primitive technique as the barrels gave the boat the buoyancy it needed to move off the sandbar: "slowly but surely, the boat began to rise." Lincoln took some paper from his coat pocket and began to sketch a buoyant boat design on his famous top hat.

Home in Springfield on a break from Congress, Lincoln went to work on a model for his creation. Walter Davis, a mechanic who had a shop near Lincoln's law office, worked with him to create a wood model. Lincoln spent hours polishing the ungainly dummy, which featured fourteen long, vertical poles on an upper deck. In theory, the poles would lower horizontal bellows positioned above the water line; simple manual insertion of

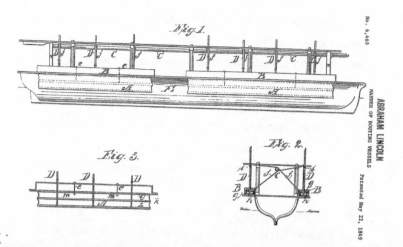

Lincoln was the only president to hold a patent. (Google Patents)

Tag from the U.S. Patent Office. (Smithsonian National Museum of American History)

Model of Lincoln's patented device. (Smithsonian National Museum of American History)

the poles, combined with the buoyant bellows, would presumably uplift the boat. Still clinging to his idea that the inconstant Sangamon was navigable, Lincoln exhibited the boat model to people who gathered in the square around the Old State Capitol. When he finished explaining the concept, he cradled the model in his long arms and walked back to his office.

Lincoln took the red-cedar model with him when he returned to Congress for a short session. Because the railroad lines hadn't been established, he took the long route to the Illinois River onto the Mississippi; then to St. Louis, picking up a steamer that went downriver to the Ohio around Louisville; and finally, overland to Washington. The mostly riverine route must have emboldened him further: When he got to Washington, Lincoln met with a patent lawyer about his invention. Preparing the drawings, description, and application, he submitted to documents to the U.S. Patent Office and was approved for Application 6,469 on May 22, 1849. The patent carried a modest title: "An Improved Method of Lifting Vessels Over Shoals."

It's unlikely that Lincoln's model was ever constructed as a working boat—railroads nigh eliminated the need for such a device—but it showed the intensity of his focus on innovation and invention, two subjects that animated his call for improvements well into his presidential terms. Lincoln is still the only US president to hold a patent.

LINCOLN V. DOUGLAS, ROUND THREE

Prosperity came into Lincoln's life and home during the height of his legal career in the 1850s. He was well respected, successful. Despite grieving the tragic death of his son Eddy, Lincoln took a wide variety of cases and looked askance at politics—until 1854.

Stephen Douglas staked out a murky and troubling middle ground for Democrats by championing the notion of popular "sovereignty." Letting new states decide for themselves whether slavery would be permitted created a new order that avoided an immediate showdown with Southern states, but opened a Pandora's box: the Kansas-Nebraska Act. Effectively nullifying Henry Clay's 1820 Missouri Compromise limiting the expansion of slavery, it compelled Lincoln to reenter politics. His political and moral maturation came at a time when the economy was globalizing.

Lincoln's "house divided against itself cannot stand" argument against Douglas during their Great Debates for the Senate did much for Lincoln's stature. Nevertheless, Douglas won reelection to the Senate in 1858; in a time in which the state General Assembly elected senators, Douglas's political machine controlled a large number of Illinois legislators. Despite that Douglas was a resident of Chicago and popular for his local boosterism, he lost the city to Lincoln during that Senate election. (Keep in mind that districting from the 1850 census does not reflect contemporary population shifts in which thousands moved to the northeastern part of Illinois and Chicago in particular.)

Douglas did not acknowledge it at the time of their debates, but he had a financial reason for bolstering the Kansas-Nebraska Act: It garnered Southern political support for an eventual rail line that would traverse Nebraska. Such a route favored a likely junction—or two—with the Illinois Central, which conveniently passed through hundreds of acres of property Douglas owned in Chicago.

The deeper moral question of expanding slavery in states where it had not previously existed tore at the country. There were symbiotic disconnects. New England and English textile mills needed cheap Southern cotton to manufacture clothing for an ever-expanding, globalized economy, increasingly enriched by steamships, railroads, and the telegraph.

In North America and Western Europe, Chinese and Indian goods were exchanged for lead mined in Illinois and Missouri. The South and the North, however, were joined at the hip economically. Annually, nearly 2 million pounds of cotton was woven into 58 million yards of textiles in places like Lowell, Massachusetts; cotton picked by enslaved people was supplied to bustling, steam-powered mills in a region brimming with abolitionists. This economic irony was not explicitly discussed by Lincoln and Douglas in their 1858 debates, but it loomed large.

The first debate, held in a capacious square in Ottawa, Illinois, attracted thousands in the sweltering heat. At the confluence of the Fox and Illinois Rivers, Ottawa thrived from commerce along the rivers and I&M Canal, which crossed the Fox in an aqueduct. It was a town Lincoln had a hand in creating. While the townspeople had some sense of his role as a legislator some twenty years prior, that conferred him no distinct advantage. Working alongside Lincoln in the legislature and later in Congress, Douglas—the incumbent senator—*also* supported the canal and railroad. The "Little Giant" had made some locals wealthy through land deals and political appointments, and was ceremoniously feted as he took the debate stage.

As one of seven debates—each in a separate Congressional district of Illinois—the two men jousted, orating on why slavery should either be left alone to wither (per Lincoln) or continue as the prerogative of new states (per Douglas). Still, Lincoln reasoned, there was no congruence between the free industry of the North and the Southern slave-based economy. Slaveholder Thomas Jefferson wrote about equality and the personal freedom to pursue commerce. Surely these freedoms would apply more inclusively in a time when labor, industry, and intellectual capital were becoming more, not less, valued, Lincoln argued.

Douglas took the offensive in the first debate, but Lincoln came back with his logical framework to argue that slavery would surely dissipate of its own accord in the coming years. Lincoln made it clear, however, that he was not an abolitionist—nor did he blame slaveholders for their practice. Nevertheless, the prairie lawyer, flatboatman, postmaster, laborer, and back bench legislator became known as *the* man of principle.

Though not an abolitionist at the time of the 1858 debates, Lincoln refined an argument that he had been developing since entering politics in his twenties. He wouldn't interfere with slavery "where it existed," but wanted to stop its expansion into Western states. And although he asserted he belonged to "the race of the superior position," Lincoln extolled another philosophy that would be eloquently articulated in his "new birth of freedom" in the Gettysburg Address: the Declaration of Independence conferred *economic* rights equally to all races. When Douglas attacked Lincoln as "Black Republican" and "radical" abolitionist at their first senatorial debate in Ottawa, Illinois, on August 21, 1858, Lincoln rebutted:

> There is no reason in the world why the Negro is not entitled to all the natural rights enumerated in the Declaration of Independence, the right to life, liberty, and the pursuit of happiness. [Loud cheers.] I hold that he is as much entitled to these as the white man. I agree with Judge Douglas he is not my equal in many respects—certainly not in color, perhaps not in moral or intellectual endowment. But in the right to eat the bread, without the leave of anybody else, which his own hand earns, *he is my equal and the equal of Judge Douglas, and the equal of every living man.* [Great applause.]

Lincoln carefully deconstructs Douglas's argument that he is in league with fiery Northeastern abolitionists. His message is tailored to an audience of 20,000 from Central Illinois, some of whom were proslavery, anti-Black, and anti-equality. Moreover, Lincoln stakes out a unique territory that he would own as president: linking the words of the Declaration of Independence with economic equality as a fundamental right. "In the right to eat the bread, without the leave of anyone else, which his own hand earns . . . he is my equal . . . and the equal of every living man." This is Lincoln's take on "the pursuit of happiness." It would form the bedrock of the Thirteenth, Fourteenth, and Fifteenth Amendments.

LINCOLN EMBRACES INVENTION

After the election in which Lincoln lost the Senate race but gained a national following, he gave a few brief lectures in 1858 and 1859 on "Discoveries and Inventions." These were hardly succinct stump speeches. He preached the power of creativity, and offered histories of steam and wind power, writing, and innovation; he praised invention in an abstruse, long-winded oration characteristic of the day:

> Man is not the only animal who labors; but he is the only one who *improves* his workmanship. This improvement, he effects by *Discoveries*, and *Inventions*. His first important discovery was the fact that he was naked; and his first invention was the fig-leaf-apron.

The "Inventions" speech itself was preachy and pedantic. One would be hard-pressed to believe the "Discoveries" speech and Gettysburg Address shared a writer. Where the Address was brief and piercing, the "Discoveries" was an overwritten, often humorous diatribe; many scholars regard it as a failure compared to the allusion, morality, and symbolism of the Address. Lincoln's "Discoveries" got little attention, and apparently did not do much to advance his political career.

What "Discoveries" has that the Address lacks is a less-celebrated side of the sixteenth president: Lincoln's curiosity and ambition for his country's deepest reserves—of intellectual capital. He saw a country teeming with inventions that would change the world. Indeed, while Lincoln cut his teeth as a state legislator, the steel plow and harvesting machines opened up a thousand-mile corridor of prairie landscape, transforming global agriculture. In another speech he gave at the Wisconsin Agricultural Fair in Milwaukee—before he was nominated for president—Lincoln applied his innovation theme specifically to agricultural research and improvement.

Like the earlier Illinois speech, his Wisconsin agriculture lecture was begging for condensation. Yet, it was a useful template for later advancements—for the Department of Agriculture and land-grant colleges, which would primarily focus on agricultural research and development at their outset. In these lectures, we see a Lincoln squarely focused on national economic and technical progress through building a new knowledge base. Up until then, farmers had general ideas about fertility, soil moisture, planting, and harvesting practices, but there was little or no science behind it. With an expanding number of states and a growing population, agriculture needed to scale up. It was an evolution that led to mega-farming, seed hybridization, and ever-greater productivity.

Lincoln saw this transformation firsthand. He was compelled, as the nation hurtled into war, to articulate how science and imagination could change history and advance civilization. Not only did Lincoln love witnessing and contemplating invention—he was ready to foment a culture that embraced it.

FREMONT EMPOWERS THE REPUBLICANS

In the national afterglow of the Lincoln-Douglas debates, Lincoln was a sought-after speaker. On February 27, 1860, Lincoln introduced himself to Eastern audiences during his Cooper (Institute) Union speech delivered in New York City. After his oration, no longer was he the unknown, frontier rube in the eyes of the adoring audience that heard his eloquent dispatch of Douglas's "popular sovereignty" and the expansion of slavery.

Lincoln was still a practicing lawyer—in early April he represented defendants in a federal "Sandbar" suit—but this would be his last appearance as an attorney, counsel in a suit wherein downtown Chicago landowners won a title contest to land that had been somewhat underwater in 1835. The parcel was worth half a million dollars, owing to its proximity to the bustling port city near the mouth of the Chicago River on Lake Michigan, a thriving commercial zone (made possible by the Illinois & Michigan Canal's opening a dozen years earlier). The case was another instance of Lincoln indirectly benefitting from actions he took as legislator in the 1830s, as a key promoter of internal improvements—one of which was the I&M Canal, with its checkered history.

Along with the status quo of the burgeoning 1840s and 1850s, Lincoln's worldview broadened. The push to "conquer" the West—and the people who lived there—was a manifest destiny of white entitlement. The popular explorer John C. Fremont (later a less-than-glorious Civil War general whom Lincoln fired twice) opened the Euro-American imagination to California and Oregon. As imperialistic fever devoured the Southwest and Mexico north and west of the Rio Grande, Fremont and others enriched themselves with gold discovered just east of San Francisco. "There's gold in them hills" was the rallying cry, creating even more impetus for a transcontinental railroad across vast Western prairies, badlands, mountains, and deserts.

Fremont mapped the expanse between the Mississippi River and the Pacific, naming the San Francisco Bay mouth the "Golden Gate" along the way. He and his wife, Jessie Benton, were among the most famous couples in America prior to the Civil War; the Golden State was the great triumph of the Fremonts' celebrity. Scarcely two years after Mexico ceded to the US, California became a state in 1850, preceded by the gold strike at Sutter's Mill two years earlier. Its promise of enormous wealth and access to Asia created a political tipping point.

The Fremonts, members of the newly minted Republican Party in the mid-1850s, opposed the expansion of slavery—which became Lincoln's *cause célèbre* and a solid plank in the new Republican Party platform. If the West remained enshrined in free labor, political balance would shift from the Southern states to the North and West. The combination of westward expansion and Republicans' anti-slavery stance in 1856 "disrupted the old political order and forced a national reckoning with it," observed author Steve Inskeep, who profiled the Fremonts. The Electoral College would give a numerical advantage to free states—if the trend continued.

Prior to the 1840s, political deals were struck to balance out the slave and free states. Clay's Missouri Compromise of 1820 allowed Missouri to permit slavery and left Maine free. Texas and Florida became slave states, while Iowa and Wisconsin did not. After those admissions, the tally was fifteen slave and fifteen free states. When California came in as a free state in 1850—with new Republicans like Fremont and Lincoln agitating for a halt to slavery's expansion—the imbalance smoldered into an irreconcilable political conflict. Adding fuel to the conflagration was the North's growing population, giving states north of the Mason-Dixon line a majority in the population-based House of Representatives.

Fremont's position to support a railroad of "stupendous magnitude" to the Pacific from the Mississippi—where Eastern lines mostly ended—hyped the idea that new free states would become more accessible, advantaging them over slave states. Indeed, Southern politicians and powerbrokers feared free states would become part of the mushrooming rail network connecting the Northeast to Illinois and the upper Mississippi Valley. This further enraged John C. Calhoun and Jefferson Davis, who saw the trend emerge decades earlier.

But even Fremont's popularity could not dislodge the slightly stronger hold Democrats had on the Electoral College in 1856. Fremont lost the presidency to James Buchanan by sixty electoral votes, preserving the explosive status quo.

As tensions mounted, Lincoln watched his terrible prophecy come true: the country's divided house could not stand the Newtonian economic forces pitting free factory labor against enslaved labor. The Industrial Revolution—even with its attendant evils of men, women, and children working for miserable wages in unsafe conditions— propelled Americans from farms into mostly Northern cities, the new powerhouses of commerce.

There was also an information revolution transpiring: In 1844, Samuel F.B. Morse first wired his telegraph system in the Supreme Court chambers, then situated in the Capitol building. Others had been working on the concept of an electromagnetic telegraph, but it was Morse—working on the invention since the 1830s—who successfully refined it, promoted it, and was awarded the patent to it (after a court battle). News that had taken days or weeks to reach far stretches of the country now took minutes. Papers that previously printed once a week became dailies. Journalists like Henry Villard, who started in German-language newspapers in Chicago and later befriended Lincoln, could "syndicate" stories to several papers at a time. News traveled at the speed of electrons (although messages received at telegraph offices had to be transported by horse riders to towns with no wire connections). Now, everything from fluctuating stock prices to breaking news in Washington could be carried by "wire." Lincoln later camped out in the telegraph room during the war, eager to receive word of the latest battle.

This profusion of infrastructural developments threatened the plantation-based Southern economy. The world was moving so much faster than it had when Lincoln entered politics as a backwoods assemblyman. The Illinois Central, which ran just blocks from his dignified home in Springfield, became the world's *longest* railroad around the close of his debates with Douglas. Rivers like the Mississippi and the Ohio, along with the Great Lakes, were indirectly connected to the East Coast and its proliferating factories. The bountiful prairie's once-impenetrable soil had long been broken and harvested at a scale previously unseen. Agriculture and manufacturing were scaled up with fewer men, horses, and oxen. Productivity was exponential. Grains, limestone, meat, and finished goods now moved effectively east and south—thanks to the canals, roads, and rails that Lincoln had fought for over the previous thirty years.

LINCOLN QUESTIONS THE GROWTH OF THE SLAVE ECONOMY

Slavery's cruel economics continued to darken Lincoln's vision of an economy and geography that could grow with free labor throughout the country, and particularly in the West.

Before the Civil War, more than 60 percent of the nation's wealth was produced by enslaved labor; 4 million humans, "valued" at $2.7 billion, had no say in their economic destiny (to say nothing of the unspeakable torments they endured). An enslaved person could not profit from their labor; someone else "owned" their life and liberty. Taking Jefferson's "pursuit of happiness" to mean that all individuals should be paid for their toil, the American house of commerce could not stand in a divided state. The plantation system was an active contradiction, entrenched from Central Texas to the Lower Mississippi to the Carolinas. Profits from America's foremost cash crop kept the slaveocracy in place. It would not be dislodged without an epic fight.

V

FIGHTING THE FURIOUS FIGHT

Infrastructure During the Civil War

"We are craftsmen and midwives and preachers and peddlers. Black hands built the White House, the seat of our nation's government. The word we. We are not one people but many different people. How can one person speak for this great, beautiful race—which is not one race but many, with a million desires and hopes for our children?"

—Colson Whitehead, *The Underground Railroad*

Lincoln was barely a few minutes into his speech in Waukegan, Illinois, when a fire broke out in the nearby Case Warehouse on April 2, 1860. Fresh from a Chicago federal court trial, he was on the presidential stump when a man burst into the Dickinson Hall assembly, shouting about the emergency.

"He's a liar! This is a Democratic trick," Waukegan's Republican Mayor Elisha Ferry barked, warning the crowd that it was a political ruse to break up the meeting from the opposition.

As it became apparent the fire was real, Lincoln stopped his speech and told the crowd: "Well, we might as well go." He reportedly manned the bucket brigade to little avail as a warehouse full of oats, wheat, and salt was engulfed, causing some $7,000 in damage.

Waukegan was about two hours north of Chicago by rail; Lincoln spoke there at the invitation of local leaders, including Mayor Ferry and abolitionist Henry Blodgett. For an audience that had never seen Lincoln, he initially presented a less-than-impressive figure for an orator of his time. The throng of mostly Yankee-emigrant abolitionist Republicans were eager to hear what the Springfield lawyer had to say on slavery as the standard bearer of their relatively new party; they initially found the lanky politician underwhelming.

"When he began to speak," relates Waukeganite J.W. Hull, "he did not impress me, perhaps because he had a squeak in his voice that was like a dash of cold water." Yet, Hull recalled the pillars of Lincoln's argument: "That we, alone, the United States, with our boasted freedom, gave [slavery] the standing of an institution, and that we did wrong. However, [Lincoln] did not blame the slaveholders; he said that most of them inherited their slaves as chattels or property, and, it seemed could not help themselves."

Repeating his familiar, quasi-biblical call that a house divided could not stand, Lincoln spoke for roughly twenty-five minutes before he realized his audience was truly leaving to fight the warehouse fire a few blocks away. Despite the interruption, Lincoln's words swept through the room like a whirlwind. He didn't take a firm stand on abolition, but an effect was still had on this small trading community, which had been connected to Chicago by rail only five years earlier. Hull continues on how Lincoln's rhetoric animated the crowd:

> The effect on me, at least, and I believe on others, was little short of miraculous. While he was speaking, such was the sledge-hammer force of his logic, that we forgot the humble appearance and the squeaky voice, and were carried away by the man's simple eloquence,

his power of reasoning and his clear exposition of questions we had all debated in our own minds.

Lincoln was making his case to mostly Yankee emigrants to the Midwest—so, to some extent, he was preaching to the choir. He wasn't an abolitionist, but he made a strong argument to men who were trying to establish free commerce on the edge of Euro-American civilization.

Waukegan, a Potawatomi word roughly meaning "Little Fort," was a trading outpost sitting on high bluffs along Lake Michigan. When French traders and missionaries first came to colonize the Western Great Lakes in the early seventeenth century, they traded with the native residents, exchanging guns, gunpowder, and silver for furs. Father Jacques Marquette and trader Louis Jolliet are said to have landed at the Dead River (near present-day Zion), a few miles north of Little Fort, in 1673.

Although there was no reliable river access to the interior, Waukegan and Lake County were blessed with other natural resources: thick oak, hickory, and black walnut forests were in walking distance of its business district, and clay from the bluffs overlooking the lake could be used as raw material for brick making. Like Chicago, it evolved rapidly—eventually becoming the seat of Lake County, which bordered Cook County to the south and Wisconsin to the north. Today, its landscape is blessed with more than 100 glacial lakes, prairies, wetlands, and forests, making it the most biodiverse county in the Prairie State.

After the Treaty of Chicago was signed in 1833, white settlers streamed in from New England, Poland, Ireland, and central Europe. Yankee farmers and merchants formed the top social strata of businesspeople, bringing with them a deep hatred of slavery. Several churches in Waukegan and throughout the county—in towns such as Deerfield, Ivanhoe, and Millburn—were stops on the Underground

Railroad, although nearly no official documentation exists of how many enslaved individuals came though seeking freedom due to the Fugitive Slave Laws.

The moral evil of slavery was apparent to most of Lincoln's audience that day in Waukegan. But little did he know that his words—and the cause he represented—would inspire the vigorous recruitment of soldiers for the war that followed. Some 2,700 men enlisted in the Union army from Lake County, of its total population of 18,000 at the time (the county had only opened to Euro-American settlement less than thirty years earlier). Northern Illinois would supply five infantry regiments and several officers, including Ulysses S. Grant from Galena, about 130 miles to the west. (Galena, a lead mining town, was one of the first in Northern Illinois to be linked to the state's burgeoning rail network.)

Illinois units went on the march, deep into the Confederacy, with Grant and General William Tecumseh Sherman—starting from Grant's first headquarters at Cairo, Illinois, at the confluence of the Ohio and Mississippi. Lake County lost many. The battle up Horseshoe Ridge at Chickamauga in 1863 saw some Lake County men perish; others survived and went on to become important county figures, like Second Lieutenant John Swanbrough, who was Lake County sheriff from 1876–86. Of the hundreds of men in the 96th Illinois Infantry, many marched with Sherman through Atlanta to the sea. Company "D" was mustered in Waukegan.

When Lincoln stayed the night at Waukegan Mayor Ferry's house, it's not known what he discussed with his host and guests. Maybe Lincoln and his hosts celebrated the growing commercial success of the "Chicago Parallel Railroad"—later the Chicago and Northwestern—that would create a vital link between Waukegan and the Windy City. South of Waukegan along its route, a wire mill would produce an innovation essential to Western farming: barbed wire. Later, diverse industries from motor manufacturers to pharmaceutical makers would build globally important businesses on the shores of Lake Michigan. Or perhaps they conversed about the active Underground Railroad running through Waukegan and Lake County churches. Maybe Mayor Ferry recounted how fugitives would be walked from barn to barn by Congregationalists, praying, under cover of darkness or during rainstorms to conceal them from those who would report them under the punitive slave laws.

Although Lincoln was invited back by city fathers, his speech was neither completed nor recovered—he never returned to Waukegan after his election later that year. Yet his pronounced, repeated assaults on the institution of slavery resounded. Lincoln questioned not only the morality of such an entrenched bastion, but the brutal economic institution that underpinned it. The two economic systems—slavery and paid labor—were like Cain and Abel. Only one would survive; only one *should* survive.

THE GREAT HORROR:
WAR BEGINS

Lincoln won the 1860 presidential election partially because two candidates—Stephen Douglas and John Breckenridge—split the Democratic Party vote, along with John Bell, Constitutional Party candidate. Douglas's centrist popular sovereignty platform somewhat appeased Northern voters, but not Southern Democrats, who would not compromise on the future of slavery. His party was fractured. Although Douglas picked up only 12 electoral votes, he garnered nearly 1.4 million popular votes, second only to Lincoln. Had the Democratic Party consolidated into one candidate, the course of history would be much different.

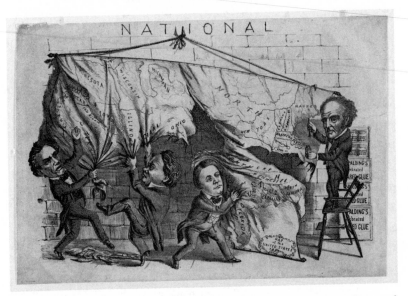

How the nation looked in 1860. The Democratic Party was split. (Library of Congress)

Rejecting Lincoln's anti-slavery (yet not purely abolitionist) stance, the Southern states could not abide "Black Republicanism." On April 12, 1861, Confederate guns fired on Fort Sumter in Charleston Harbor. Many thought the war would brief at its outset, including President Lincoln, who had to sneak into Washington to avoid assassination.

At war's outbreak, the twenty-three free states enjoyed a robust economy and advantages in manufacturing and population. They also had a more advanced rail and water transportation network. The country's longest railroad system allowed Lincoln to move troops from Chicago and the Upper Midwest to Cairo, and further south and east to the mouth of the Tennessee and Cumberland Rivers. Yet, as war unfolded, Lincoln struggled with the Union's incompetent or reluctant generals, the fiercely intelligent Confederate military command, and the logistical challenge of capturing thousands of miles of territory from Virginia to Texas.

The South had its own strategic benefits over the North. In 1861, it had access to all of its ports, controlled most of the Southern Mississippi, and held the crown jewel of marketplaces: New Orleans. At the onset of the conflict, the South could still ship cotton to England for income and supply its nimble troops through rail lines that did not exclusively depend on Northern connections to operate. Though distinctly disadvantaged in manpower, the Confederacy also had the geographic upper hand: Most battles would be fought on Southern soil across mountains, rivers, piedmonts, and forests. Southern soldiers knew where best to ford rivers, hide in the woods, and resupply their troops. At first, no Union river traffic could move south of Vicksburg, which became a formidable fortress commanding Mississippi River bluffs, amply armed with cannons that rained hell upon river boats. There was no continuous rail line connecting the industrial heartland with Southern ports. The Union army had to conquer the river one well-fortified citadel at a time.

The South also enjoyed a perversely symbiotic connection to a global economy; it was not entirely cut off from European markets. Global consumers and producers benefitted too well to divest from the enslaved economy. Cotton prices had fallen to 10 cents a pound—by a factor of three from 1790 to 1860, making cotton clothing much more affordable for an increasingly industrialized world—a cost advantage that made it cheaper than wool. Coupled with a (brutally wrought) 400 percent productivity gain in cotton picking from 1800 to 1860, the South was going to battle to preserve its enormous and inhumane profit margins. Edward Baptist, who studied the slave labor economy, describes how the cotton profits created a powerful political incentive:

> And those gains created a huge pie, from which many other people across the world took a slice. Lower real cotton prices passed on gains in the form of capital invested in more efficient factory

equipment, higher wages for the new industrial working class [in the mills] and revenue for factory owners, enslavers and governments. Thus productivity gains in the cotton fields also translated into benefits for consumers of cloth.

"Big Cotton" in 1860, in terms of its size and importance relative to the US economy, was an enterprise analogous to automaking in the 1960s. It brought capital to Southern plantations from financiers backing English and New England textile mills; and, of course, "the Northern economy's industrial sector was built on the backs of enslaved people," an irony Baptist calls out. Capitalists across the cotton supply chain resisted impairing the profits from this industry. It had a momentum that sought expansion like a natural force. Southerners envisioned its commerce headed West. Lincoln, his fellow Republicans, and some Democrats foresaw it dying a natural death of attrition, freeing the West from the stain of enslaved labor and allowing farmers to own the land they tilled. Nevertheless, Southerners embracing the "King Cotton" economic model rightly suspected that Northern state legislators were eager to impose tariffs on their exports, thus slashing profits. In a commercial system that favored one economic model over most others, hurting cotton profits beckoned financial ruin for plantation owners, slave traders, middlemen, and clothing manufacturers.

What the North had in abundance, other than its larger population of free laborers, was infrastructure: Rail and telegraph networks connected Washington to all major points north of the Mason-Dixon line. Rail did not extend far west beyond the Mississippi, but it didn't have to: Most of the war was fought east of the Mississippi and south of the Ohio River. The North could also mass produce nearly everything it needed. New England was home to a robust gun and armaments industry; commodities like grain, coal, and pig iron were shipped via the Illinois Central to Cairo. The tiny river town became a key staging point for General Ulysses S. Grant's battalions, soldiered by tens of thousands of volunteering Midwesterners.

Moreover, the 1860 rail network favored shipping commodities— a thoroughly diverse mix from meat and grain to coal and timber— east to west, *then* south. A rail system connecting the Wisconsin forests to Chicago favored the Upper Midwest, which supplied nearly everything a modern army needed. In 1860, historian William Cronon writes, "all roads led to Chicago." Of the nation's 30,000 miles of railroad track, Illinois had more than 2,500 miles. Chicago formed the eastern terminus of the network, supplied by the productive fields of eastern Iowa, Illinois coal mines, and timber lands adjacent to the Upper Mississippi. Thus what the Union lacked in competent generals in the war's first years, it made up for in the logistical ability to provision itself through an established, growing supply chain. The North out-manufactured the South in armaments, processed food, clothing, ships, wagons, and the latest technology of advanced warfare.

The Union also had the growing power and reach of a communications network—telegraphy—established years before rail linked coast to coast. Samuel F.B. Morse developed Morse code in the 1830s during the canal era. He spent decades convincing the infrastructure-shy federal government to set up a telegraph network; his demonstration of the technology, the "What Hath God Wrought" message from Washington to Baltimore in 1840, secured some $30,000 in federal funding. After that, the world shrunk as a combination of telegraph messages and horse riders conveyed through the new Associated Press "wire service" news of the Mexican War to Washington. Telegraphy quickly made the legendary Pony Express mostly obsolete.

By 1860, the passage of the Pacific Telegraph Act would eventually extend lines from the East Coast to as far as Nevada. San Francisco was connected the following year. Abraham Lincoln received the first "cable" from the Golden Gate city, a political message:

> On Oct. 24, 1861, with the push of a button, California's chief justice, Stephen J. Field, wired a message from San Francisco to President Abraham Lincoln in Washington, congratulating him on the transcontinental telegraph's completion that day. He added the wish that it would be a "means of strengthening the attachment which binds both the East and the West to the Union."

Lincoln, intensely devoted to telegraph missives throughout the war, cradled the technology—and others he supported—like few other presidents. As chief executive (and an inventor himself), he was also chief innovation officer, and often visited the Naval Yard on the Potomac to see the latest weapon or ship technology. As much as any other significance it held, the Civil War was a technological arms race. Armies needed to move faster, more efficiently. The time-consuming muzzle-loading process needed to be streamlined. Over time, it evolved from gunpowder horns and cumbersome, hand-stuffed lead bullets to factory-made cartridges and rifles that could fire repeatedly. Lincoln encouraged such improvements, though most of the major innovations in the Civil War came near its end—and couldn't yet be produced on a mass scale. He regularly "inspected" new armament innovations and met with inventors and generals who championed them.

Politically, Lincoln was deeply aware that he garnered less than half of the popular vote in 1860; more than 60 percent of it went to other candidates. Attitudes in Lincoln's own state were more reflective of the institutional racism that propped up the economy and culture of the entire country. "Black laws" deprived freed Black people of exercising their full constitutional and economic rights. In the decade before the Civil War, both Illinois and Indiana changed their state constitutions to restrict freemen from settling in their states. Often, Black farmers would be required to post egregious bonds—ranging from $100 to $1,000 (an outrageous sum, even at the time)—signed by white residents, "attest[ing] to their good behavior." Even Illinois, deemed a free state by the 1787 Northwest Ordinance, passed a law in 1819 requiring Black folks to register and obtain a certificate in the county they resided. "Every negro without this certificate was considered a runaway slave," according to Grace Humphrey's early history of Illinois. The Dred Scott decision, in concert with the Fugitive Slave Law, made it clear that African Americans were not entitled to the same legal rights as white Americans. Many in the Northern states still believed them to be property.

DOUGLAS REVERSES COURSE TO BACK LINCOLN AND THE UNION

Scarcely a month after Confederate cannons roared in South Carolina, Lincoln's rival Stephen Douglas was on the stump again—this time *supporting* his old debating opponent. On May 1, the Little Giant took the podium at the Chicago Wigwam where Lincoln had received the Republican nomination a year earlier. Stalwart Democrat Douglas, who incensed Lincoln with his Kansas-Nebraska Act, did his best to trumpet the moral high ground: "There can be no neutrals in *this* war. There can be none but *patriots and traitors!*"

The stout senator wobbled as he let loose his hammering rhetoric. It would be his last speech, as Douglas succumbed to typhoid fever on June 3, 1861. His last words were an urgent missive: "Telegraph the president and let the column move on. *Death! Death! Death!*"

A year after he died, Douglas's Chicago Oakenwald estate acquired a dark history: It became the site for "Camp Douglas." Confederate prisoners sent directly north to Chicago on the Illinois Central were interned at the notorious site. What became the largest military prison in the North—holding up to 26,000 men—was a festering patch of hell, as there was never enough space in the camp for the sheer numbers of prisoners captured by Grant's forces in Tennessee. More than 4,000 Rebel soldiers died on the Chicago estate of the man who soft-pedalled slavery as a matter of self-determination. The South had a counterpart, it should be noted: Andersonville Prison, which was equal or superior in its brutality against Union prisoners of war.

Sanitation was appalling at Camp Douglas, where one in seven died from the pestilent conditions. Countless prisoners, not given much—if any—medical care died of the same disease that felled Douglas. The contemporary water system was hopelessly foul, as the Chicago River was a turgid channel of offal and excrement that ran directly into Lake Michigan, the city's main water supply. When summer heat blazed down on the city, typhoid and cholera ravaged it. Deadly waves of infectious disease were not unique to Camp Douglas: More soldiers died of "camp fevers" than battlefield wounds in a war that took more than 700,000 lives. And there were no cures for the many maladies. Public health professionals still blamed epidemics on "miasmas" or bad air; the germ theory of disease, large-scale public sanitation, and the antibiotic revolution was about eight decades away.

Camp Douglas was more than what the US Sanitary Commission called "a soil reeking with miasmic accretions." It was an epic failure of infrastructure that plagued nearly every city at the time, exacerbated by substandard housing and a punishing climate. Theoretically, Chicago had an abundance of fresh water, but it was consistently polluted—lacking a viable sewer and filtration system. The filtering wetlands that bordered the lake had long been eliminated; the city was literally built on mud and wet soil.

Progress cursed the humble, sluggish Chicago River. What had become a superhighway of commerce from the 1848 opening of the I&M Canal turned into a putrescent open sewer, receiving everything from animal carcasses to storm water. Flowing directly into the tideless lake—and drinking water intakes—it took thousands of lives over the years. Not until 1900, when engineers "reversed" the course of the river (that is, made a "deep cut" into the limestone bedrock and ancient glacial valley to create a "Sanitary and Ship Canal"), did Chicago begin to address its water problems. It was no small coincidence that the new, wider canal—parallel to the I&M Canal—began only blocks from where Camp Douglas once stood. Until the Chicago Metropolitan Water and Reclamation District created modern sewage treatment systems in the 1930s, the city's waste flowed into the Illinois and down the Mississippi River (starting in 1900). St. Louis residents, realizing that they would be the recipients of the Windy City's effluent, sued Chicago in 1900 when the canal surreptitiously opened—but by the time the suit got to a judge, fetid water was flowing south and could not be stopped. The Sanitary District of Chicago, created in 1889 (now called the Metropolitan Water Reclamation District of Greater Chicago), later built the Stickney water treatment complex of seven plants along the canal in the 1930s (and later expanded into a larger system of six plants and 22 pumping stations). The complex became the largest such water reclamation facility in the world.

Chicago, along with most major industrialized cities, gradually built the infrastructure it needed to address water filtration and sanitation, but such efforts are not universal. Many large cities in developing countries still struggle with polluted water that yearns for modern public works. (As for Douglas, the park named after him on the South Side of Chicago would be renamed "Douglass" Park after abolitionist leaders Frederick and Anna-Murray Douglass, as this goes to press.)

RAILROAD MEN AND ENGINEERS BECOME GENERALS

Since most extensive railroad networks were in the North, it was no surprise that Lincoln tapped railroad executives and engineers for their perceived expertise. Some, like General George McClellan—who proved to be an ineffective and sheepish warrior—had been Illinois Central executives. Military engineers were also well represented in the top ranks of both armies, from the Union's Henry Halleck and George Meade, defender of Gettysburg, to the Confederacy's Robert E. Lee, Joseph Johnston, and P.G.T. Beauregard.

Union army engineers were often called on for their expertise in building and rebuilding railroad bridges, constructing forts and breastworks, digging tunnels, laying explosives, and fording rivers. Some of their engineering was stunningly innovative in its conception, since there were no steel or iron bridges over the many rivers in the South. In 1862, six pontoon bridges were built to cross the Rappahannock River in Virginia under withering enemy fire. A 2,000-foot bridge was constructed across the James River in 1864 as the Union Army of the Potomac marched toward Petersburg.

In the early years of the war, the North—even with its logistics of transport and telegraph networks—was often no match for the superior tactical brilliance of Southern Generals, who could often move troops quickly and to greater advantage on home turf. Often outmanned and outgunned, the Confederate tacticians were nimble in movement and quick to seize any strategic advantage. And their numbers were constantly overestimated by Union generals, particularly McClellan, who many a time were too reluctant to move their massive armies.

The one exception was General Ulysses S. Grant, who bulldogged his way down the Mississippi Valley to split the Confederacy, take its most vital ports, and then push east—winning the war. Grant worked his engineers and soldiers beyond their limits as he employed any opportunity to move them forward, repeatedly at great cost.

GRANT AT VICKSBURG

Little of his undistinguished service in the Mexican War prepared Grant for what was needed on the Western front during the Civil War. In prior service, he didn't have the commission to move tens of thousands of troops down and across massive rivers like the Mississippi. Rather, during the Mexican War, Grant answered to commanding officers like Zachary Taylor and Winfield Scott—who were reasonably competent and captured huge swaths of territory in a relatively short period of time. To boot, there wasn't much engineering needed (relative to the Civil War) to defeat Mexican General Santa Ana.

Emerging from military retirement and his father's leather goods business in Galena, Illinois, Grant was a failed farmer and a lackluster merchant. Although a highly skilled horseman, he was known to take wild, unhinged rides under the influence of his nemesis: alcohol. Normally taciturn, unassuming, and dogged, Grant disdained attention and wore a private's uniform even when he was a top commanding general.

In appearance, Grant was the opposite of the Napoleonic George McClellan, who spent a great deal of energy looking the part of a dashing, nineteenth-century officer. Even so, Grant had an innate sense of what it took to become the ultimate warrior—prosecuting "total" warfare that focused on destroying the enemy's will, supply chain, and ability to replenish the staples of war. Reviled and envied by other generals—including many above him in rank—Grant applied every tool he had to win. His ability to make war ruthlessly all-consuming was formidable.

A most perfect example of human creativity, experimental engineering, and brutal persistence intersecting in operatic fashion is Grant's repeated attempt to capture and control Vicksburg, the city that dominated the lowest reaches of the Mississippi. The town was on a promontory where the river took a sharp bend. It would have been an ideal place for a medieval castle, with the quirky river acting as a moat. Vicksburg was also connected by rail to Jackson, Mississippi, to the east and was a gateway to Baton Rouge and New Orleans.

Lincoln knew this city, having been through this river chokepoint four times; it doubtless stuck—like trying to ride a liquid prairie road in the spring—in his mind. Vicksburg was an essential strategic junction: river traffic needed to pass through the notorious river bend to reach New Orleans. More importantly, to take Vicksburg would be to cut the Confederacy in two. Raiders in Missouri, Arkansas, Louisiana, and Texas would find a horrendously daunting challenge in resupplying from the East because there was no bridge spanning the river that far south, where the river was wide and the delta shores wet and impassable. There were no railroads yet going west from the southwestern Confederate states—California was nearly 2,000 miles away—so opening the Mississippi meant the Union army could focus its efforts on Richmond and the Eastern front.

Grant was a man of singular focus when he chose to be, resourceful and undeterred by the elements—political or geographical. In that way, he had much in common with Lincoln. Not much of a merchant and a questionable officer in 1861, President Lincoln and the Union army gave him a second chance with a significant command, but few thought much of Grant when he started down the Mississippi into Tennessee.

The first year of the war went abysmally for the Union, whose army beat retreats in the First Battle of Bull Run (Manassas); Wilson's Creek and Lexington, Missouri; and Ball's Bluff, Virginia, where many federal troops drowned trying to cross the icy waters of the Potomac. Up against sterling Confederate tacticians like Stonewall Jackson and Joseph Johnston, the Union forces pulled back to reinforce Washington, DC, only a stone's throw from Virginia.

Success against the Southern rebels finally came in 1862 when Grant pushed his way into Tennessee, taking Forts Henry and Donelson at the mouths of the Tennessee and Cumberland Rivers. At Fort Donelson, he earned the nickname "Unconditional Surrender" Grant—attracting the attention of the president, who defended the general against stories of his intoxication and persistent sniping by other commanders. Lincoln empowered Grant to execute an overall strategy of shutting down the Confederacy's Western front, part of an "Anaconda" plan conceived by Winfield Scott, who advised Lincoln at the war's outset to choke off the rebels by enveloping it. The wartime president commissioned Grant not only to shut down the Confederacy's access to the river, New Orleans, and the Gulf of Mexico, but to open up the vital route for the Union. The railroads that paralleled the river would also be freed to operate for the North. Such invaluable infrastructure would be a turning point for Lincoln—if Grant could pull off the coup, deep in enemy territory.

After winning the battle of Pea Ridge in Arkansas on March 8, 1862, the Union army was able to move south and east—to begin its assault on southern Mississippi. March 8 and 9 saw the new ironclad ships *Monitor* and *Merrimack* fight to a draw at Hampton Roads,

Virginia. Both ships were of a new chapter in naval warfare that introduced heavy armor plating, but the Union's *Monitor* had an additional innovation: a cannon turret that could turn 360 degrees, giving it more flexibility when firing, much like modern tanks. James Eads, engineer and salvage diver, helped design and build the *Monitor*. (After the war, he designed one of the most famous bridges across the Mississippi to St. Louis.)

Shortly after the iron clads' square-off, Grant secured a victory at Shiloh (Pittsburg Landing) on the Tennessee River, barely fending off a Confederate counterattack. Grant's army was saved by some 25,000 reinforcements—in addition to the nearly 40,000 troops he had when the battle began—but casualties were heavy. More than 20,000 soldiers across both armies were killed, wounded, or missing, one the war's biggest blood baths. Ten days later, Union gunships under Admiral David Farragut's command took New Orleans; Grant was pulled back to the Mississippi, concentrating on Vicksburg so as to completely free the river to Union traffic.

The road for the Northern army would be filled with misery in late 1862 and early 1863. Despite a Union victory at Antietam, the Confederacy won Mechanicsville, Fredericksburg, and the Second Battle of Bull Run, blocking multiple Union attempts to advance to Richmond. The North was disheartened and turning against Lincoln by January 1, 1863, when his executive order for the Emancipation Proclamation became effective (having been issued on September 22 the year previous after the stalemate at Antietam)—freeing enslaved individuals in Confederate states to join the Union cause. Frederick Douglass, among countless other critics, attacked the Proclamation for not going as far as to abolish slavery, which did not happen until 1865 with the Thirteenth Amendment. The Emancipation Proclamation—which enabled the Union army to recruit enslaved men—did not free anyone in the border states.

Grant started planning his ultimate attack on Vicksburg early in 1863, conferring with his commanders and engineers on the best way to conquer its river fortress—which posed some of the war's most perilous military challenges. Vicksburg itself was perched on high bluffs and surrounded by water on three sides. The Confederate army was well fortified by cannons and protected troops sheltered in clay grottos on every side of the citadel. Delta muck, poisonous snakes, and tributaries like the Yazoo, throttled with low-hanging branches and turgid streams, cut off alternate approaches. Full-sized gunboats could not be run anywhere but up and down the Mississippi, where Confederate cannons mercilessly pummeled anything coming around its bend, as they did many times when Union gunboats tried to run the gauntlet.

Grant and his engineers tried multiple tactics, which became agonizing, time-consuming failures during attempts to breach the geographic advantages Vicksburg conferred the rebel army. On the Louisiana side, Grant endeavored to cut a channel from Lake Providence to deepen streams that flowed into the Mississippi—thinking it possible to then go east and downriver from Vicksburg, drawing supplies from New Orleans. After two months, it became apparent that plan was a bust.

Grant also attempted cutting a levee above Vicksburg that would allow troops to float down the Yazoo tributary, which would put his army right on top of the city. Gunboats made it to the point where they encountered Fort Pemberton, which had commanded the river because it was surrounded by water. Grant abandoned that plan, since he could move no farther. A final engineered solution—moving gunboats on small streams leading into Vicksburg—proved to be a near fiasco, according to Bruce Catton: "the fleet narrowly escaped destruction. It finally got back to the Mississippi, but it demonstrated that this route to Vicksburg was no good."

By May of 1863, Grant revised his plan to concentrate on logistics. One of his main problems was getting enough supplies south to where he could keep an army working around Vicksburg. Union troops built roads and bridges while Admiral David Porter moved his gunboats closer to the city. As Grant fought skirmishes to the south, he abruptly moved his army fifty miles east to the state's capital at Jackson. The move to capture the city bewildered Confederate General Pemberton—and Union commanders like Joseph Hooker—but revealed Grant's genius in cutting off Confederate supplies and rail connections. It also blocked General Pemberton from reinforcing Vicksburg, which was Grant's goal. What had appeared to many to be a distraction was a stunningly brilliant feint. Grant received reinforcements from Tennessee, which eventually controlled North-South rail lines of the Mississippi Central, Mobile, and Ohio. Grant hoped that Jackson and Vicksburg would be effectively blockaded from the Confederate army to the east. After several smaller battles, Grant returned to Vicksburg in late May, where he attacked again, retreated, and rethought his battle plan.

With Confederate forces unable to regroup or resupply, Grant dug in at the foot of Vicksburg with 75,000 troops, who laid siege to the city in an unrelenting barrage. By July 4, the starving army and city residents, pounded with seemingly endless fusillades from below in the punishing heat, surrendered. Grant was generous in his terms: he allowed the rebel soldiers to go home with a single side arm and personal possessions. While he could've chosen to ship some 37,000 soldiers to nightmarish prisons like Camp Douglas, he wanted to spare them humiliation and remove them from combat, freeing Union troops to head east.

Lincoln heralded the victory, redeeming Grant from his status as the "butcher" of Shiloh: "The Father of Rivers again goes unvexed to the sea." Freeing control of the entire length of the nation's Western highway to the Gulf, the General cleaved the Confederacy in half. Cattle and other supplies from Texas and Arkansas could not reach the eastern half of rebel territory. Their largest port was completely in Union hands. Lincoln had never met his fellow Illinoisan at this point in the war, but he sent Grant a letter admitting he was wrong to doubt the general's strategy to attack Jackson. In contrast to Lincoln's incompetent eastern generals, Grant was a winner with a combination of pluck, resourcefulness, and resilience that appealed to the president's nature. Grant later became Lincoln's top general, although it would be another two years before Grant reached Appomattox. In a Napoleonic comparison, biographer Ron Chernow called Vicksburg Grant's "masterpiece, the pre-eminent campaign waged by any general during the war."

THE FURY CONTINUES

With Lee's defeat at Gettysburg, the slaughterous tide of the war had turned, albeit slowly and tortuously. The comprehensive war machine piloted by Grant and William Tecumseh Sherman would concentrate their horror on dismembering the Confederacy infrastructure. Telegraph and rail lines were disabled. Farms were burned. The "March to the Sea" in Georgia cut off the last of the Southern ports. Engineer-generals like Herman Haupt moved Union troops to battlefronts with increasing efficiency and success.

Although the Union army repelled General Lee's bold incursion into its territory, Union commanding generals were once again hobbled by indecision and reluctance. After the victory of Gettysburg, which resulted in a shocking 55,000 casualties, General George Meade refused to chase and execute what was left of Lee's impaired army. An incensed Haupt boarded a train to Washington, urging his commanders to pursue Lee, but Meade rebuffed him. Having been instrumental in repairing roads, bridges, and rail lines to ensure the Union victory, Haupt recounts in his autobiography: "if Meade had acted [to chase and destroy Lee's Army] . . . Lee would have doubtless have been captured and the Rebellion ended."

VI

THE MORRILL ACT

Creating an Intellectual Infrastructure

"Please don't misunderstand. We had been mothers, fathers. Had been husbands of many years, men of import, who had come here, that first day, accompanied by crowds so vast and sorrowful that, surging forward to hear the oration, they had damaged fences beyond repair."

—George Saunders, *Lincoln in the Bardo*

I t was near midnight when Lincoln arrived to meet Professor Jonathan Baldwin Turner, one of the most distinguished academics of his state, who happened to sport a truly biblical beard. The scholar and progressive reformer had come from Illinois College in Jacksonville, where Stephen Douglas got his start in local politics. Lincoln always warmed when Prairie State friends came to visit. They brought needed relief from the war, and from domestic turmoil at Lincoln's cottage residence, the Soldiers' Home, where he escaped the swampy misery of a Washington summer. At the hillside retreat he could be himself, tell stories, and hear what was happening back home.

"Everything was doleful and discouraging," as Turner greeted his friend, who was reeling from yet another Union defeat that had emboldened the Confederate army to cross the Potomac and threaten Washington.

Despite the dismal state of the country, the old friends chuckled while reminiscing over one of Lincoln's many jobs before his law career—as a field hand harvesting crops for a widowed neighbor. Lincoln first encountered Turner when he read one of the professor's books on English, likely acquired when he was a freelance farmhand in the early 1830s. Turner recalled in his memoirs that despite the war's turmoil and the president's frustration with his generals, Lincoln "had never stood out before me in such grand, overwhelming proportions as during that midnight interview."

While vying for his party's presidential nomination in 1860, Lincoln talked with Turner after speaking in Decatur, Illinois. Lincoln thought he would receive the nomination, and without hesitation, addressed one of Turner's requests: a national plan to establish federally supported universities in every state.

"If I am [nominated]," Lincoln told Turner, "I will sign *your* bill for state universities."

Shortly thereafter, Turner met Stephen Douglas on a train to Peoria. The Democratic presidential candidate also pledged his support of Turner's legislation. Turner was in the rare position of support from two leading, opposing candidates before either was even elected.

Turner was known as an "evangelist of ideas" in Central Illinois. Well-versed in biblical history and literature, he saw industrial and liberal arts education as a societal necessity. As a botanist, he championed the establishment of agricultural research stations. The polymath was also a Christian missionary and a student of classical literature at Yale. A professor at the newly formed Illinois College in 1833, Turner promoted the planting and propagation of Osage Orange trees, which acted as durable, natural fences before the days of barbed wire (also invented and manufactured in Illinois). Thousands of Osage Orange trees still grow throughout the Midwest. Others of his ideas were less popular, however—not for non-sectarian industrial colleges, nor his abolitionist views. Enemies burned down his farm in 1853. Yet Turner promoted his educational opinions with a religious zeal, addressing the needs of the growing "working class."

Like many of his fellow New Englanders who moved to the Prairie State, Turner was a vocal abolitionist, editing an anti-slavery paper in Jacksonville and assisting in the Underground Railroad. It was a perilous role in Central Illinois, since many of its settlers had arrived from slave states and despised abolitionists. Former residents of the Southern states were often sympathetic to slavery in pre-Civil War times, even supporting the Black Codes that prevented free families from settling and farming in Illinois.

Like Turner, Vermonter Justin Smith Morrill had several things in common with Lincoln. The well-read son of a blacksmith, he could not afford a formal education and was largely self-educated.

A portrait of Justin Smith Morrill. (Library of Congress)

He started out young as a store clerk, later buying his own general merchandise shop and retiring wealthy at thirty-eight. A supporter of college education for the masses, Morrill brought an open mind and an almost scientific view of progress to Congress.

Like many of his contemporaries, Morrill observed that growing certain crops—like tobacco—resulted in decreased agricultural productivity over time. In the late eighteenth and early nineteenth centuries, farmers and large-scale planters typically just bought more land in the face of this issue. This did nothing to solve the problem of soil being perennially depleted of nutrients. Robust agricultural science did not exist on a meaningful scale, so most farmers were unaware of what would increase productivity. Indeed, Morrill observed that tobacco planting in Vermont declined by a million bushels from 1840 to 1850; in the tobacco-rich state of Virginia, 18 million fewer pounds of the crop were grown than during the previous decade. Contemporary practices were not increasing productivity—a major problem in a growing country. A concerned Morrill asked the same question as a contemporary policymaker and farmer: "Does not our general system of agriculture foreshadow ultimate decay? If so, is it within our constitutional power and duty to provide an incidental remedy?"

As was the case throughout the first half of the nineteenth century, the burden to create a research and development infrastructure largely fell on the states, which had neither the capital nor the broad public support to scale up agricultural research to a meaningful degree. States *did* have millions of acres, so land grants formed the basis of their capital. Moreover, states had a handful of agricultural colleges and "normal schools" to educate teachers, but not nearly enough to meet population needs that were burgeoning due to expanding cultivation and commerce.

Historians often dispute whether Morrill was working with Turner or had developed his land-grant plans independently—but documents show that Turner first contacted Morrill in 1855, a year *after* Turner introduced a resolution in Illinois for land-grant colleges. It was Morrill's first year as a Vermont representative. The House of the Illinois General Assembly, led by Lincoln's friend Elihu Washburne, had presented resolutions calling for "the establishment of industrial universities for the encouragement of practical and general education among the people in several states of the Union." Behind this legislative directive was the Illinois Industrial League, which Turner founded to promote the idea of public universities—specifically, the institution that would become the University of Illinois at Urbana-Champaign. Turner had extensively published and promoted his Industrial University proposal prior to Morrill's introduction of his land-grant bill in Congress. One Turner paper—"A Plan for an Industrial University for the State of Illinois"—was published in 1851.

Although the nation had its share of established private colleges in the nineteenth century (Harvard, Princeton, and Yale, to name a few), many had limited curricula, were dominated by specific religious denominations, and denied enrollment to students of lower classes. The idea of Washburne's "industrial" universities was to promote widespread education in the practical arts, such as engineering ("mechanics") and agriculture, to a broad class of Americans. If the nation was to make agriculture and industry more efficient and productive for a growing population, it would need institutions to provide the necessary research infrastructure. Canals, roads, and rail lines alone would not sustain steady growth.

There were a handful of land-grant colleges operating before the Civil War, but only a few states supported them. Two notable examples were the Michigan Agricultural College, now Michigan State, and the Agricultural College of Pennsylvania, now Penn State. In 1855, both were state chartered.

Education became a linchpin for universal economic progress during the war. When Frederick Douglass first called on Lincoln, the president ushered him immediately into his private chamber. Besides allegiance (to differing degrees) to the cause of ending slavery, the two men had one powerful bond: education. Both thought universal public education was essential for the country. Douglass, who learned to read while enslaved despite laws and cultural dictums prohibiting it, repeatedly promoted the connection between freedom and democracy: "Education means emancipation . . . It means light and liberty . . . Once you learn to read, you'll be forever free." Douglass wrote, "Knowledge makes a man unfit to be a slave." Sadly, the majority of colleges did not admit African Americans or women prior to the Civil War or immediately after it. Public higher education, such as it was in the middle of the nineteenth century, was not available to most who lived in the country.

During the Civil War, the bill that would become the Morrill Act creating public land-grant colleges hit a few roadblocks before it became law. Although Turner and other advocates had forwarded extensive materials to Morrill in 1857 and 1858, the legislative push was hobbled in committees. President James Buchanan vetoed Morrill's first land-grant bill in 1859.

Morrill's first speech laying out the principles of the proposal—delivered on the floor of the House of Representatives on April 20, 1858—argued that the United States had already made provisions for patents, internal improvements, and land grants to railroads. It seemed eminently logical that the federal government should do the same for land-grant educational institutions:

> Our naval architecture is a subject of national pride. Our engineers are doomed to no merely local fame. Our agricultural elements are beyond the reach of competition. Yet, while we be in the advance of the civilized world in many of the useful arts, it is a humiliating fact that we are far in the rear of the best husbandry in Europe; and notwithstanding, riding here and there on an elevated spot, our tendency is still downward.

Morrill was indignant that the country that produced the steel plow and the mechanized harvester was lagging Europe in cultivation and livestock breeding. Citing plentiful statistics that showed declining agricultural yields throughout the states, he judged the current system "unproductive and ruinous." The contemporaneous agricultural practices simply exhausted the soil of essential nutrients, although there was little fundamental knowledge or applied science to solve the problem. Farmers knew it by observation alone. And annexing new territories and creating states would not address the "exhaustion of the soil," either. New lands to cultivate would acquire the same issue of soil becoming "depleted and stationery." With rapidly expanding populations demanding their own land to till, the response—or lack of one—from the United States government was *unsustainable* (although Morrill does not use that word).

Morrill was not able to get his bill passed under President James Buchanan and the Democrats, but one point of his argument must have made an impression. At the time of his 1858 speech, some 25 million acres had been granted to the states for railroads, creating 9,000 miles of track. Why not also dedicate public lands to non-military colleges that would educate students on improving agricultural yields? Was that not in the best interests of national commerce, and in the spirit of Jefferson and Jackson, nonetheless? Morrill attempted to appeal to his Democrat colleagues, and he did not use an exclusively soft approach. Many of those Democrats in power, like Stephen Douglas, made a fortune from speculating with the lands they acquired—creating a "prolific source of corruption." With an inventory of more than 1 million acres of public land, even after the donation for colleges, Morrill concluded that the US government would still be "the largest landholder in the world, while confessedly we are not the best farmers. Let it never be said we are the 'greatest and meanest of mankind.'"

It would be four more years before Morrill had presidential support and the votes to pass his land-grant act. Its passage addressed far more than agricultural improvement: The Morrill Act indirectly tackled class warfare and economic inequality. Those Euro-Americans who had started out as subsistence yeoman farmers could "ascend the ladder"—Lincoln's phrase—and become farm managers, doctors, engineers, and even lawyers. More wealth would be distributed to the middle class, making a difference in America's rigidly stratified society; in New York City, for example, some 61 percent of wealth was held by 1 percent of the population. Higher education would massively contribute to flattening the curve of income distribution, particularly as the country moved beyond the Gilded Age into the Progressive Era and the twentieth century.

LINCOLN SUPPORTS MEDICAL RESEARCH INNOVATIONS DURING WAR

Lincoln's personal and intellectual conflicts with his cabinet members are well-known; perhaps less known is that he appointed like-minded officials who worked in the background to support his agenda of innovation and research. When he appointed William Alexander Hammond as Surgeon General on April 25, 1862, he did so over the objection of Edwin Stanton, his autocratic Secretary of War, who had just fired Hammond's predecessor. After only a year in the Union army, Hammond had been promoted to its top rank of medical officers; a brilliant researcher and surgeon, he had graduated from New York University at the age of twenty and taught at the University of Maryland at Baltimore, becoming one of the first specialists in neurology.

Lincoln's appointment of Hammond as Surgeon General led to several important Army Medical Corps reforms. Hammond expanded the number of hospitals and established the Army Medical Museum, which later became the Armed Forces Institute of Pathology. He modernized the use of Army ambulance wagons and banned calomel, an ineffective mercury compound that was harmfully administered as a "miracle drug" in the nineteenth century. Battlefield mortality dropped significantly during his tenure, although medicine was still in the dark ages: Off the battlefield, some 400,000 soldiers died of diseases. In camps, they succumbed to dysentery—which felled 95,000 combatants on both sides—as well as typhoid, pneumonia, measles, malaria, and tuberculosis. Most doctors were unaware that unsanitary, cramped conditions perpetuated such maladies, caused by microbes they did not even know existed. Air or waterborne disease caused by microorganisms such as bacteria and viruses would not become established as scientific knowledge until near the end of the century.

Hammond's founding of the Medical Museum was a landmark in the history of science. Under its first curator, John Brinton, the army collected thousands of tissue samples for later research. The Surgeon General's seminal 1862 "Circular No. 2" pamphlet provided for the Medical Museum's establishment, laying out the importance of pathology for future research and development: "illustrating the injuries and diseases that produce death or disability during war, and thus affording materials for precise methods of study or problems regarding the diminution of mortality and alleviation of suffering in armies."

In the field, Hammond asked army surgeons to collect "sanitary, topographical, medical and surgical reports, details of cases, essays and the results of investigations and inquiries," all of which formalized medical reporting. The Institute also became a global storage facility and clearinghouse for pathology samples: At its height, it held some 55 million glass slides and 500,000 tissue samples, and would later process some 50,000 research requests globally every year. Critically, the Institute held lung samples of the 1918 flu pandemic, which killed between 50 million and 100 million people. That one collection helped researchers study the virus in detail and attempt to answer the question of why it was so deadly. Future great institutions such as the National Institutes of Health, Walter Reed Army Hospital, and Centers for Disease Control can all trace their lineage to Civil War Army research facility.

In addition to grim yet lifesaving procedures such as embalming and amputation, and the novel 1860s use of disinfectant in army hospitals—which Lincoln personally endorsed—other reforms Hammond undertook began the centralized collection of research and formation of a network of hospitals, such as Walter Reed. The Army Medical Museum—at one time housed in Ford's Theatre, the site of Lincoln's assassination—would even hold the bullet that killed him, fragments of his skull, and pieces of his hair. Army Museum staff performed Lincoln's autopsy.

After the war, Hammond became professor of nervous and mental diseases at Bellevue Hospital in New York, writing several medical texts and founding the American Neurological Association. He died in 1900. And although the Armed Forces Institute of Pathology closed in 2011, its legacy lives on in mammoth institutions such as the Bethesda Naval Hospital and the myriad Institutes of Health. Its foundational research contributed to countless advances in infectious diseases and medical research.

AIDING INNOVATION ON A LARGER SCALE

The Morrill Act and land-grant institutions were built on a prairie culture of innovation. Turner's original 1850 "Plan for a State University for the Industrial Classes" resulted from more than twenty years of research while he was at Illinois College, a few miles west of Springfield. As he witnessed technology's role in the opening of prairie lands to larger-scale agriculture, he realized the need for higher education that would support its development much more comprehensively.

Beginning in the 1830s, bootstrapping inventors like John Deere and Cyrus McCormick revolutionized agriculture in quantum leaps with their steel plows and agricultural innovations, but the steam age demanded more. A new class of farmer-merchants, trades people, and professional middle-class Americans—like Lincoln—was emerging. The more enlightened politicians of the time agreed with Professor Turner, gradually pledging their support over a period of more than two decades. Illinois Senator Lyman Trumbull, a friend and supporter of Lincoln's, wrote to Turner of his idea: "I have re-read the pamphlet in regard to industrial universities. The idea is a grand one, if it could be carried out and made practical."

While lobbying for support for his land-grant proposal on the cusp of its passage, Turner worked to convince one more correspondent, Stephen Douglas—who had earlier said he would vote for Turner's bill. Seeking to confirm his advocacy, Turner sent Douglas a summary of the bill, which the senator insisted he would introduce.

Douglas was effusive about the legislation's potential: "This educational scheme of Professor Turner's is the most democratic scheme of education ever proposed to the mind of man," the senator wrote, requesting a full copy of the proposal in June 1861. But when Turner's son went to the post office to mail Turner's expanded proposal letter to Douglas, a telegram was waiting for him: Douglas had died in Chicago. Morrill himself took up the measure in the Senate (based on his earlier bill in the House), and Lincoln signed it into law on July 2, 1862.

The Morrill Act was a masterwork of legislative direction in creating a new system of pedagogy, disseminating and spurring knowledge that has improved over time and often been imitated in other countries. "One of the most progressive pieces of legislation passed in the [nineteenth century]," Robert Hormats observes in *The Harvard Business Review*, "this act broadened educational opportunities in Western states and ultimately throughout the nation, thus reinforcing the role of government in promoting upward mobility."

Economic progress was the solid ballast of public higher education, but it was on a small, slowly sailing ship. Women, Native Americans, and Black Americans were largely or entirely barred from the boat of economic progress. Discrimination against Jews and immigrants was pernicious well into the twentieth and twenty-first centuries. Yet, there is undeniable significance to how the Morrill Acts (and companion laws bolstering public education) created a fertile political environment for educating a larger swath of the American population.

GETTYSBURG:
A NEW BIRTH OF FREEDOM

Roughly when Grant was culminating his final paralyzing siege of Vicksburg after months of failure, General Robert E. Lee thrust into a little Pennsylvania town: Gettysburg. Lee was hoping to exploit weaknesses in Union army leadership and march to Philadelphia to cripple Northern resolve. His plan seemed possible in the first hours of the battle, with the Union army led by General George Meade back on its heels.

After enduring a frustrating series of indecisive and ineffective commanding generals—who lost battle after grinding battle in Virginia—Lincoln needed a breakthrough. The wartime sentiment was turning against him. With an election coming up the following year, 1864, even his own party had doubts. Gettysburg—the bloodiest battle in America's most gruesome war—unexpectedly provided a turning point.

Lee's attack was ferocious, but Meade's troops—more than 86,000 of them—held their ground, and later received essential reinforcements while occupying several hills. Lee had barely 60,000 soldiers, and repeatedly marched them uphill into withering cannon fire. All told, more than 50,000 died or were wounded in that singular confrontation, along with more than 3,000 slain horses and mules. Lee retreated into Virginia, and Meade chose not to follow. The war continued.

It's difficult to imagine the extent of the slaughter at Gettysburg in the first three days of July 1863. More than 20,000 injured soldiers came through the field hospitals. The verdant fields of southeastern Pennsylvania became covered with decomposing bodies. It would take months to bury all the corpses; every nearby farm and field became plots in a vast, ghastly cemetery. It is more difficult still to fathom what Lincoln said on November 19, 1863, when he came to consecrate the hallowed ground four months after the battle. How does anyone reconcile such a senseless slaughter? Lincoln chose to embed in the speech's eloquence his "new birth of freedom."

To classical scholars like Garry Wills, the elusive phrase echoes the oration of ancient Greek and Roman speakers. Wills also sees Lincoln's durable thread of the battle's significance echoing the original intent of the Declaration of Independence. Although Lincoln respected the Constitution's groundwork, the document permitted slavery, violating Lincoln's ideals of economic freedom and progress. Its writers and founding fathers, Jefferson especially, wrote with moral intent but were clearly conflicted in practice. Their wealth—and that of all global slavery-based commerce—depended upon immoral bondage, perpetuated to preserve their capital and power. Wills argues using the lens of Lincoln's interpretation:

> If all men are created equal, they cannot be property. They cannot be ruled by owner-monarchs. They must be self-governing in the minimal sense of self-possession. Their equality cannot be denied if the nation is to live by its creed, and voice it, and test it, and die for it. All these matters are now contained in the pregnant formulae of the Address.

Most scholars agree that Lincoln's guiding principle in the Gettysburg Address was to reassert the egalitarian ethos of the Union, and the American Republic at large, while memorializing the "last full measure of devotion" of the soldiers who perished. Yet there is another message lurking in the text. Government is not just "*of* the people" and "*by* the people." It should be "*for* the people"—that is, truly serving everyone it governed.

Historian Harold Holzer emphasizes that "for the people" meant something pragmatic. Indeed, Lincoln directed government to take "an active role clearing the path for its citizens to advance economically. It was a belief he had already put into practice as an Illinois state assemblyman, when he had promoted the construction of roads and canals and education for its citizens." The Address succinctly embodied what Lincoln had worked toward ever since he emerged from the Indiana woods and entered politics to better his life and that of others. He wanted to build an economically robust and equitable society, a country of landowners who managed their own property free and clear, unlike his father in Kentucky. His "new birth of freedom," Holzer added, "was to be an economic as well as political liberation for all citizens, both African Americans and white Americans. It was a new essential element in sustaining the exceptionalist middle-class society envisioned by the founding fathers."

Lincoln's vision also articulated a powerful holistic plan he put into place during the war's darkest days. Economic freedom meant tending your own homestead, the ability to start anew. It meant shipping the fruit of your labor across the continent efficiently and at low cost. It meant being supported by a government that provided the physical, intellectual, and social infrastructure for your economic success. And it meant life in the United States would be further bolstered by public education and technological development. These ideas may not be mentioned by name in the Address, but Lincoln's "new birth" sowed American ideals that we continue to examine and debate.

THE DARK SIDE
OF THE MORRILL ACT

Without question, Lincoln's wholehearted endorsement of the Morrill Act was a fundamental tool to elevate many Americans above their station. He called it a "right to rise." But granting land to states meant appropriating property from Native Americans, in many cases illegally.

Research from the Pulitzer Center tracked the use and ownership of land granted in the original Morrill Act that covered "approximately 10.7 million acres taken from nearly 250 tribes, bands and communities through over 160 violence-backed land cessions, a legal term for the giving up of territory." The Center found that universities and states made money speculating on land value, often paying not a cent to the tribes from whom it appropriated the real estate:

> To extinguish Indigenous title[s] to land siphoned through the Morrill Act, the United States paid less than $400,000. But in truth, it often paid nothing at all. Not a single dollar was paid for more than a quarter of the parcels that supplied the grants—land confiscated through outright seizure or by treaties that were never ratified by the federal government. From the University of Florida to Washington State University, from the Massachusetts Institute of Technology to the University of Arizona, the grants of land raised endowment principal for 52 institutions across the United States.

In effect, the Morrill Act often resulted in massive, immoral land grabs that funded the endowments of several leading public universities. Pulitzer researcher Tristan Ahtone found that "by the early [twentieth] century, the grants had raised $17.7 million for university endowments, with unsold lands valued at an additional $5.1 million." Adjusted for inflation, the grants totaled roughly half a billion in today's dollars.

The Pulitzer Center's findings indicate a need for a more comprehensive evaluation of how universities built their endowments over time. Some institutions, such as Georgetown, have acknowledged profiting from slavery and committed to "engagement with the members of the Descendant community, collaborative projects and new initiatives, and learning and research . . . [and to pursue] a path of memorialization and reconciliation in our present day." Much more work needs to be done to establish a national accounting and reconciliation process with Native Americans and the descendants of enslaved Black Americans.

WHAT THE MORRILL ACT WROUGHT: MODERN URBAN SOCIOECONOMIC IMPACT

The growth of public higher education under Lincoln's administration did not end with the Morrill Act. Subsequent legislation funded additional universities, research, and "extension" programs that would educate farmers on the local level in each county. By 1873, there were twenty-six land-grant colleges throughout the United States. More than a quarter century later there were sixty-five; by 1975, seventy-two. Now there are more than 100.

Congress continued expanding the land-grant system well into the late nineteenth and twentieth centuries, seeded by the Hatch Act of 1887 and the second Morrill Act of 1890, which established "separate but equal" colleges for African Americans—creating seventeen schools throughout Southern and border states. Both laws created sustainable funding streams for land-grant universities, which also financed practical science programs such as agricultural research stations. More than a dozen subsequent federal laws sustained the expansion, creating Native American colleges and Cooperative Extension programs.

Since land-grants proved effective in building higher education infrastructure, the system spread to other countries, particularly in the developing world. Land-grant universities work globally on today's agricultural, environmental, and educational issues. A team of plant scientists from Indiana, Pennsylvania, and Florida, for example, worked with farmers in Colombia to plant sustainably harvested cacao crops after fifty-three years of their civil war. Because many of the world's poorest people live in rural areas, land-grant researchers help to identify appropriate crops and wild foods. They also employ current data on climate change impact to determine the best farming practices.

URBAN BENEFITS
OF LAND-GRANT UNIVERSITIES

In cities, to which most of the world's population is migrating, land-grant universities play a large role. Although originally created to bolster agricultural research, universities today engage in multiple engineering and manufacturing ventures. Chicago's Discovery Partners Institute, for one—cosponsored by the University of Illinois System (which was first championed by Turner)—"prepares students and workers to step into high-demand tech jobs."

Moreover, Lincoln was spot on with his underlying sentiment that widespread education would lead to enhanced economic progress, particularly when it came to research universities—the bulk of them land-grant institutions by the twenty-first century—which yielded large urban benefits in the nation's burgeoning cities. According to a Brookings Institution study by Scott Andes, "downtown universities punch above their weight as economic anchors for both the regions in which they are located and the nation." The Brookings report found the below:

University research and innovation leads to economic growth. A dollar increase in university expenditures has been shown to lead to an increase of 89 cents in average income within a city. Put another way, the overall multiplier effect of university activity is 1.9—the university's own dollar plus the external effect. Universities create thousands of jobs, internships, think tanks, and outreach programs today—all of which bolster local economies.

Universities located in urban areas produce more patents, corporate partnerships, and startups. Downtown schools produce significantly more licensing deals (and income from them), patents, and new businesses, respectively, than their rural, suburban, and college town peers. This isn't to say that universities situated in college towns don't do their part in innovation. Many, if not most, harbor their own research parks, business incubators, and related facilities that generate economic activity.

Universities located within "innovation districts" build on existing urban assets. Research universities are best positioned when they cluster near firms, entrepreneurs, venture capitalists, and other resources that utilize technology into their markets. This relationship is more efficient and more likely to generate economic value when universities are geographically proximate to cities.

Research drives urban vitality and growth. While downtown universities make up only a quarter of the nation's research universities, they account for one-third of university R&D expenditures and invest more than twice as much in R&D per student as their peer universities not based in cities: $22,044 per full-time student versus $12,633.

By signing the Morrill Act and promoting public education, Lincoln was the facilitator of progress and economic activity through broad-based education. Land-grant colleges not only enabled millions to climb the economic ladder, but added value to countless commercial and scholarly activities, from planting corn to the creating of the internet.

LINCOLN'S ULTIMATE AIM

Throughout the Civil War, Lincoln refused to lose sight of his higher objective for an activist government. Without opposition from seceded Southern states he accomplished a great deal. Education was always close to the president's heart, "the most important subject which we as a people can be engaged in." The Morrill Act's land grants of 30,000 acres per state congressional district empowered every corner of the country to build colleges that would address educational needs, all the while conferring local control on the institutions. Each would have its own officers and board of trustees. While each college later received federal funding for research, their own governance would decide how to spend it. The new institutions also had the power to hire and fire its own administrators and professors, and to select a promising student body. Most would develop professional schools for accounting, engineering, law, and medicine. Lincoln's aim to create a universal education system transcended wartime grief and destruction by elevating knowledge and training above the fractured economic system of slavery.

Yet such a knowledge infrastructure would not be completed in Lincoln's time; indeed, it is still a work in progress. Lincoln's desire to link the country coast to coast in one transportation network also gained political currency during the war, along with the opportunity provided by open land to settle and farm. There was more work to be done, his potent pen at the ready.

VII

MOVING WEST

Creating a Link to the Pacific

"I see the tracks of the railroads of the earth,
I see them in Great Britain, I see them in Europe,
I see them in Asia and Africa.
I see the electric telegraphs of the earth,
I see the filaments of the news of the wars, deaths, less, gains,
passions, of my race."

—Walt Whitman, "Salut Au Monde!" *Leaves of Grass*

Connecting the North American continent was an all-out obsession throughout most of the early and mid-nineteenth century. Anyone who ventured west of the Mississippi River swiftly concluded that a better route was needed to get from the East Coast to the Pacific. John C. Fremont championed the cause as he explored the Rockies and California. Settlers trudging west in Conestoga wagons reached their homesteads in treacherous discomfort. From Washington to Lincoln, every president wanted a better trade route "to the Orient," which could shave months off a dangerous voyage from the East Coast around Cape Horn to Pacific ports.

Like other national transportation initiatives, it took more than half a century to build rail tracks from the Atlantic to the Pacific. Politics played a large part. Southern states wanted a route through Arkansas, Texas, New Mexico, and California; they opposed a northern route that would link the upper Midwest to California and Oregon. One of the first surveyors was Jefferson Davis.

At the height of the Civil War, Lincoln's pen was poised to reshape the country far beyond the reach of the Emancipation Proclamation and Gettysburg Address. The impending Homestead and Pacific Railway Acts would transform land from the Mississippi River to the Pacific Ocean, displacing thousands of Native Americans along the way. The economic destiny of land-seeking Euro-Americans would be exponentially enhanced.

THE PACIFIC RAILWAY ACTS

Only six weeks separated Lincoln's signing of the first Pacific Railroad Acts and the Homestead Act, which came first in 1862. As Union troops struggled in nearly every battle, it became clear that the war wouldn't be over in a year. Yet Lincoln kept his focus on economic progress. The Transcontinental Railroad was the link between the Midwestern-Eastern rail network and the West Coast; getting from Omaha to California, though, would be a Promethean task. Several mountain ranges, including the Rockies and Sierras, had to be crossed. There were streams and rivers to bridge. Great deserts and plains challenged the imagination, resources, and stamina of the mostly Chinese and Irish crews hoping to meet at Promontory Point in Utah.

It took two pieces of "Railway Acts" legislation to fund the rail expansion to the West. The first, in 1862, provided rights of way, ten sections, and government loan bonds to start the project. The second, in 1864, enabled railroads to sell their own bonds while doubling the size of the land grants. (These private bond issues were later found to be the object of financial speculation.)

The Homestead Act and the Transcontinental Railroad were twin drivers of the westward push for "free" territory. As part of Lincoln's platform (that of the expansionist Republican, and earlier Whig, parties), these twin pillars were overshadowed by Lincoln's unpopularity leading up to the last year of war. One cartoon from 1863 depicts Lincoln pulling off a mask, revealing a kinglike devil. The model of virtue and self-reliance Lincoln stood for in 1860 was demonized throughout the South and some parts of the North, dubbed a "backwoods rube" and a "gorilla." Even his cabinet had issues with him—its members thought the uncouth, loquacious Westerner was inferior and unqualified for the presidency in every way. Yet Lincoln became a profoundly influential leader because of his ability to navigate a host of conflicts, ultimately imprinting a "moral purpose and meaning upon the protracted misery of the Civil War."

Much like his riverboat journeys impressed upon Lincoln the need for canals, what he saw when he defended the Rock Island Bridge Company only a few years earlier inspired him to champion the Transcontinental Railroad. Yes, the Mississippi could be spanned and the continent conquered by a combination of innovative engineering and ceaseless labor. It should be a public endeavor, Lincoln ordained; the federal government would only oversee it and grant land to the railroads, who would have to raise much of the capital themselves.

While Lincoln knew little about *building* railroads, he had extensive knowledge on how to finance them, having been one of the original sponsors of the Illinois internal improvements laws of the 1830s. Indeed, his many railroad legal cases were profitable, allowing him to add a second story to his modest Springfield home. One of his first cases involved the Alton & Sangamon Railroad. When later representing the Illinois Central, he was not directly employed as corporate counsel. Because more than half of his 5,500 legal cases involved personal debts, per historian James Cornelius, he gained a deep understanding of money issues—gaining diverse insights on how to best apply capital on large scale. While Lincoln was not a "railroad" lawyer in the strictest sense, he had a deep understanding of corporate and debt financing.

The Pacific Railway Acts effectively doubled track mileage in the decade from 1860 to 1870. Railroads gained tremendous advantages; on either side of the tracks, they were granted generous rights of way. Channeling his legislative experience with the Illinois Central, Lincoln ensured that the Pacific Railroad was the most solid plank of his party's platform in 1860. There was little doubt what path the Central and Union Pacific would take: the northern line through Iowa, Nebraska, Wyoming, Utah, and Nevada, into Sacramento, California. The eastern terminus, in Council Bluffs, Iowa, was near property Lincoln owned and visited in 1859 as a candidate. He was there, he claimed, to inspect seventeen parcels offered as collateral for a personal loan to his friend Norman Judd. (The loan was for $3,000, repaid to Mary and Robert Lincoln in 1867—with $2,400 in interest.)

Lincoln had another interest in Council Bluffs, perched on the eastern shore of the Missouri River. As the county seat of Pottawattomie County, it looked across the river at a key city: Omaha, Nebraska. As the nation's geographic center—along with its population—moved west, Omaha became an important gateway to the Pacific route, one Jefferson Davis would've disparaged in early surveys for the western railroad. Lincoln stayed some four days in Council Bluffs, the longest period of time he sojourned anywhere west of the Mississippi. While in town, he had a chance meeting with local railroad man and engineer Grenville Dodge, later a Civil War general. Their discussion turned to the Pacific Railroad: Both men apparently agreed Council Bluffs would make an excellent terminus for the eastern line.

Of Lincoln's questionable corps of commanders, Dodge was reliably brilliant, serving in a number of roles; perhaps most significantly, he was one of Lincoln's cadre of experienced railroad engineers. When the Confederacy formed, not only did it seize telegraph lines, it "nationalized" the rail lines and post offices in the South. The seizure disrupted the country's entire postal rail network—which, by the 1850s, had carried more mail than by steamship and stagecoach combined. In response, Lincoln's government created an innovative Railway Mail Service, which expanded the logistical reach of the post. This move was vitally necessary: The Confederacy had taken over 40 percent of post office routes and 30 percent of its offices.

Dodge knew railroads well; he had surveyed them as a civil engineer. Born in Danvers, Massachusetts, in 1831—when Lincoln was making his way out of Indiana and exploring river piloting—Dodge settled in Council Bluffs, Iowa, and became a respected member of the town's council. Sent to Washington to obtain arms for Iowa volunteers at the beginning of the war, he was rewarded with a commission as colonel in the Iowa infantry. Wounded at the battle of Pea Ridge, Dodge's commanders decided that he would be more useful to the Union army building and repairing railroads rather than shepherding troops into cannon fire. He was promoted to Major General by 1864 and accompanied General Sherman to Atlanta as a corps commander. After the war, he resigned his commission to become chief engineer of the Union Pacific—the eastern leg of the Transcontinental Railroad running from Omaha that would connect to the Central Pacific in Utah.

Dodge was one of the war's most resourceful Union generals, acquiring skills that built his knowledge and confidence for when he would tackle the Pacific Railroad. He was often tasked with building railroads from scratch; one such line went to Corinth, Mississippi, and was sixty-four miles long. General Grant wrote that Dodge was a "most capable soldier . . . he had no tools to work with except those of the pioneer—axes, picks and spades." Driven by ingenuity, Dodge faced herculean challenges: He once had to repair eighteen bridges and rail lines torn up by Confederates with little in the way of modern equipment. When the Pacific Railway Act was passed, Lincoln fondly recalled their meeting in Council Bluffs. Dodge disagreed with Lincoln on one point—Dodge believed the government should finance the *entire* project—but the two men agreed that the Nebraska section should follow the flat Platte River Valley route.

A PUBLIC-PRIVATE PUBLIC WORKS PROJECT EMERGES

As Lincoln remained occupied with financing and winning the war, he saved some focus for his plan of a public-private rail partnership: The federal government would provide extensive land grants while private corporations raised the capital for labor, rails, and ties on their own ("cross" ties were laid on the road bed under the track). Yet before Grenville Dodge could jump back into railroading, he was shot in the head outside of Atlanta in 1864. Word circulated that he died, but two days later he regained consciousness and Grant asked him to take command of one of Sherman's divisions back in Georgia. Dodge's doctor advised him to resign from the army and return to railroading. Instead, at Grant's request, Dodge went to Washington to meet with Lincoln, who was glad to see him; the president pressed Dodge on Grant's likelihood of taking Richmond and ending the war. Dodge assured Lincoln that Grant was on the right path to victory.

"You don't know how glad I am to hear you say that," Lincoln said with a smile, then sent Dodge off to command the Department of the Missouri in St. Louis, far away from the front. When Lincoln won re-election and the war ended, Dodge started his work with the Union Pacific with more than a plan in mind: He would finish Lincoln's "great enterprise," knowing he already had the confidence of generals

Grant, Sherman, and Philip Sheridan, powerful allies in completing what would become the largest public-private entity of that century.

Of course, linking the two railroads north of Salt Lake City (Mormon leader Brigham Young was an investor) would require dedicated stamina and creativity that would test the wills of the railroad executives, including president of the Central Pacific Leland Stanford. Thousands of Irish and some 20,000 Chinese workers endured forbidding conditions in frigid mountain passes and blazing deserts. By 1865, some 90 percent of railroad workers were Chinese; badly treated and underpaid, they worked six days a week for $26 a month. Assigned the most dangerous jobs—such as laying explosives—their white coworkers were paid 50-70 percent more. Although exact records are lacking, it's estimated that some 10,000 workers died building the railroad.

When some 11,000 Chinese laborers went on strike in 1867 for better pay and shorter hours, management cut off their food and supplies. The strike ended unsuccessfully. Work continued. What the laborers endured is hard to imagine today; the leg from Sacramento through the Sierra range alone involved blasting thirteen tunnels and round-the-clock work to meet deadlines. They were literally digging into mountains to lay down the track.

At the outset, the railroads raised money through stock subscriptions. Executives and engineers were appointed, with Dodge heading the Union Pacific's team. Financing and construction were perilous affairs, but the work was finally completed—at great cost, in terms of human lives and suffering—in 1869. When the final spike was driven at Promontory Point in Utah, history had few equals in engineering feats. More than 3,500 rails were laid on 25,800 ties. Two oceans were joined by an iron highway. Commerce and transportation flourished, yet a multitude of workers were never acknowledged. While Irish laborers were honored in a parade in Sacramento—far more credit than they received when the I&M Canal was completed in 1848—Chinese workers' names were not recognized or even recorded.

The unprecedented achievement also changed the world in ways society still struggles to catch up to globally. The wealth from the railroad's financing and income flowed to a handful of people, fueling the age of the "robber barons," predominantly white, Protestant men. Stock and bond markets began stampeding in opposite directions at the first hint of collapse or overnight wealth. Land speculation, seeded in the canal-building era of the 1820s and 1830s, became an insular industry unto itself. It was best mastered by manipulators who had avaricious motivation and fraudulent intent. Nevertheless, what blossomed was a harvest of *laissez-faire* capitalism, in the most superficial sense. Lincoln and Clay's American System fulfilled some of its promise to elevate a greater portion of Americans to prosperity, though wealth-building was limited to a precious few individuals in the waning days of the nineteenth century. Author Stephen Ambrose observes the historical impact:

> Alexander Hamilton and Henry Clay had wanted American manufacturing to grow, but they could not imagine anything like what happened after the Civil War. Nor could Lewis and Clark, who had led the way in which the Union Pacific and Central Pacific created a precedent for government aid to business, or how the government could create a new class of capitalists. Men of great fortune, tied to the Republican Party. Men ready to take great risks and then accept great profits.

Considering that the Transcontinental Railroad was built within two generations of Lewis and Clark's exploration of the Louisiana Purchase, the American Industrial Revolution is even more remarkable. Although it was girded with commercial intentions, it stimulated countless other industries and their subsequent jobs and income. In a narrow sense, the public-private structure of Lincolnomics worked on a large scale. Public investment (offered through land grants) made a profound difference for all when married to a culture of innovation.

GROWTH CREATED BY BETTER TRANSPORTATION NETWORKS

When the railroad system finally knitted two coasts together, it spurred commercial growth unprecedented in human history. At the beginning of the war, only 16 percent of America's economic output was manufactured. By war's end, the economy had grown, spurred by wartime demand. Charles Morris, who analyzed the growth of American industry in *The Dawn of Innovation*, found that certain industries enjoyed a comparative advantage; they grew because of the ready availability of raw materials, labor, and transportation to market. Booming industries had a dramatic impact on the American economy, in what he calls the "real American system, or perhaps the American ideology of manufacturing." Those that grew the most and the workers who benefitted included the below:

> They worked in grain milling; meatpacking; lard refining; turning logs into planks and beams; iron smelting and forging; and making steam engines and steamboats; vats and piping; locomotives; reapers and mowers; carriages; stoves; cotton and woolen cloth; shoes; saddles and harnesses and workaday tools.

The rail and postal network's growing reach fueled many of these industries, which mostly emerged near sources of water power such as fast-flowing rivers. Yet when railroads began transporting coal from Appalachian fields, it didn't matter whether your plant was near a river. What you needed was a rail siding to receive coal and supplies. This is why Chicago became a leading manufacturing center, lumberyard, and "hog butcher to the world"; why Cleveland and Pittsburgh became major iron and steel producers; and why Detroit later evolved as a maker of "horseless" carriages. Even inland cities, like Ohio's Akron and Dayton, Indiana's Indianapolis, and New York's Schenectady, would eventually become manufacturing centers. With the Transcontinental Railroad opening vast new markets west of the Mississippi, factories in every industry needed to scale up. This increased demand for manufactured goods forced factory owners to apply new, more efficient methods of production.

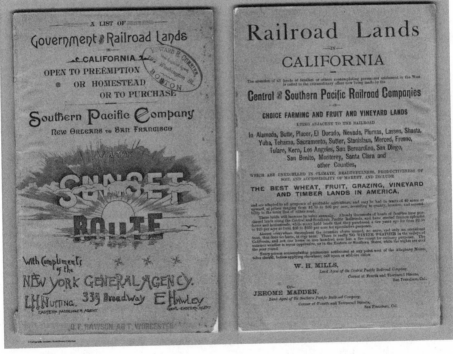

1886 pamphlet advertising government expanded railroad lands in California as "the best wheat, fruit, grazing, vineyard and timber lands in America." (Digital Public Library of America)

Economic growth also led to better living standards. By the end of the 1870s, the US population had grown by 25 percent—yet benefitted from better food, more productive farms, better education (in great part from land-grant colleges), and more in-home comforts like stoves, washtubs, and consistent sources of heat and clean water. The Homestead Act resulted in the Euro-American settlement of 10 percent of the total American territory; it also formed some of the basis of our modern economy by creating mass consumer demand. Farmers who staked their claim in the Great Plains, and prospered— if they survived its unforgiving winters—wanted better tools, farm implements, and home supplies. Through the growing rail network, they were able to order anything they needed—and have it delivered. By the early twentieth century, farmers could even order entire homes that could be assembled on site.

NATURE DESTROYED
AND PRESERVED DURING THE WAR

Lincoln, shaped by the wilderness in his youth, had a unique relationship with it. As a boatman-woodsman-poet, he saw its splendors and experienced the rigors of its forests and rivers. His upbringing in the woods of Kentucky and Indiana required that he know his way around different kinds of trees, log cabins, split-rail fences, axes, mauls, and the many uses of wood. As a boatman, he built his craft from scratch with available lumber. (His father was a carpenter, in addition to a hard-scrabble farmer.) More than half of Lincoln's life, wood was the basis of nearly everything structural— from bridges to rail cars. Locomotives also burned copious amounts of wood before they converted to coal—some three to four million cords a year.

The great North Woods (hundreds of miles north of Chicago) in Wisconsin, Michigan, and Minnesota were ravaged for the massive railroad and building boom during Lincoln's era and well into the twentieth century. Timber came into Chicago's gargantuan depots along the Chicago River, many of them in the "timber district" of Bridgeport at the northern terminus of the Illinois & Michigan Canal. Mass cutting of trees like white pine made Chicago the largest such port during its height in the middle to late nineteenth century.

Before the industrial, scaled-up mass production of pig iron, and later steel—after the war—nearly every railroad bridge was constructed of wood, and so were easily destroyed. The metal revolution would not make wood obsolete until the 1870s. The same was true of rail cars, which consumed some 50 million board feet of wood annually, as estimated by George Pullman, whose Chicago plant dominated the business and employed Robert Lincoln (Abe's eldest) as president in the last decades of the century.

But by mid-century, the single largest use of wood was for railroad cross ties per Eric Rutkow, who researched the history of America's forests from first European colonization to the present. In the decade after the Civil War, about 30 million railroad ties were needed every year, requiring wood from 150,000 acres. The timber-gorging trend—at least for railroad use—likely peaked around 1880, when most major rail lines had been built.

The massive war on forests enraged conservationists like Henry David Thoreau, who had significant bonds with specific trees around his home in Concord, Massachusetts. Like his fellow transcendentalists Ralph Waldo Emerson and Nathaniel Hawthorne, Thoreau cursed the outsized gluttony of the iron horse. A broad-based conservation movement emerged from that period and grew over the next two centuries. John Muir championed the forests and mountains of the High Sierras, among other sacred places; Theodore Roosevelt, immersed in the tradition of Lincoln's progressivism, later followed suit.

Yet it was Lincoln himself, during the war's bloodiest year, who signed the 1864 Yosemite and Big Tree Grant Act. While it did not directly create today's national park, it ceded federal land and the Mariposa Big Tree Grove to the State of California for "public use, resort, recreation for all time." The law became the template for nearly every major park to follow. Rutkow notes:

> This was the precursor to every national park in the country: the first time that the federal government stepped into protect natural resources (even if done obliquely through state transfer); the first time the government recognized a non-commercial value in land; the first time that concern for the commons triumphed over private development.

Was Lincoln the Railsplitter a tree hugger? Doubtless he was the country's greatest advocate for economic development, and was lobbied to set aside Yosemite in a land grant swap, one of his favorite tools. While we don't know if he felt about trees the same way Thoreau or Muir did, perhaps it was part of his inner spirituality—which was frequently questioned by his critics.

THE HOMESTEAD ACT
OPENS UP LAND

For $12 and a simple registration, the US government *gave* you 160 acres, free and clear. This was the basic contract underlying the Homestead Act, which Lincoln signed into law on May 20, 1862. All an individual had to do was to stay on the land—and hopefully cultivate it—for five years, and it was theirs after paying a $6 "proving fee." Lincoln and Congress worked carefully on the language to ensure that homesteaders could acquire the land and resulting title quickly and uniformly. Haunted by his father's exile from Kentucky over a vague land title, lawyer-turned-president Lincoln wanted to guarantee that sod busters would not be kicked off their land. In his view, ownership was essential: "It is best for all to leave each man free to acquire property as fast as he can."

Like many initiatives shot down by Democrats prior to Lincoln's election, the Homestead Act sought to change the economic balance in favor of middle- and lower-class Americans. Freed of indentured servitude or enslavement to landowners, with no previous prospect of earning their own income from property, homesteaders were given real estate to farm or pasture as they pleased. Little in European history provides a precedent to this seemingly heroic giveaway meant to encourage financial independence. The Act was somewhat Jeffersonian in conception, as it sought to create prosperous farmers with significant plots of rural land. While Northern and Eastern states continued to industrialize at a furious pace, Lincoln encouraged generations of dispossessed Euro-Americans to cultivate the plains' fertile soil. Turning property into a productive economic asset for individual farmers was the bedrock of his plan. Even before the war ended, Lincoln could claim that the Homestead Act was a roaring success for Euro-Americans settling the West: Some 1.5 million acres were sold in the region by the end of 1864.

Demonstrating his faith in the future of productive, independent agriculture, in 1861 Lincoln signed legislation establishing a Department of Agriculture to oversee the expansion of farming. Although not a cabinet-level agency, the fledgling department distributed seeds and cuttings and offered an agricultural library to aspiring farmers. He called the agency "peculiarly the people's department." The move proved successful: Despite the ongoing war, agricultural output of mostly Northern and Western farms doubled from $707 million to $1.4 *billion* in 1864. For his part, Lincoln did not benefit from westward expansion in a personal capacity, though he held a warrant to purchase land in Crawford County, Iowa—compensation for his participation in the Black Hawk War. He never exercised the warrant.

In spite of harm inflicted on Native Americans dispossessed of their ancestral homes, the Homestead Act had far-reaching impacts that reshaped the country for millions who had no access to land. According to Lincoln Presidential Library historian Jacob Friefeld, "in many ways, the Homestead Act was a progressive law by nineteenth century standards." There were no restrictions on what you could do with your 160 acres, although you'd have to be able to subsist on it in all kinds of unforgiving weather. Friefeld heralds the Act's lack of titling restrictions, which also allowed many who were previously prevented from owning land to secure "free and clear" ownership:

> By allowing "heads of household" to claim land, it opened the way for single and widowed women to claim land in their own names. The act also encouraged immigration to the United States, allowing immigrants to claim land as long as they became U.S. citizens before they 'proved-up'—both proving-up and filing for citizenship required five years of residency. The act also included no overtly racial language. With the passage of the Civil Rights Act of 1866 and the Fourteenth Amendment that secured full citizenship for African Americans, they, too, were free to homestead.

They did so by the thousands in the Southern homesteading states and the West.

The majority who homesteaded gained title to their land, which expanded agriculture in the West: Between 1863 and 1900, homesteaders started two-thirds of new Western farms. Homesteading was free from the onerous Jim Crow restrictions to come, and thousands of African Americans headed west to start farms, including Illinoisan Oscar Micheaux. The South Dakota homesteader became the first African American to a produce a feature-length film, entitled *The Homesteader* (1919). He went on to produce forty-four movies, write novels, and found the Lincoln Motion Picture Company in Chicago, which was the birthplace of motion pictures before the industry moved to Hollywood in the 1920s.

SIMON POKAGON MEETS LINCOLN

The Transcontinental Railroad was certainly one of the nineteenth century's greatest engineering achievements, enabling millions of Euro-Americans to cross the continent. It also came at severe cost to Native Americans. By one estimate, from early colonization to 1887, Indigenous people ceded some 1.5 *billion* acres to colonial and American governments (according to a University of Georgia study). Pushed off their ancestral lands onto reservations and "compensated" through annuity payments, American practices of exile and genocide were charted by the government's "Bureau of Ethnology" in 1899. Homesteading and the reach of the railroad only exacerbated the plight of the tribes, who were victims of institutional segregation.

MOVING WEST

Simon Pokagon, the son of one of the chiefs who ceded what became the city of Chicago in 1833, spoke powerfully for Native American interests in the mid-to-late nineteenth century. Born in Southern Michigan, he became chief of his band of Potawatomi, decrying the reservation system and disparaging the "treaty" his father signed in Chicago. He twice appealed to Lincoln during the war and later to President Grant. Lincoln was reportedly respectful to Pokagon, but his government's policies further obliterated tribes' demands for freedom and better treatment, during the war and well into the remainder of the nineteenth century. Still, Pokagon pressed his cause, noting that his tribe wasn't paid their annuity from Washington for the Chicago treaty:

> I went to see the greatest and best chief ever known, Abraham Lincoln . . . .I told him how my father long ago sold Chicago and the surrounding country to the United States for three cents per acre and how we were poor and needed our pay. He said he was sorry and would help us what he could to get our just dues. Three years later I again visited the Great Chief; he excused the delay in our payment on account of the war. He seemed bowed down with care. At this time, Grant was thundering before Richmond for its final overthrow, while Sherman was making his grand march to the sea. Some time after this visit, we were paid $390,000.

Pokagon spent the rest of his life advocating for Native Americans. Educated at Notre Dame and Oberlin Colleges, his eloquent prose was on display in his novel *Queen of the Woods*, and his speech and pamphlet "The Red Man's Book of Lamentations," presented at the 1893 World's Columbian Exposition in Chicago. By that time, the American government's horrendous outright slaughter of Native Americans was essentially over. Thousands of troops that fought for the Union went west to murder and subjugate thousands of Indigenous people. Many "insurrections" were crushed by Union generals like John Pope, Phil Sheridan, William Sherman, and Grenville Dodge.

THE ROBBER BARON ERA EMERGES FROM RAILROAD EXPANSION

The unnerving boom and bust of capital markets was another outgrowth of homesteading and rail expansions. While the land provided for railroads was effectively free due to grants, the rail lines themselves were funded by private capital from the East Coast and Europe. There was no limit to how much stock and bond money could be raised for private companies, and there was little to no regulation of the markets channeling that capital to investors and operating companies. This post-Civil War *laissez-faire* environment led to rapacious profiteering and speculation.

Henry Villard, a war correspondent who befriended Lincoln, was an innovative journalist when he met the president. Originally from a wealthy German family, he came to Chicago, changed his name, and started working for German-language newspapers in 1853. Like many immigrants of his time, Villard employed his many skills to find a better life. During the Civil War, he reported from the battlefront, sending his dispatches back to Northern papers like the *Chicago Tribune*. Well-respected, he had access to Lincoln and his top war generals, and personally witnessed horrible battles such as Petersburg. Seeking to broaden his reach, Villard created one of the first newspaper syndicates, publishing his battle accounts in multiple newspapers simultaneously.

Bad health eventually sidelined Villard from warfront reporting; he needed to find another way to make a living. As a well-traveled reporter, Villard knew where to go and whom to interview to obtain valuable information. Leveraging connections he made in the German financial community, he acted as an on-the-ground researcher for German financiers interested in investing in American railroads. Bondholders wanted to know how their money was invested, and if they would lose capital in the race to build western railroads.

Offering his services as an agent for German investors, Villard first became involved in railroad securities as a broker for Wisconsin Central bonds, the acting intermediary for Frankfurt bankers. In a few years, Villard became an executive himself: untangling the knotty financial affairs of railroads such as the Kansas Pacific—then investing in them. By May 1876, he was president of the Oregon & California Railroad Company, another link in a new transcontinental line that extended to the Pacific Northwest. Through brokering fees, dividends, stock sales, commissions, and interest, he became a multi-millionaire in the decade after the Civil War. The one-time newspaperman was now a railroad baron.

Building a palatial New York mansion, Villard was at the top of his game until financial pressures forced him to resign as president of the Northern Pacific in 1884. He soon rebounded, financing a promising inventor, Thomas Edison, and the Edison Lamp and Machine Works companies (which he consolidated into the Edison General Electric Company in 1889). A young Edison protégé, Samuel Insull was hired to run the manufacturing arm of the Edison empire, which J.P. Morgan merged into General Electric in 1893. In the years leading up to his death in 1900, Villard came full circle, buying newspapers and philanthropizing.

Witness and chronicler of his era—from the Lincoln-Douglas debates to the Civil War battlefront to the railroad boom—Villard engaged with some of the greatest figures of the century, from Lincoln to Otto von Bismarck. Although the wealth he acquired came from a mostly closed loop of financiers, he was one of few visionaries of his time. He remarks in his memoir that he was "a firm believer from the outset in the availability of electricity as a motive power for transportation," among other applications, such as replacing steam in factories and powering entire cities. Through his discrete recognition of innovation, Villard's hand in extending the transcontinental rail system helped finance the Second Industrial Revolution, which would create a new class of entrepreneurs and financial dealers when the railroad boom ended.

Men of their time, Villard and Lincoln approved of the marriage of technology, economic progress, and entrepreneurism. What bound together those relationships was the flexibility that free labor offered. One wasn't destined to be a hired hand for their entire lives; Lincoln was living proof. Even before the war, Lincoln had formulated this philosophy, articulating it at a Wisconsin Agricultural Fair speech in 1859:

> Even in all our slave States, except South Carolina, a majority of the whole people of all colors, are neither slaves nor masters. In these Free States, a large majority are neither *hirers* or *hired*. Men, with their families—wives, sons and daughters—work for themselves, on their farms, in their houses and in their shops, taking the whole product to themselves, and asking no favors of capital on the one hand, nor of hirelings or slaves on the other.

Although Lincoln's economic vision did not exactly create a robust class of free entrepreneurs, the combined gains from public education, agricultural research, and land grants opened countless doors for farmers, merchants, and financiers.

However, the Gilded Age—which mushroomed during and after Reconstruction—also created wild speculation frontiers for rapacious financiers. While Wild Bill Hickok played his last hand in Deadwood, Wall Street metastasized into an unfettered incubator for swindlers, trusts, and plunderers. What began as a promise for widespread property ownership became a free-for-all in the unregulated world of ever-growing monopolistic capital, where scoundrels like Jay Gould bought and sold stocks with abandon, vying for corporate control—against financiers like Villard. Many hapless investors were ruined by stock manipulations and operators. President Grant managed to steer clear of Gould only to be ruined financially by his son's mischievous investment partner, Ferdinand Ward, who put all the president's money into a Ponzi scam. (Impoverishment forced Grant to make money for his family by writing his timeless autobiography while dying of throat cancer, urged on by *The Gilded Age* coauthor Mark Twain.)

It was a reckless time, fortunes made and lost overnight as railroad barons added track, overbuilt, and speculated their way across America. Congress and the Republican Party—dominant until the Progressive Era—largely ignored the financial shenanigans. Regulation did not come into play until the century's end, and remained light until Teddy Roosevelt's "Square Deal" antitrust reforms and Franklin Delano's 1930s-era New Deal. As powerful corporations and tightly controlled trusts, railroads exerted their financial muscle at every turn. Lincoln and his party's overly generous support of railroad growth with little to no initial oversight created an unruly, spoiled monster of an industry by the 1880s. As Robert Hormats notes in his *Harvard Business Review* analysis of the Pacific Railway Acts:

If there is a caveat to the extraordinary expansion of America's railroad network, it involves the absence of regulation to accompany the government's generous support for the railroads. The railroads successfully resisted—in court and in Congress—curbs on their growing economic power. The resulting unregulated competition led to overbuilding, stock market crashes, corruption and ultimately an oligopolistic industry.

Moreover, little-strings-attached policies such as the Railway Acts emboldened corporate power cartels well into the twenty-first century. The J.P. Morgan "money trust" and its affiliates would control entire industries; John D. Rockefeller's "oil trust" would ruthlessly dominate the growing petroleum industry.

Robert Hormats, wading through a hands-free era of American expansion, lands us in the present: A mere handful of companies dominate retail and tech. "The American experience with railroads is a good lesson in the dangers of providing government support for an industry without also putting in place sufficient or effective regulation," Hormats concludes.

Had he lived beyond 1865, could Lincoln have navigated the epic confrontation between overconcentrated capital and a consumerist society? Many elements of corporate power had their genesis in his time. While he profited from defending corporate interests, evolving economic disparities that hurt the growth and sustainability of the middle class would have troubled him. Lincolnomics was about spreading the wealth, not concentrating it.

VIII

PAYING FOR IT ALL

Financing Lincolnomics in the Nineteenth Century

"Political activity alone cannot make a man free. Back of the ballot, he must have property, industry, skill, economy, intelligence, and character."

—Booker T. Washington

Before he was martyred and globally admired, America's sixteenth president had a legion of vicious detractors, even those he knew before and during the war. Lincoln endured a significant amount of abuse during his late political career, especially in the last years of the war.

Nineteenth-century invention royalties were often litigated for years after the patents were filed. In one such 1857 Cincinnati patent infringement case, Lincoln was asked to represent Cyrus McCormick, one of the inventors of the mechanized reaper; McCormick filed against John Henry Manny, who invented a reaper of his own. Also representing McCormick was the bullheaded co-counsel Edwin Stanton (later Lincoln's capable Secretary of War), who was apparently incensed that Lincoln was even considered for the legal team.

"Where did that *damned, long-armed creature* come from and what can he expect to do in this case?" Stanton reportedly blurted when they met in Cincinnati for the trial. Lincoln was humiliated, withdrawn, and sidelined for its duration. Stanton likely knew little about Lincoln—except that he was a "Western" lawyer. Had he known Lincoln was an inventor himself, and an admirer of innovation and likely of McCormick, he may have changed his attitude.

When Treasury Secretary Salmon P. Chase and Secretary of State William Seward lobbied to have Stanton (then a Democrat) added to the cabinet as War Secretary, a position he assumed in 1862, Lincoln put his reliable gauge of character above personal grudges. As for Stanton, he was hardly a fan of the president when the war began. In June 1861—before joining the cabinet—Stanton wrote that due to Lincoln's "painful imbecility," Confederates "would be in possession of Washington within thirty days"; it was a reasonable assumption given the lack of martial mastery Lincoln's Virginia commanders exhibited in the war's first two years. Yet Lincoln focused on Stanton's intellectual and leadership abilities, setting aside his old colleague's criticism.

With war raging, President Lincoln needed an experienced ally who could champion complex financial legislation, someone with a flexible skill set and pliable personality. (His cabinet was composed of many men who thought themselves superior to the Illinois lawyer.) The era's fiscal drains—principally the Civil War, and costly but necessary infrastructure—begged for major financial innovations by figures who understood how to navigate politics, legislation, and national economic policy. Although the war's bloodshed and slavery's questionable future dominated national attention, Lincoln and his Congress needed to pass the nation's first income tax and "greenback" paper dollar system. The war was costing the Union some $2 million a day. Washington desperately needed a way to pay for it.

Lincoln respected both Secretary of State Seward and Treasury Secretary Chase, whom he later entrusted with enormous wartime responsibilities. Chase particularly embodied a unique role in Lincoln's inner circle and grew to respect the president. As Secretary of the Treasury, he needed to invent mechanisms to finance the war, under pressure of threats by rebel forces crossing the Potomac to potentially attack Washington.

Somehow Lincoln managed the complex dynamic of men who had once despised him—and competed with him—on the political frontier of the Republican Party. Chase was a peripatetic example; he switched parties multiple times in hopes of garnering political nominations. Settling in Cincinnati, the Dartmouth graduate practiced law there; a fierce opponent of slavery, he wrote early and often about the peculiar institution, at one time joining the Ohio "Free Soil" Party. Like Lincoln, he was vitriolically opposed to Stephen Douglas's Kansas-Nebraska Act and slavery's Western expansion. Chase was an early progressive Republican as governor of Ohio, supporting public education, women's rights, and prison reform. What he shared with Lincoln—other than the status of being an anti-slavery Republican lawyer—was a relentlessly cruel trail of familial grief. Chase lost three wives and three daughters. This doubtlessly accounted for his "habitually grave" personality.

While Chase wasn't an ideal fit for Treasury Secretary, Lincoln knew he was principled. In Chase, he saw a man who acted decisively with an embedded passion for fairness; he was one of few lawyers who defended escaped slaves in local and federal courts. But like Stanton, Chase was not completely loyal to Lincoln politically. In 1864, he resigned his post as Secretary of the Treasury to run for the Republican nomination against Lincoln—who, again, did not take it personally. When Chase lost, Lincoln unexpectedly appointed him Chief Justice of the Supreme Court (where he later presided over the impeachment trial of Andrew Johnson, who sought to block Reconstruction efforts after Lincoln's death). What Chase accomplished—at Lincoln's bidding—in his few years in the cabinet was nothing less than essential and groundbreaking, and so justified Lincoln's faith in the Ohio lawyer.

While Lincoln did not ask him to manage surly, sheepish generals or the war's expanding tableau, during its middle years Lincoln charged Chase with raising tens of millions of dollars to fund the federal army, which stretched from Arkansas to the shores of the Potomac River. Prior to 1864, the federal government had little revenue beyond the tariff system implemented generations ago largely to protect domestic production, one of the pillars of Clay's American System. To boot, the Union lost that income from Southern states, so Lincoln and his cabinet needed to be creative. The president was literally building and expanding one of the world's largest armies; he needed capital to pay for supplies, from cannons to camp tents.

Chase quickly got to work, realizing that the Union—and the country as a whole—would need its own paper currency. And those government-issued "greenbacks" would need something to back them up, which would eventually be the debt or "full faith and credit" of Washington. Throughout the nineteenth century, it was mostly up to states to issue their own currency, run chartered banks, and fund infrastructure projects. This made sense when the country was small and did not have much of a population beyond the Appalachians. With Western expansion, the need arose for a national banking system along the lines of what Alexander Hamilton proposed in the republic's early days. Such a system would need to issue credit and settle debts. Capital was necessary for funding everything from bridges and turnpikes to canals and railroads.

New state residents west of the Appalachians and in the South had little faith in a banking system based in Washington. When populist Western politicians like Andrew Jackson attacked the idea of a national banking system in the 1830s, it stirred up populist sentiments: Jacksonians revolted against the idea of a powerful central bank. Those in Western and Southern states saw that cronyism and corruption determined who got credit—often denying them it. The potential for a national currency and banking system languished until Lincoln needed to uniformly print and raise money in the 1860s. By establishing greenbacks and creating the National Banking Act, Chase was instrumental in crafting a revised system of national finance. The notes Washington issued ensured that the Union army would have the capital it needed. Although Chase wanted to resign several times during the war, his economic leadership was invaluable.

CREATING THE FIRST INCOME TAX

Chase had a key role in establishing the nation's first federal income tax, which provided a steady and sustainable source of capital. The political landscape—with its Republican-controlled Congress and White House—certainly favored Lincoln's financial innovations, but the new tax was so transformative as to still be a hallmark in government financing. No longer were tariffs a prime source of federal income. Individual earnings would be taxed, so every working citizen would have a stake in financing the government's operations—this case, fighting a horrendous war to upend an immoral economic system.

Signed on August 5, 1861, the Revenue Act created the income tax, imposing a flat 3 percent levy on earnings. Farmers swiftly claimed it placed an unfair burden on them, and a year later Congress revised the law, graduating it with wide income brackets: The 3 percent rate would apply to incomes between $600 and $10,000, and 5 percent to earnings above $10,000. Many thought the tax itself was outrageous—it impacted most of the working population—but it was an innovation for the time. As a progressive tax (that is, based on one's ability to pay), its underlying principle was equity. You made more, you paid more. A 1872 Supreme Court decision would strike down the tax, but nonetheless it became a template for twentieth-century taxes funding government (or not). Moreover, it later provided the Treasury a pool of money with which to build the country. Harold Holzer highlighted its political significance, hardly lost on Lincoln during the worst years of the war:

> Over time, Lincoln had learned the efficacy and inherent fairness of the graduated tax system . . . Lincoln understood that the public needs to believe that America operates on the moral principle of fairness. Americans must view their government as pursuing policies that are fair to all citizens.

While the doctrine of fairness in taxation has been severely challenged and revised in recent years, how taxes are applied—and to whom—is still a dynamic part of our national dialogue.

GOVERNMENT SPENDING GROWS THE WARTIME ECONOMY

There was a drawback to the 1860s currency, banking, and tax laws: their scope was not truly "national." They did not apply to the Confederacy, which had its own (shortly worthless) currency. It's a fair assumption that most Jacksonian Southern congressmen and senators would have opposed the national measures, had they not seceded.

Until Union gunboats shut down major Southern ports two years into the war, the Confederacy had plenty of sugar and cotton to ship and sell, financing the war through its export economy. When the Union controlled the Mississippi and New Orleans—and later shut down Mobile, Savannah, and Charleston—it was a different story. The North, reaping cash from its newly imposed income tax in the war's last two years, stimulated its economy while financing its army's needs. Holzer found that Union tax revenues allowed "government expenditures to grow year by year . . . the result was a great boom from 1863 to 1865, and ordinary Americans enjoyed the benefits." Indeed, because the government could also invest in infrastructure, a stimulus was in place to finance the Second Industrial Revolution benefitting the manufacturing economy.

Dubbing Lincoln "the principal architect of the expanded American economy during the war," Holzer notes that his domestic policies "provided the first clear example of the positive role that could be played by the federal government to encourage the economic growth of the nation." The president's program provided a government stimulus that the private sector was unlikely to generate. The income tax redistributed capital for a large segment of the population: As factories and businesses grew, they employed more workers, who paid more in taxes, which led to more government investment. Lincoln indisputably created jobs in a time of crisis.

Indeed, a group of financiers told Lincoln that by approving the banking legislation, he had "wrecked the economy"; in fact, it was the opposite. Allen Guelzo found that the Northern economy's gross domestic product actually grew—despite the loss of the Southern states—to $3.8 billion by 1864. The Legal Tender Act authorized the sale of $500 million in bonds and issued $150 million in paper money.

While the flood of greenbacks raised the Northern cost of living by 80 percent, "the economy grew nevertheless."

HOW PAPER CURRENCY
GAINED POPULAR TRUST

The greenback, which became America's national paper currency, had an unusual origin. Paper money was rarely a trusted vehicle of exchange in the nineteenth century. Even today, some contend that bills are of dubious value—preferring gold, silver, and even virtual digital currency to US dollars, which are based on credit.

When Chase and Lincoln worked together to issue greenbacks, it was imperative that they instill widespread trust to the people using the currency for daily transactions. After all, the federal government was trying to establish a durable medium of exchange. Religion was important to a vast degree of the nation, so many suggested that some acknowledgment of divinity be imprinted on the currency. After sifting through a few suggestions, Chase came up with "In God We Trust," which has been printed on the American dollar ever since. Since Chase was in charge of the operation, he vainly doubled down, placing his own picture on the first dollar bill to endorse the greenback.

Americans became accustomed to having God, Chase, and other national symbols printed on bills. George Washington's image eventually replaced Chase's handsome, confident visage on the one-dollar bill. Andrew Jackson, who owned slaves and hated the idea of a national bank in his time, somehow ended up on the twenty-dollar bill.

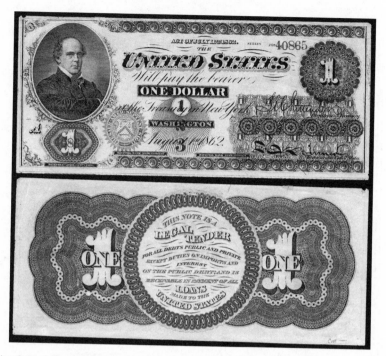

The first dollar bill from the Series 1862-1863 greenback issue, with Salmon Chase's image on its face. (Smithsonian National Museum of American History)

The Federal Reserve system was created in 1913, its logo added to bills along with unique serial numbers. Later, the eagle emblem of the Great Seal of the United States was added; it's interesting to think public approval might have been undermined if greenback designers had used Benjamin Franklin's preferred symbol for a national bird: a turkey. Yet more symbolism was designed to inspire the people's confidence: the mysterious pyramid topped by an eye adorned greenbacks, along with *Novus Ordo Seclorum*, a Latin phrase meaning "new order of the ages" (the phrase was used as early as 1782, but did not appear on the dollar until 1935). On either side of the eye is "*Annuit Coeptis*," or "favor of our undertakings."

The pyramid phrase subtly implies that not only was the republic founded by God-fearing people—they were especially blessed in history for doing so. This spiritual idea was important in politically winning the people's trust; most didn't like the idea of paper currency in the first place, given its literal status as a government-issued debt instrument. If that implication is not enough, the Treasury reminds us on every bill that "this *note* is legal tender for all debts, public and private." In order for currency to be trusted and used, it has to be universally accepted.

Illustrating presidents on bills helped inspire faith in greenbacks. It's no coincidence that Lincoln would appear on the five-dollar bill and Grant on the fifty-dollar note. Alexander Hamilton, the nation's first Treasury Secretary, remains on the ten. Yet the bills' denominations seemed to have nothing to do with the men and their various statures in history. Benjamin Franklin, who was never president, curiously appears on the hundred-dollar bill—whereas Chase made an encore appearance on the rare $10,000 note when he was bumped from the dollar—and replaced for a time by Martha Washington. (Her brief 1880s appearance makes her the only woman depicted on a bill to date, which was actually a certificate for silver.) Years later, Chase's name was added to "National" to form the "Chase National Bank," superimposing the idea that the Treasury Secretary had something to do with the bank's security and dealings. Chase wasn't a banker, nor an investor in the bank; the addition of his name was to honor him and somehow inspire confidence in the underlying institution, which has become one of the largest banks in the world.

As for the eye on the top of the pyramid, there are myriad explanations. It's possibly the "eye of providence"—that is, the symbol of an omniscient entity watchfully overlooking and protecting the republic. Or it could be a veiled reference to freemasonry. After all, Washington and many other founders were part of that secret order. Add it all together and you have a note rich in symbolism that hopefully instills trust of the government in those using the currency.

BANKING REGULATION GROWS DURING THE WAR

Examiners of the Civil War years' impact habitually miss that some proto-progressive legislation emerged under the conflict's shadow. Both the National Currency Act of 1863 and the National Bank Act of 1864 began the first wave of national banking organizations. Prior, states regulated banks within their borders—often loosely. State houses, which were far more pliable to financial concerns than a national assembly such as Congress, bent to the will of local commercial and political powerbrokers (a prime example: Stephen Douglas and the Democratic Party in Illinois). Even today, some banks receive state charters while others are accountable to federal entities such as the Comptroller of the Currency—the first truly national banking regulator created by the National Bank Act. This is why banks still include "National" and "State" in their titles. These are legal designations indirectly revealing which entity the bank is regulated by.

More importantly, the dual banking system reflected an ongoing clash that has never been fully resolved: Which units of American government would have more regulatory power, the states, or Washington? Since the Republic's beginning as a confederation of states, the issue of the whole—the *union*—has been an ongoing source of conflict.

At first, it made sense for the young nation's more commercially advanced states to have their own bank and currency systems, but when the economy and population expanded westward, state-centric models made much less sense. If one traveled from Kentucky to Illinois, or traded goods from Indiana to New Orleans, operating under the old system was inefficient. Nevertheless, with strident voices turning "nullification" and "state's rights" into rallying cries—sounded by firebrands like South Carolina's John C. Calhoun before (and long after) the war—the issue has never disappeared from the American political dialogue.

As Mehrsa Baradaran documented in the 1619 Project, weak banking oversight overall would later disproportionately hurt African American communities during the 2008 financial crisis, an indirect consequence of Antebellum banking history:

> After the war, states were allowed to keep issuing bank charters of their own. This byzantine infrastructure remains to this day and is known as the dual banking system. Among all nations in the world, only the United States has such a fragmentary, overlapping and inefficient system—a direct relic of the conflict between federal and state power over maintenance of the slave-based economy of the South.

As a Whig-Republican working under the mantel of Clay's American System, Lincoln was keenly aware of these tensions and sought to unify the country under one economic model. He did so by supporting an infrastructure national in scope, and a financial-economic system that would follow suit. What Lincoln sought in the 1860s—indeed, what congressmen would futilely seek well through 2009—was a coherent way of regulating banks. But banks can still choose their own regulators—often on the state level, which varies dramatically state to state. The insurance industry, for one, has never been federally regulated and is subject to individual state insurance regulators. The overall result is a hodge-podge of often ineffectual oversight over one of the most powerful industries on the planet, a flaw that has its roots in pre-Civil War divisions.

POLITICAL EQUALITY AND ECONOMIC OPPORTUNITY EXPAND SLOWLY, PAINFULLY

The core abstract principle of Lincolnomics was to offer Americans an equal *chance* at economic progress. If a nation "conceived in liberty" were to fulfill its promise, workers would need to have growing opportunities to ascend the ladder through their "labor"; and "capital"—meaning commercial interests—would also have the chance to expand, but not necessarily at the expense of the emergent working class.

Until 1865, slavery was the main barrier impeding Lincoln's ideal, particularly if it was allowed to flourish west of the Mississippi. How could a wage-earning person or business compete against an entity that exploited enslaved individuals? In his first Annual Message (today's equivalent of a State of the Union address), Lincoln tackled the labor-capital conflict, making his intentions clear:

> Labor is prior to, and independent of, capital. Capital is only the fruit of labor, and could never have existed if labor had not first existed. Labor is the superior of capital, and deserves the much higher consideration.

In these words, Lincoln's economic manifesto is clear. In the debate over respect for workers' priorities, he saw a clear conclusion: Laborers should get primary consideration in the country's economic policy. Although most eyes were focused on the war's progress, Lincoln's views reflected a global struggle. Workers hardly gained the upper hand as millions of them moved from the countryside—where they subsisted on their farmland and made some extra money in "cottage" industries—to the grim, "satanic mills" (in the words of poet William Blake). Living conditions, health care, and wages grew dismal as city populations swelled. The Industrial Revolution introduced the anti-worker conditions of "wage" slavery; working people could be imprisoned or exiled for unpaid debts, regarded as dark stains on their moral characters. As a young man who incurred debts—and worked them off—Lincoln was especially motivated to elevate labor above capital.

A Lincoln contemporary who would change the world with his economic thinking was the German economist and *Das Kapital* author Karl Marx. Watching industrialization unfold and envelop workers throughout Europe, Marx documented multiple injustices in working society. Because workers could not control the means of production, working conditions, or wages, they would be forever preyed upon, Marx concluded. He took note of Lincoln's Emancipation Proclamation and his reelection in 1864; along with a group of pro-labor activists called the International Workingmen's Association, Marx drafted an address that he sent to Lincoln. The worker's group expressed its optimism that Lincoln's policies, along with a Northern victory, would reaffirm the primacy of free labor and herald "a defeat for the most reactionary capitalists who depended on slavery and racial oppression."

History does not know if Lincoln read the Workingmen's letter: Charles Francis Adams, US Ambassador to Great Britain, replied for him. Adams thanked Marx and his group for their support in spite of the war's trade blockage disrupting the British textile industry. Lincoln likely knew of Marx, as the German had contributed more than 500 articles to *The New York Daily Tribune*—a powerful Republican paper at the time. The two men held diverging views on the role of capital, but they agreed on one thing: workers should ultimately be free to pursue a prosperous economic destiny. Where they differed is Marx's belief that workers could not fulfill their destiny until they controlled businesses outright, and were granted full autonomy to limit their working hours, improve workplace conditions, and enjoy free, public education. Only then would workers be truly "emancipated," in Marx's view.

As the labor movement grew in Europe, it struggled through fits and starts in the United States. After Lincoln's assassination threw the nation "under the gloom of calamity," as Emerson eulogized, President Andrew Johnson was nearly impeached over his multiple efforts to quash Reconstruction. Only the presence of federal troops in the South prevented mass bloodshed against freedmen—at first. Later, lynchings and segregationist "Jim Crow" laws permeated the institutions and culture of the South like a metastatic cancer. Nothing akin to Marx's ideal of a "bourgeois democratic republic" emerged in the former Confederacy.

Although the Thirteenth, Fourteenth, and Fifteenth Amendments conferred inalienable federal rights upon Black Americans, the Southern aristocracy preserved its white supremacist agenda, consistently and defiantly ignoring the Fourteenth Amendment's "equal treatment of all persons" clause. As the nascent labor movement painfully gained ground for eight-hour workdays in the North through the 1870s into the 1890s, the South moved backward when Reconstruction ended. Federal troops that had been protecting freedmen from the Ku Klux Klan were dispatched to break up the Great Railway Strike of 1877, leaving Black Americans undefended. Republican-led government turned *against* labor, a trend that would continue in the robber baron era as the Republican Party began to move in lockstep with capitalists, until the Progressive Era in the early twentieth century.

Lincoln was not a Marxist, but more of a bootstraps economic political philosopher. He represented railroads, appreciated free enterprise, and gave away millions of acres to capitalists to create development. There's little evidence that his overall philosophy was akin to that of Marx, who was deeply concerned over the exploitation of factory workers. And, in fact, Lincoln never definitively said that Black Americans were equal to white Americans. David Herbert Donald observes in his landmark biography:

> Lincoln's version of the American Dream was in some ways a curiously limited one. Confident that advancement was open to all who worked hard, he was untroubled by the growing disparity of wealth between the poor and the rich . . . Though Lincoln regularly represented railroads, the largest corporations in the country, he thought of economic opportunity primarily in terms of individual enterprise. In his analysis, he gave scant attention to the growing number of factory workers, who had little prospect of upward social mobility.

Still, Lincoln's legacy continued to expand the reach of economic freedom for an ever-larger group of Americans—and throughout the world. Eric Foner, our foremost scholar on the Reconstruction Era, finds that "by 1865, the war had vindicated the social vision of free labor essential to the Republican Party's outlook since its founding." The Thirteenth Amendment had expunged the institution of slavery from the Constitution. Forms of indentured servitude still existed after the amendment was passed—"peonage," or debt slavery—but it did create a new foundation for the *respect* of free labor. There was a greater agenda afoot before and after Lincoln: That democracy could be perpetuated in tandem with free labor. Foner highlights the ambition of this doctrine:

> The Republicans [of Lincoln's era] saw their anti-slavery program as one part of a worldwide movement from absolutism to democracy; aristocracy to equality; backwardness to modernity and their

conviction that the struggle in the United States had international implications did much to strengthen their resolve.

Lincoln earlier articulated this view succinctly during his campaign, when he made his Cooper Union address in New York City in 1860: "Right makes might." Free labor had moral gravity because it meant economic progress and freedom. Or, as William Seward stated, such a premise would "renovate the condition of mankind." That is still the hope of liberal democracy, although history is still climbing that treacherous road, and there would be plenty of switchbacks in the ensuing twentieth century.

IX

LINCOLN'S
INFRASTRUCTURE
OF OPPORTUNITY

"The figure of Lincoln is sui generis *in the annals of history. No initiative, no idealistic eloquence, no bushkin, no historic drapery. He always presents the most important act in the most insignificant form possible."*

—Karl Marx, 1863

L eon Czolgosz lurked in the crowded receiving line to meet President William McKinley at the Pan American Exposition in Buffalo on September 6, 1901. A new era had dawned; the world was becoming electrified, as fully showcased in the fair. Only a few years ago, Nikola Tesla engineered the hydropower of nearby Niagara Falls, creating a grand torrent of electricity to power entire cities. Industry, transportation, and commerce were profoundly changing; greater efficiency produced more goods. Electric lighting could extend the workday indefinitely. Electric trolleys connected cities with suburbs. Housework could be reduced since rugs no longer needed to be beaten by hand (with the advent of electric vacuum cleaners). Incandescent and arc lighting illuminated dark streets, rendering dangerous gas and kerosene lamps obsolete. Reading at night wouldn't make you blind. You could plug in progress: it cooled you, cooked your food, heated your home.

Yet there was a dark side to all this light. Factory workers were subjected to longer hours and more dangerous working conditions. Cities were noisier, more polluted. Immigrants lived in abject tenements and labored under poor working conditions. In reverse of Lincoln's dictum, labor was clearly inferior to capital at the turn of the century.

There was something volcanically unhinged in former steelworker Czolgosz's mind as he waited for his turn to see McKinley, an avatar of the Republican Party's unquestioning embrace of big business and industry. Czolgosz seethed: in his anarchistic haze, he saw McKinley reigning like a tyrant as workers increasingly toiled in unforgiving factories without labor rights or fair compensation, working hours, and benefits. When McKinley extended his hand, Czolgosz shot him twice. The president died eight days later of a massive infection. His assassin was executed by electric chair.

Standing in the background of the Buffalo exhibition was Robert Todd Lincoln, acting president of the Pullman Palace Car Company in Chicago, scene of the deadly Pullman Strike only seven years earlier. The president's oldest—and only surviving—son was also present at the scene when President James Garfield was shot and killed in 1881 (he was working for Garfield at the time). Neither presidential assassination was the first Robert witnessed: he had watched his father expire in a house across from Ford's Theatre in Washington, succumbing to John Wilkes Booth's shot to his head in 1865.

Despite witnessing firsthand epic violence against three presidents, including his own father, Robert Lincoln—having been solicited to run for president several times—was quietly content to amass wealth as a diplomat, investor, and Chicago lawyer and executive while tending to his grief-stricken mother, whom he committed to an asylum in her last years. Though he did not participate in politics as an elected official, Robert Lincoln remained in the inner circles of the Republican political echelon, and was familiar with the upper-class progressives active in the era to come.

Portrait of Robert Todd Lincoln, eldest son of the sixteenth president, circa 1865. (Library of Congress)

When Theodore Roosevelt became president after McKinley's death, the country fully morphed into the Progressive Era, during which the people—and a new branch of Lincoln's Republican Party—challenged corporate power, fighting for improved working conditions and more hospitable urban life. At the center of this movement was a group of social advocates that included Jane Addams, whose father was a friend of Lincoln's.

HONEST ABE REVIVED IN CHICAGO DURING THE EARLY TWENTIETH CENTURY

Chicago's sociocultural progressive movement included reformers, artists, and leaders who reverently beheld Abraham Lincoln's ideals. Jane Addams, a toddler during Lincoln's last years, often wrote of the link she felt to the president. She appreciated his endurance through a difficult childhood in Cedarville, Illinois, the state's Northwestern corner. Her father, John Huy Addams, owner of a prosperous milling operation, was a colleague of Lincoln's when he served in the state legislature; Addams would often proudly show his young daughter letters he'd received from the sixteenth president. Long after Jane Addams became one of the most influential social reformers of the twentieth century—winning a Nobel Peace Prize—she referred adoringly to her father's Lincoln letters. An entire chapter of her memoir, *Twenty Years at Hull House*, was devoted to him.

Jane Addams was one of the key figures who built a network of social change and artistic innovation on Abraham Lincoln's principles of equal economic progress for all. When Addams and Ellen Gates Starr co-founded the Hull Settlement House in 1889 to accommodate poor immigrants on Chicago's west side, there was no social safety net for the influx of millions streaming from Europe, and after World War I, from the Deep South. They needed proper food and education, to learn English and skills that would help them transcend the rat-infested tenements that first housed them. Inspired by a visit to Toynbee Hall in 1887, Addams saw the need to provide social services directly to the poor.

Hull House served the Chicago immigrant community well, hosting more than 9,000 residents in a complex of thirteen buildings. Its programs included a boys' club, kindergarten, art, theatre, and health and language classes. When Teddy Roosevelt visited in the early 1900s and befriended Addams, he won her support for his

Progressive agenda, which she embraced long before they met. During his later run for president under the "Bull Moose" Progressive Party, Addams seconded his nomination—the first woman to do so. After what proved to be an unsuccessful campaign, Roosevelt telegrammed Addams, lauding her: "I prized your action not only because of who you are and what you stand for, but because of what it symbolizes for the new movement."

Along with Roosevelt, Addams campaigned for women's right to vote, the eight-hour workday, and to outlaw child labor—three hallmarks of the era that echoed Abe Lincoln's phrase, "labor is superior to capital."

Italians, Jews, Greeks, Slovaks, and Poles came to America to work in the early twentieth century, arriving from countries in which acquiring land—and surviving on it—was, for most, an impossibility. European immigrants had a lot in common with young Abe. But when they made it through Ellis Island, they discovered streets stained with cruel inequality and nativist Americans who thought them backward, stupid, and dirty—only suited for the lowest forms of work. They were recruited to factories run by robber barons who sought cheap manual labor. Most immigrants weren't Protestant, either, making life even more difficult; the Anglican ruling class was prejudiced against "non-Natives" (never mind about Indigenous peoples), Catholics, and Jews. This cultural bigotry was so powerful that many changed their names. Shortly after McKinley's assassination by Czolgosz, *anyone* with a Slavic name was suspect; it wasn't much better for other ethnic groups whose names hadn't been anglicized.

The Progressive Era's fight against discrimination of foreign cultures and laborers fueled, among other things, a fresh look at Lincoln and his social legacy. A frenzied wave of writing focused on his life and times in the early twentieth century, much of it put to paper during the Chicago Renaissance from around 1900 to 1930. In addition to cultural change, it was truly a time of aspirational economics: If you worked in a factory, you deserved better wages, working conditions, and benefits. You had a right to expect that the *government* would respect your labor instead of bowing blindly to capitalism. The Midwestern and Chicago sectors of this movement included Theodore Dreiser, Sherwood Anderson, and Sinclair Lewis; and later, Ernest Hemingway, F. Scott Fitzgerald, and Saul Bellow, who lived briefly in Chicago.

Even William Jennings Bryan, serially unsuccessful candidate for president, espoused better circumstances for average people (particularly farmers). Reared in Jacksonville, Illinois—where Stephen Douglas got his start in politics—Bryan's memorable 1896 "Cross of Gold" Democratic Convention speech in Chicago was one of the hallmarks of populism, though he later lost the election to a well-funded McKinley campaign. He was nominated twice more for president, losing to McKinley and William Howard Taft, respectively, in subsequent elections. Bryan's final public drama was perhaps his most famous: prosecuting teacher John Scopes for teaching Darwin and the theory of evolution in the "Scopes Monkey Trial" of July 1925 in Dayton, Tennessee. Although Bryan technically won a conviction of Scopes, hewing to an anti-Darwin biblical tact, Chicagoan defense attorney Clarence Darrow later got the fine and conviction over-ruled. An exhausted Bryan died six days after the trial. Although Bryan was a failure as a political candidate, his populist sentiments reflected those of struggling farmers and rural Americans, which Lincoln would have appreciated.

As the Progressive Era continued to unfold, Lincoln's stature as a godfather of aspirational and spiritual economics grew, enhanced by leading reformers like Addams. At the core of Addams's beliefs was her father's admiration and recognition of Lincoln, recounted in her memoirs:

My father always spoke of the martyred President as *Mr.* Lincoln, and I never heard the great name without a thrill. I remember the day . . . when at my request my father took out of his desk a thin packet marked 'Mr. Lincoln's Letters,' the shortest one of which bore unmistakable traces of that remarkable personality.

Addams cultivated an elite group of friends who desired progressive change not only in social institutions, but also in literature and the arts. They reimagined architecture, poetry, fiction, biography, and urban planning in a truly American—and many a time, uniquely Midwestern—vernacular. While Addams's work was respected and celebrated well into the 1940s, scrutiny was often leveled against the "socialists and other radicals" she invited to Hull House for meetings and lectures.

One such avowed socialist was the young newspaperman, speechwriter, and poet Carl Sandburg, who arrived in Chicago from Milwaukee looking for steady work. Having served as an aide to Milwaukee's socialist mayor, he was imbued with the contemporary progressive zeal to help working people, who were struggling to organize since the disastrous Pullman Strike. Sandburg covered Chicago's race riot of 1919 and wrote for various labor journals; he knew the toils of working people, which he profiled in his volumes of "prairie" poetry.

Sandburg dedicated years to a six-volume biography of Lincoln. Written untraditionally in prose poetry, it won him international acclaim and a Pulitzer Prize. Sandburg became known as Lincoln's most extensive biographer at that time; he also wrote blank verse poetry evoking images of the prairie and Chicago's industrial leviathan, coining indelible phrases like "city of big shoulders" and "hog butcher to the world."

The Chicago poet was part of a group of artists bolstered by the city's renaissance, which was anchored by Harriet Monroe—founder of *Poetry* magazine—who published emerging voices from Sandburg to Ezra Pound, Vachel Lindsay, and T.S. Eliot. Monroe came to Chicago to establish the magazine in 1912, introducing the work of

Midwestern poets such as Edgar Lee Masters, a lawyer-poet whose law partner was Clarence Darrow. Each of these literary masters shared an intense reverence of Lincoln. According to Mark Pohlad, "Monroe was instrumental in shaping the modern literary treatment of Abraham Lincoln. She revered his memory and advanced the careers who engaged Lincoln as a subject in their work."

Monroe's time was ripe for a reappraisal of Lincoln. She started writing and editing only two decades after his assassination. By 1909, the centennial of his birth, the entire world—most notably through literature—was celebrating Lincoln's legacy. Many who knew him were still alive at the beginning of the twentieth century; Monroe had met Generals Ulysses S. Grant, William Sherman, and Philip Sheridan in the 1870s while she attended boarding school in Washington, DC.

When Monroe came to Chicago, she befriended Addams and frequently joined meetings at Hull House, giving copies of Carl Schurz's Lincoln biography to its residents. Another friend of hers was the legendary muckraking journalist Ida Tarbell; in addition to penning exposés on nefarious power trusts like Standard Oil, Tarbell wrote a two-volume Lincoln biography. Pohlad notes that Tarbell's writing on Lincoln was "wildly popular . . . she emphasized Lincoln's common rather than degraded origins, his idealism, and his successful navigation through the real world." Indeed, Tarbell celebrated the humble roots of the Prairie State president: "Where other biographers had downplayed or excoriated his frontier origins, Tarbell celebrated them as a contributing factor in his greatness."

Writers like Tarbell and other artists of the era more comprehensively injected Lincoln's rhetoric and beliefs into the creation of the modern age. An illustration from the *Chicago Daily Tribune* in 1909 depicts Lincoln sitting in front of a smokestack-crowded backdrop. The caption reads: "Lincoln's Vision: Chicago, the Capital of the Great West." The Pacific railroad would entitle San Francisco "capital of the West," but the sentiment nonetheless points to seeds sown from Lincoln's legacy.

Examinations of the romantic side of Lincoln also blossomed during Harriet Monroe's stewardship of prairie poetry. One of the most successful poets in her orbit was Edgar Lee Masters, whose *Spoon River Anthology* gave voice to Lincoln's early days in New Salem and his tragic sweetheart Ann Rutledge. *Spoon River* sold so well—eleven printings in its first year—that it became the bestselling book of poetry "in the history of American literature up to that time," Pohlad observed. Despite the resounding success of *Spoon River*, Masters burned bridges with a disparaging 1931 biography of Lincoln, which many rejected.

Lincoln's role as a social fulcrum of the Progressive Era even had a hand in reshaping architecture. Another friend of Addams and Monroe—who gave one of his first public lectures in Hull House—was a young architect envisioning buildings in a new light.

Frank Lloyd Wright came to Chicago to lead a revolution. When the central city burned to the ground in 1871, great minds like John Root, Daniel Burnham, and Louis Sullivan did more than rescue it from ash and rubble: they created a new playbook for urban architecture and planning. Architects were freeing their industry from neo-Classic or "beaux arts" constraints that imposed European formality on facades lined with Corinthian columns. The Art Nouveau and Arts and Crafts movements infused an organic sensibility. Buildings could look more natural, decorated with tangled oak leaves and vines instead made to appear like staid Greco-Roman temples.

Wright established his studio in Oak Park, Illinois, a prosperous suburb west of Chicago; the area hosted a hotbed of merchant and professional clients who could afford custom-designed homes. Establishing his practice only a few blocks from where Ernest Hemingway was raised, Wright started out with conservative, Queen Anne, and mock-Tudor designs, but soon moved to a more personal, "prairie" style as the twentieth century beckoned.

When Addams invited Wright to speak at Hull House in 1901, he read his revolutionary essay "The Art and Craft of the Machine," an obtuse manifesto of the new school of architecture. Wright looked forward to when machines would better serve artists like himself who were revisioning interior living spaces and the philosophy of the built world. At the time, Wright—who started at and was later fired from architect Louis Sullivan's prestigious architectural firm—championed an organic architecture that morphed into his prairie aesthetic. Victorian homes with their gables, sharp angles, and frilly ornamentation ceded to more streamlined, "democratic" lines; its clean, horizontal lines were embellished by glorious stained glass and front entrances that beguiled and challenged visitors. Although he loved motor cars, Wright hated gutters, sloped roof lines, and garages.

His timeless twentieth-century masterpiece, the Robie House, on the University of Chicago campus in Hyde Park (on the city's South Side), looks more like an elegant, cubist luxury yacht than a private residence. Inspired by Japanese architecture and the work of William Morris, English artist and leader of the Arts and Crafts architectural movement, Wright strove to merge a new aesthetic with a greater sense of humanity. Interior spaces were capacious and resplendent with wood trim, generous electric lighting, welcoming fireplaces, and custom-designed furniture. Wright's structures were designed to harmonize with their building sites; at Robie House, the prairie's abstract, horizontal plane. Window designs flowed with light and color based on abstract prairie grasses.

"I hope to prove, that the machine is capable of carrying to fruition high ideals of art—higher than the world has ever seen," Wright told the Hull House audience. From the Gilded Age through the Second Industrial Revolution past World War II, there is little question that Wright used the mortar of "high ideals of art" to build some of the most famous twentieth-century structures: New York's Guggenheim Museum, the Pennsylvania "Falling Water" home, Wisconsin's Johnson Wax complex, as well as countless unbuilt designs such as a mile-high skyscraper and an urban plan he called "Broadacre City."

Wright and his contemporaries were in the right moment of history to begin and execute a revolution in urban (and suburban) architecture and planning in Chicago and its environs. Wright's mentor Sullivan notes:

> Chicago grew and flourished by virtue of its pressure from without—the pressure of forest, field and plain, the mines of copper, iron and coal, and the human pressure of those who crowded in upon it from all sides seeking fortune.

Indeed, a port city built on wild, unfettered land speculation, trading, and commerce was wide open to the economic imperative of entrepreneurial efforts—which extended throughout Chicago during that explosive age. The city was little more than a mud puddle a few short years after its founding, in 1837; only some 4,000 Euro-Americans lived there. By 1880, still frenetically rebuilding after the 1871 Great Chicago Fire, the city had 500,000 residents. By 1890, when Wright emerged as an independent architect, one million resided within city limits—working the mills, lumber yards, and bustling docks. Wealthier merchants and professionals moved to Oak Park and Riverside to the west, and to North Shore enclaves like Evanston, Lake Forest, and Wilmette. Wright followed the money to clients willing to part with their cash to make bold, new statements via their suburban abodes. Thorstein Veblen's "conspicuous consumption" was in full bloom. If you had wealth, a unique home design put it on full display for all your neighbors.

Wright designed high-end custom homes, although mass production techniques were slowly being applied to houses, factories, and labor. The Chicago architect would later adopt this ethos for a series of "American System-Built" homes that were partially pre-assembled. It's unlikely that Wright borrowed their name from Henry Clay, although Lincoln was certainly a lodestone in Wright's childhood and early adulthood. Less than a dozen System homes were built (mostly in Milwaukee and Chicago's Northern suburbs in the 1910s, prior to WWI); they signaled an increasing need to make homes affordable, an idea Wright later readopted in his more compact "Usonian" homes some twenty years later. Having designed a bevy of luxury homes for private clients, Wright frequently eyed lower-cost construction techniques that made his blueprints more accessible to working people. While his American System-Built homes were hardly bargains, they were intended to be sold to middle-income clients.

In his youth, Wright was drilled by his domineering mother and inspired by his family's liberal Unitarian faith. His uncle Jenkin Lloyd-Jones, a gifted preacher and Unitarian minister, moved from southwestern Wisconsin to Chicago just like Wright had. Jenkin came to the city to establish a church and an "Abraham Lincoln Center" that his nephew had a hand in designing for his uncle, whom he mildly characterized as a "difficult client."

"Uncle Jenk" and family were "passionate admirers of Lincoln," Wright biographer Meryle Secrest writes. Jenkin had fought in the Civil War; his brother Thomas made money as a "country architect." Frank Lloyd Wright's father, William—a preacher, administrator, and itinerant businessman who frequently abandoned his family—reportedly gave a mesmerizing eulogy when he heard of Lincoln's assassination (Secrest describes it as an "appropriate and elegant address"). As his mother Anna raised him, she constantly told Frank that "the world demanded greatness from him and that he should emulate Lincoln and Christ." For the Wrights and Lloyd-Jones, Lincoln was a family affair.

LINCOLN'S INFRASTRUCTURE OF OPPORTUNITY

Frank Lloyd Wright attempted to bring Lincoln's values and his unique aesthetic to the big city. When Uncle Jenk and nephew set up in Chicago, they became enmeshed in the circle including Addams, Susan B. Anthony, Sandburg, Booker T. Washington, and William Jennings Bryan. It was quite a crowd: charged with perpetuating Lincoln's legacy and spouting new ideas on social justice, reform, literature, and politics. Frank's cousin Richard Lloyd-Jones would even bid for Lincoln's Kentucky boyhood home when it came up for auction, raising $400,000 for a granite memorial in 1905. No less than Teddy Roosevelt laid the cornerstone.

IDA B. WELLS FEARLESSLY LEADS CHICAGO MUCKRAKERS

The Progressive Era ignited a new wave of activist journalism targeting corporate greed, worker abuses, and economic hegemony. One heroine of that time stands out for her undaunted courage: Chicago-based journalist Ida B. Wells.

Born a slave in Mississippi in 1862, in her thirties she began reporting on lynchings and institutional racism for Southern papers. After a white mob burned down her office, she headed North to continue her work. Wells moved to the South Side of Chicago, just a few blocks from Stephen Douglas's Bronzeville estate. She led a crusade against a wave of lynchings in the South that began in the 1890s, documenting the murders for decades: "She faced a lot of danger, a lot of criticism and a lot of loss during her lifetime, in exposing the truth about the brutality and the extent of lynching," says Michelle Duster, her great-granddaughter.

When she came to Chicago in 1893, Wells organized a protest of the World's Columbian Exposition's failure to recognize African Americans; the fair sponsored pavilions for advances in transportation, the arts, and commerce, and for nearly every major country in the world. The fair's organizers thought the Haitian exhibit would be a suitable representation for African Americans. Frederick Douglass, the fair delegate for the Haitian government, was similarly aggrieved; he and Wells published a pamphlet entitled "The Reason Why the Colored American Is Not in the World's Columbian Exposition." Fair officials offered a compromise, sponsoring a special "Negro Day" for African Americans. Although Wells and many other African Americans considered the gesture inadequate, Douglass did not push the issue further, and chose to highlight other problems that Black people faced during the time. Wells continued her muckraking journalism and began writing an autobiography, which she was unable to finish due to her untimely death from kidney disease.

"She left a firsthand document behind for us to be able to read about the realities of what was going on in our country during that tumultuous period of 1870 to 1930," Duster told *The Chicago Sun-Times*. "Some would argue those struggles continue. But I think she created an example of how to document information in a way that is indisputable, letting the facts speak for themselves."

To honor her legacy, the Chicago City Council renamed Congress Parkway (between Columbus Drive and the Eisenhower Expressway) "Ida B. Wells Drive" in 2018. Although Wells received little recognition from the mainstream press in Chicago—she died in 1931 at the age of sixty-eight—she was honored with a special Pulitzer Prize citation in 2020.

ROBERT LINCOLN'S WORLD

The Second Industrial Revolution—seeded in part by the sixteenth president's legislative legacy—became Robert Lincoln's new reality as steam locomotives rolled right into the heart of hectic downtown Chicago, spewing cinders and toxic haze. On the South Side, smoke-billowing foundries and mills turned upper Midwestern iron ore, coal, and limestone into steel for the cities and railroads. At the time of the World's Columbian Expo in 1893, Chicago was grossly polluted by the industrial effluence of the manufacturing and transportation upheaval.

Despite societal advances and the reexamination of Abraham Lincoln's political and economic aims, cities at the beginning of the Progressive Era were mostly dark and crowded, unhealthy and unbearably sooty. Few could afford to live in sparkling new Chicago suburbs like Frederick Law Olmstead's Riverside, where Wright built some of his spacious jewels. Those of the lower classes lived in grim, industrial districts near factories. Noisy, polluting trains were everywhere. Homes were dimly lit by dangerous gas or kerosene.

How did Robert Lincoln view his role in carrying his father's legacy into the twentieth century, even as his contemporaries elevated Abe's iconic status to a social force? He certainly knew that his father traveled in Pullman's earliest rail cars and defended two of Illinois's largest railroads. As a boy, he traveled with his father, even enjoying an I&M Canal excursion. When Robert started his own law firm in Chicago, his social network included many firms and city leaders who would be involved in rebuilding downtown after the Great Chicago Fire of 1871. Architects like Sullivan and Burnham were part of his cadre, men who would reshape how cities looked and operated across the world. (Burnham's firm designed New York's striking Flatiron Building and Union Stations in Washington, DC, and Chicago.)

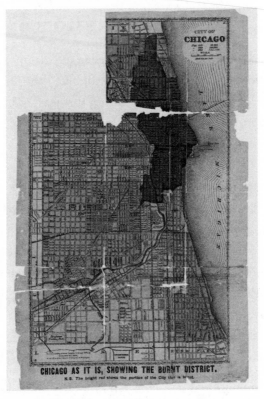

Most of Chicago's downtown core burned to the ground in 1871. (Library of Congress)

Robert's law firm—Isham, Lincoln and Beale—represented future titans who were reimagining civilization. Widespread use of electricity, which first came to urban centers in the late nineteenth and early twentieth centuries, rooted in Chicago like no other city. At the turn of the new millennium, Chicago was the world's fastest-growing metropolis. It was also America's warehouse and distribution center, thanks to its port, rail hub, and central location between three coasts (by then, the Illinois Central reached all the way to New Orleans). Sears and Montgomery Ward based their mammoth catalog operations in Chicago, shipping goods by rail. Steel mills, foundries, and machine shops sprung up all around, manufacturing everything from rails to sheet metal. The meatpacking, food processing, and candy-making industries—and, later, pharmaceuticals and telephone equipment companies—all made vast industrial complexes in the Chicago area their homes.

One of Robert's most notable clients was Samuel Insull, whose name is somewhat lost to history. As Thomas Edison's secretary and one of the first executives of Edison General Electric (initially backed and financed by Lincoln's friend Henry Villard), Insull learned the electrical distribution business so well that when he came to Chicago in 1893, he seeded an empire of his own—merging smaller electrical generation companies. Insull quickly consolidated the tiny power companies Chicago Edison and Commonwealth Electric into Commonwealth Edison (which still operates today as part of Exelon), building his empire on the alternating current technology of Nikola Tesla—the Serbian engineering genius who harnessed Niagara Falls and worked for Edison in 1884. The two men became friends in their Edison days; Insull sent Tesla money when he was down on his luck in the early twentieth century. Both blossomed at the dawn of the new age.

Tesla demonstrated his technology to glorious effect at the 1893 Chicago Fair, which some 28 million Americans (nearly half of the country's 63 million) attended. What they saw was a luminous flowering of the contemporary age: Electric lights provided by Westinghouse and Tesla's generators illuminated the beaux arts buildings. Trains ushered attendees directly onto the fairgrounds, which featured a giant Ferris wheel, the music of Scott Joplin, and the boxed treat "Cracker Jack." Most importantly, the sinewy might of electricity was everywhere: powering motors and demonstrating how it would change life from the factory to the domicile.

Insull's utility holding empire would include a gas company, three railroads, and the corporation that eventually became Exelon, still one of the nation's largest utilities. He marketed electrical power the way

Armour sold beef, Wrigley sold Juicy Fruit, or Pullman sold sleeping cars. Stock in his "public utility" companies was sold door to door. Insull gave away electric flat irons from electric trucks to housewives, who would demand their husbands pay up to wire their homes with Insull's systems.

Nearly all of Chicago knew Robert Lincoln, Insull's lawyer, who befriended his client when he came from New York after Edison's companies were consolidated by J.P. Morgan into the General Electric Company. When Insull's companies filed for bankruptcy after the crash of 1929, the utilities baron fled to Europe, fearing prosecution. He was later extradited and tried for fraud in three trials—and acquitted each time. Unlike today's accused executives, Insull lost everything, including his palatial country estate. Robert Lincoln was untouched by Insull's demise; he died a wealthy man in 1926, at the height of the Roaring Twenties.

In Abraham Lincoln's day, railroads connected barely half of the nation. By the time his son started his law practice, the iron highways spanned the continent with freight and people. It was no coincidence that Pullman and other manufacturing giants like Cyrus McCormick, founder of International Harvester—which later expanded into trucks and construction equipment—chose Chicago as their headquarters and main manufacturing bases. The city sat at the nexus of the continent's most vibrant rail hub.

An idyllic American state, however, would not emerge from the Progressive Era. Although tremendous advances were made on the fronts of labor, industrial productivity, and economic stability, they were often punctuated by horrible reversals. A massive recession followed the 1893 Columbian Expo. World War I took the lives of tens of millions while it shredded the Hapsburg, Prussian, Russian, and Ottoman Empires. The 1917 Russian Revolution installed the Bolsheviks and later Soviet Stalinism. A flu pandemic took the lives of perhaps 50 to 100 million people worldwide following that war. Then another recession, fascism's rise, the Great Depression, and World War II. Imagine what life was like for those who lived from the dawn of the twentieth century to just 1946: They witnessed unprecedented destruction, followed by an eventual rebirth in North America, Europe, and Japan. Even during the booming 1920s—which, of course, ended badly—social critics like Lewis Mumford grasped vainly for utopia.

"In the economic foundations of the Republic," Mumford wrote in *The Story of Utopias* in 1922, presaging British economist John Maynard Keynes, "we look in vain for a recognition of the labor problem. Now the labor problem is a fundamental difficulty in our modern life." A supporter and friend of Frank Lloyd Wright, and an incisive observer of the increasingly technocratic world, Mumford was referring to Plato's classic, *Republic*. America was far from a utopia. There was still a dearth of decent housing, living wage labor, and land for people to transcend subsistence living—a pronounced issue in the 1920s and today. Mumford's perennial labor problem supposed that workers should earn enough to retire in dignity from a life of honest toil.

Other major problems loomed between the wars. Cars and trucks began clogging country roads and narrow city streets by the million, but it was still difficult to get from one city or region to another. The infrastructure simply was not there for rubber-wheeled vehicles. Building upon the Transcontinental Railroad, the idea of national roads stumbled out of the Progressive Era—a notion that eventually gained momentum despite numerous political potholes.

X

BUILDING UPON LINCOLN'S LEGACY

Infrastructure to Date

"In those days, we were not sure it could be accomplished at all. Nothing of the sort had ever been attempted."

—Dwight D. Eisenhower on crossing the US in a military convoy

A young army lieutenant colonel came through the "Crossroads of America" on July 19, 1919, part of a massive military convoy testing the feasibility of moving men and material across the continent. Where the Lincoln Highway crossed the Dixie Highway is a little-known national landmark in Chicago Heights, Illinois. Theoretically, you can drive to all three coasts from there, although your vehicle might not have made it in the year after the Great War. Roads were perilous, where they existed at all. The elements made them virtually unpassable during the wet months. Older roads were built on trails such as the Vincennes, which linked the Wabash Valley to the Sauk Trail, used by Native Americans to travel from the Detroit area to the Chicago region.

The convoy—280 soldiers, sixty-three trucks, ambulances, and trailers—was greeted with resplendent fanfare. The city welcomed them with bands playing and sirens sounding, flags draped from the streets in the year after the "War to End All Wars" ended in 1918. The convoy was treated like royalty; visitors streamed through the nearby grounds where they were temporarily camped, treating the soldiers to hot coffee, showers, and home-cooked dinners. The dusty dough boys were on a special mission: They were collecting data on the *military* value of the road and researching how the federal government could construct a national policy on national highways.

Col. Dwight D. Eisenhower, stopping in Chicago Heights with the army convoy as part of a sixty-two-day ordeal, came to learn about mass-scale logistics more than two decades later as Supreme Allied Commander when he and Allied Forces invaded Europe along two different fronts and fought the Japanese Empire across an impossibly wide ocean. Germany's well-constructed *Autobahn* seemed logical and efficient, Eisenhower later observed. His home country lacked anything remotely like it, even though it was thousands of miles across. Ike traversed the country only to discover the gross inadequacy of its national road system. It was an irony not lost on the future president.

When the colonel made his trek on the cusp of the Roaring Twenties, the country had national roads (such as the Lincoln and Dixie Highways), but their routes were more suited to romantic adventures than for use as viable transcontinental motorways. As mass production of rubber-wheeled vehicles powered by internal combustion began, the country—and world—was ill-prepared for the advance of the vehicular machine age. Other than railroad expansion, little had been done to create modern, all-weather roads—save for the first traffic light, erected in

1868 outside of the British Parliament. Modern transportation demanded much more than the old miracle of the Transcontinental Railroad, signed into law by Lincoln in 1861 and completed in 1869. Nearly a century later, there was no decent, continuous coast-to-coast thoroughfare.

Roads were nearly all rough because they were not designed for the new generation of vehicles, nor were they ever suitable for efficient travel by trucks, much less by horses. The old stagecoach routes and Indian trails' surfaces were always changing. Travelers needed roads built of a durable material that could stand up to precipitation, cold, heat, and varying weather the whole year through. The innovation called *macadam*, named after Scottish roadbuilder Loudon Mac-Adam, was first introduced on an English turnpike in 1816. Laid on a smooth, dirt bed, the macadam surface combined a ten-inch layer of stone compressed by a horse-drawn roller. Later iterations added more layers of finely crushed stone and a sticky, petroleum-based substance called asphalt, which bound the stone into a somewhat uniform surface. This "water-bound macadam" was later renamed "tarmac." These formulae variations evolved into modern asphalt; concrete also came to be used as a longer-lasting material. It would be decades, however, before a workable formula could be mass-produced and applied to American roads.

Scarcely a decade before Ike's eye-opening 1919 journey, few roads in the US were paved. Driving hundreds of miles west of Chicago led a hapless driver onto old pioneer trails and through mountain gaps, like the infamous Donner Pass through the Sierras. At the end of the twentieth century's first decade, there were 2.2 million miles of state and county roads. Only a miserable *8 percent* of total road length was "improved" by some modest form of paving or concrete. Most were primitive dirt or gravel paths that followed ancient trails. Concrete covered just nine miles.

FISHER AND THE LINCOLN HIGHWAY

Because there was no dedicated, robust federal funding for multi-state road improvements prior to the 1950s Interstate era, most funds came from states, counties, and townships—the initiative to build national highways was first raised by the private sector. Carl Fisher, entrepreneurial builder of the Indianapolis Speedway in 1908, created the Lincoln Highway Association: a private entity formed to raise money for a road that would connect New York's Times Square to San Francisco. The vehicle boom was mushrooming; 250 automakers a year introduced new advances to make the gasoline-powered "horseless carriages" more powerful, durable, and safer. Fisher, a brilliant promoter who would develop (and lose) his fortune on developing Miami Beach, was at first ridiculed for the "Indy" speedway. But he was right on top of the zeitgeist: Americans were falling in love with cars and the freedom they offered.

Cars and trucks offered Americans a quicker route to the promise and perils of the twentieth century. Before the mass electrification of the 1890s, street trolleys were mostly pulled by equine labor, littering cities with horse manure. The four-legged locomotives deposited some 60,000 gallons of urine and 2.5 million pounds of manure on New York streets *daily* in the trolley days of the late nineteenth and early twentieth centuries. The waste contributed to disease and the general unpleasantness of city life before the traction age.

Fisher became the avatar of the "Good Roads Movement" advocating for decent city streets and highways. It was a ripe time for that Progressive Era branch to flower, as former Civil War General Roy Stone stated in 1893: "Americans have the worst roads in the civilized world," imposing a "crushing tax on the whole people, a tax the more intolerable in that it yields no revenue." Having committed to free rural postal delivery in 1896, the federal government needed passable roads to make good on that promise. It wasn't until 1913—when

Fisher formed the Lincoln Highway organization—that America's awareness of its road problem came squarely into public view.

Ironically, even well into the twentieth century, many states were *prohibited* by their constitutions from contributing to internal improvements—the underlying political theme that motivated Lincoln to run for office in the 1830s. A nascent federal highway program did not emerge until 1916, and would not gain meaningful funding until the Eisenhower era. World War I delayed any serious legislative consideration of the program. Undaunted by Europe's Great War, Fisher called for a "coast-to-coast rock highway" on May 1, 1915. He severely underestimated its cost at only $10 million. Despite raising some $1 million from friends in the auto industry, he couldn't convince Henry Ford to contribute, as he insisted that the *government*—not private citizens or companies—should fund road building.

Dedicating it to Abraham Lincoln, Fisher renamed the "rock" highway the Lincoln Highway, and a massive project was born. Country-wide celebrations—carefully coordinated by Fisher and the Lincoln Highway Association (LHA)—introduced prewritten sermons preaching that "such a highway would be a most fitting and useful monument to the memory of Lincoln." Indeed, thousands of markers along what would become US Route 30 trumpeted Lincoln. The sixteenth president's iconic deeds were once again invoked, this time while connecting the continent in the motorcar era. After Ford rolled out the mass-produced Model T in 1908, America was irrevocably smitten.

As if the Lincoln memorialization of a century wasn't enough, there was another link to the president: Henry Bourne Joy, then president of the Packard Motor Company, also became an executive of the LHA. His father, James Frederick Joy, was an Illinois railroad man; like Lincoln, James was a railroad lawyer, serving as general counsel for the Michigan Central Railroad. As a "Free Soiler" and a Republican, he claimed to be a "close friend, confidant and supporter" of Lincoln.

They likely met and conferred during Lincoln's famous defense of the Illinois Central.

Henry Joy felt it his personal mission to educate the public on how wretched America's roads were, since he had driven over them on many excursions in his exquisitely styled Packard sedans. If he was successful, he thought, Americans would *demand* better, more durable roads from their government. From the aspirations of private businessmen like Joy and Fisher derived the onus of building public infrastructure. Improved roads meant more car sales and growth in industries like refineries, "filling" stations, and roadside restaurants and lodging. A national road program was the first big kiss of America's tempestuous affair with wheels and the open road.

Despite its glorious name, the Lincoln Highway Association first sold "certificates" to fund the colossal undertaking it proposed. President Woodrow Wilson was assigned "Certificate #1" for his generous contribution of five dollars. Teddy Roosevelt and Thomas Edison also contributed. Yet Henry Ford, who revered Edison, was right about the LHA's mission: It would not come anywhere close to raising the billions needed to build a true intercontinental highway system. The initial East-West route was 3,400 miles, about half of it considered to be improved (a bold overstatement). Joy straightened out the route to 3,100 miles, but it would still have to cross brutally challenging mountains, deserts, and rivers, following older routes such as the Mormon Trail and Pennsylvania Pike. Its original course crossed or ran over some 250 named trails.

With much work to be done, bonfires and fireworks feted the dedication of the Lincoln Highway route on October 31, 1913. Fisher's first official "Trail Blazer" semi-passage occurred months earlier, starting in Indianapolis on July 1, 1913. It took an exhausting thirty-four days to arrive in San Francisco. The convoy of seventeen cars and two trucks battled deep mud in Iowa, sand drifts in the deserts of Utah and Nevada, and suffered a number of cracked axles, exploding radiators, and flooded roads. They took the train to Indianapolis on the return trip.

After World War I, a modest amount of highway construction began, including a high-quality "Ideal Section" of poured concrete between Dyer and Schererville, Indiana, in 1920. The Roaring Twenties, which saw a great deal of urban road development, would see little progress on national highways—although standards would be put in place for long-distance roadbeds.

As America grew richer, its lust for the open road became more intense. Establishing a numbering system for longer highways assigned older roads numerals that became famous: The Lincoln Highway became Route 30, and Dixie Highway eventually became Route 41. In 1926, US Route 66 was born. As the "Mother Road," Route 66 started at Lake Michigan in Chicago and terminated in Los Angeles. Not coincidentally, it ran right through Springfield and parallel to the I&M Canal, southwest of the city—a route Lincoln often traveled.

After the 1929 crash, most federal dollars in the New Deal alphabet soup programs went to job creation. While the country struggled to regain its economic footing—building rural roads, improving parks, expanding electrification outside of cities—the national highway system was mostly sidelined. Franklin D. Roosevelt's "Federal-Aid Highway Act of 1938" was a major step forward. It called for the feasible building and funding of a national road system. Fisher died the following year, having been ruined by the stock market and real estate crash, which was most damaging in southern Florida.

INTERSTATE SYSTEM EMERGES FROM THE LINCOLN HIGHWAY MOVEMENT

The mental notes Ike took when traveling the Lincoln Highway in 1919 (and later during WWII, decent German roads) reemerged as goals of his administration when he served as president in the 1950s. He was flummoxed by resistance to building a world-class transportation infrastructure in America following history's most devastating world war. Europe and Japan were rebuilding while Congress dithered on how to link the nation's cities.

Several legislative attempts to fund an intercontinental highway system were mired in special-interest politics. Trucking companies did not want a tax on diesel fuel to pay for it. Automakers lobbied against a gasoline tax because they believed it would hurt car sales. And there was still the vexing question of how a federal government rebuilding after WWII—and shelling out for the Korean War—would finance the initiative.

Yet the Interstate Highway System was emblematic of what could be done with publicly financed infrastructure. Seemingly everyone with a car, truck, or business benefitted from this amenity. What would it cost, though? The concrete and asphalt ribbons, bridges, overpasses, clover leaves, and tunnels of a vast continental system would need ongoing repairs, expansions, and rebuilding, amounting to hundreds of billions of dollars of capital.

In recovery from a heart attack at his home in Key West on January 5, 1956, Eisenhower announced in his *in absentia* State of the Union address that he would support "legislation to provide a modern, interstate highway system." The president also addressed the difficulties of getting such a bill through Congress in the past year, pivoting to a deeper appeal: such a system was "needed for the personal safety, general prosperity and national security of the American people." The Lincoln Highway convoy still embedded in his memory, conquering general and president Ike was hard to resist. He repeated the dispatch in his budget message eleven days later, emphasizing "our mounting traffic problem."

Ike and Congress succeeded, of course, in funding the Interstate System with tens of billions of dollars collected from fuel taxes deposited in a Highway Trust fund (and additional appropriations). This financing mechanism worked for decades; in recent years, it's fallen short of the demand for highway improvements. Suburbs and roadside developments created during the Interstate Era led to an even-greater demand for infrastructure. Public urban and interurban transportation networks have not kept up with the need to keep a growing number of cars off the road. As more retail deliveries are dispatched by truck overnight—and brick-and-mortar retail establishments die in the "etailer age"—traffic increasingly clots every road and highway.

Nevertheless, economic development that grew from the Interstate System is one of the great success stories of public infrastructure in modern history. The Romans certainly built some great roads and aqueducts, but they achieved nothing close to the US Interstate System: Its initial 41,000 miles girdled the globe in sheer distance. Though the system cannot accommodate the more than 250 million vehicles on today's roads—cities are choked by traffic and pollution—it is still a marvel of mass engineering and public financing, a model that needs to be thoughtfully reimagined in the era of climate change.

MODERN FAILURES TO EMULATE LINCOLNOMICS

Eisenhower's Interstate System incorporated Lincoln's spirit in more than just the aspiration of the project. It was the ultimate internal improvement: rivalling the scope of the Transcontinental Railroad while elevating the economic status of every town and city along the way. Lincoln was never far from Ike's mind and heart, particularly as he rested in his farm home adjacent to the Gettysburg battlefield. The two men won wars that exacted horrible tolls, and led to global societal changes and massive rebuilding—work that continues, an ongoing legacy.

Enshrined in Lincoln's dream was a radical American goal: If the nation committed to funding infrastructure *and* pursuing equality (through Constitutional amendments and federal laws), the collective impact would create more economic opportunity for the greatest number of Americans. There's been severe backsliding on that prospect in recent years; it's important to ask why America has been moving away from the rich future of Lincolnomics.

For millions, progress in agriculture, employment, and manufacturing meant escaping the back-breaking, life-shortening labor of Lincoln's day. Industrialized labor wrought specialization and better wages for Americans with higher-level skills and college educations. Those ascending the ladder were solving what economist John Maynard Keynes called "the economic problem": captivity to constant work that pays bills—the "struggle for subsistence." Unionization efforts across industries, supported by New Deal policies in the 1930s, led to collective bargaining for better wages, benefits, and working conditions.

In 1930, Keynes referred to "technological unemployment"—loss of jobs to machines—when predicting mankind would achieve a dramatically improved standard of living that would *solve* the "economic problem." Then, other worries would occupy us, such as what to do with our lives without work in them. In theory, machines would handle the drudgery, and we would be free to discover the meaning of life and find purpose in our existence. To an extent, this has come to be—a high degree of mechanization has taken over mining, manufacturing, and the most labor-intensive industries, eliminating hundreds of thousands of jobs along the way.

But Keynes failed to predict the overall impact of the rising cost of living in a consumer-focused society. Escalating consumer costs have made living-wage work, and fringe benefits like retirement plans and health care, a necessity for most middle-class Americans so that they might be able to avoid poverty. Social Security, the crowning last achievement of the New Deal era, is not enough to finance a dignified retirement. And Medicare doesn't apply to anyone under sixty-five, unless they have a severe medical condition or are permanently disabled. Out-of-pocket health care is dramatically costlier than thirty years ago; college educations often run six figures or higher. It would be nirvana if Keynes was right about a universal shift from work to leisure pursuits. He was prescient about so many things in his time—and ours.

Then, there's the existential question of capitalism. Work gives us a purpose to get up every morning, something we need in a spiritual sense. Keynes's original optimism has a bittersweet conclusion: "If the economic problem is solved," Keynes wrote, "mankind will be deprived of its traditional purpose."

Keynes's optimism about vastly improved standards of living has been contradicted in recent decades. Jobs that paid relatively decent, defined-benefit pensions offered to many blue-collar workers (and throughout the white-collar world) are hard to come by. Now, 401(k)-type plans featuring voluntary contributions are the standard. Union power and collective bargaining is diminished. Tens of millions of Americans struggle on hourly wages with few benefits, largely on their own with health care—a painful point proved by the novel coronavirus pandemic.

There were signs of modest economic progress through 2019 (mostly in income), but for most of the twenty-first century, middle-income workers have lost ground (the COVID-19 pandemic is causing ongoing massive economic disruption as this goes to press). From 2000 to 2018, median household income fell 2.3 percent (for nonelderly households) and 6 percent for median African American households, according to Census Bureau figures. This eighteen-year period included two recessions and the massive credit meltdown of

2008, in which most middle-class Americans suffered from job loss or depletion of home equity, or both. The 16 percent poverty rate for children showed no change over that period. (At the time of this writing in late 2020, income and employment statistics are much more disheartening.) Meager boosts for people on the ragged edge of middle-class life included programs like Social Security, unemployment insurance, Supplemental Nutritional Assistance (food stamps), and refundable tax credits, which keep an estimated 38 million people out of poverty.

Much of the stagnation in middle-income economic growth can be attributed to the lack of jobs paying more than $20 an hour. Wages simply have not kept up with inflation and the rising cost of health care, housing, and higher education. Debt, an avoidable sinkhole for many trying to pay their bills, has overwhelmed Americans on this treadmill: US households held more than $14 trillion in total debt in 2019; $1.6 trillion was for college loans, and more than $444 billion was on credit cards.

HOW LINCOLNOMICS COULD WORK TODAY

How might a massive Lincolnomics-guided infrastructure plan help Americans advance beyond mass unemployment, wage stagnation, and debt? Such a program would be a broad, Keynesian jump-start toward better jobs with higher incomes. The economist championed government creation of jobs during the Great Depression, which became part of Franklin Delano Roosevelt's "New Deal" plan to revive the economy. This kind of national stimulus was, in fact, proposed by President Barack Obama in 2009—and in his seven subsequent budget requests through the end of his second term. Congress, controlled by anti-Obama Republicans from 2009 through 2016, blocked his every effort to enact a broad-based infrastructure program.

Such a fifty-state infrastructure revival plan, however, would dramatically impact family incomes, particularly those stuck in the hourly economy: Better-paid workers would have more disposable income for services and goods. They'd pay higher income taxes, which would support more infrastructure on every level. Workers would rebuild roads, schools, bridges, and public amenities at prevailing wages for skilled and semi-skilled jobs. The public works and social programs trend, unfortunately, has moved in the other direction for the last several decades.

According to a report by the Economic Policy Institute, public infrastructure spending parallels the decline in real income over the past decade (after inflation is subtracted), a trend that began in the late 1960s. This inverse relationship hurts middle-class Americans' economic well-being. "Overall spending on infrastructure as a share of gross domestic product (GDP) has been in long-term decline," author Josh Bivens notes. What would happen if a serious national infrastructure program was enacted? There's little debate that it would create higher-paying jobs, increase private investment, and boost productivity. Bivens adds:

> If the fiscal boost of infrastructure investment were accommodated by monetary policymakers, each $100 billion in infrastructure spending would boost job growth by roughly 1 million full-time equivalents (jobs) . . . The rate of return to infrastructure investment is large; the median and average estimates of a review of dozens of studies on infrastructure indicate that each $100 spent on infrastructure boosts *private-sector* output by $13 (median) and $17 (average) in the long run.

But recent federal and state administrations have ignored the promise of Lincolnomics. There's a disconnect between economic progress and the jobs needed to fulfill that promise. Even in the recovery years after the 2008 collapse, significant and ongoing investments in infrastructure were not made, sidelined by partisan politics. More focus was placed on the temporary nature of financial markets and tax breaks. In its wake, "the American dream of rags to riches, the Horatio Alger story, was largely a myth," observed Joseph Stiglitz, a Nobel Prize-winning economist. "Economic mobility was extremely limited." The days of Lincoln-like ascension from the Kentucky backwoods to the Oval Office were long over.

Stiglitz found that "many investment opportunities in the public sector with very high economic and social returns" were abandoned in favor of revising the tax code to favor the ultra-wealthy. The effects of this poor tradeoff impair the nation's economic future: "Eventually such underinvestments in the public sector will hurt returns to investment in the private."

This is a moment when one thinks back and sighs, "What would Lincoln do?" Based on his philosophy and politics, Lincoln would endorse a way forward that revisits the American Dream through a collaborative model. Reflecting the diverse interests of his cabinet, the wartime president had to work with incompetent generals, slow battlefield progress, and the politics of overseeing a bloody, unpopular war. His collaborative model succeeded through it all, and the Thirteenth, Fourteenth, and Fifteenth Amendments passed after he was assassinated—and Reconstruction-hater President Andrew Johnson was impeached (but not removed) from office.

In forecasting the "Future of American Politics," *New York Times* columnist and author David Brooks invokes a decidedly Lincolnesque strategy that abandons political tribalism. Just as Lincoln governed a fractious electorate, the underlying power of his leadership style was collaboration based on diverse opinions. He regularly courted Frederick Douglass's views on equality and read letters from families who lost loved ones in the Civil War. Although he could be at odds with powerbrokers like newspaper mogul Horace Greeley, he wanted to know what they thought. When the war was going poorly in its early years, Lincoln had a lot of enemies; similar anxieties that tore the country apart during the Civil War still fester and divide. Brooks notes that "some of our institutions, like Congress, have been completely subsumed by tribal warfare." He suggests "reforming institutions so that they encourage collaboration."

For that to happen, we would need a new leadership culture. Infrastructure rebuilding would be an ideal purpose for this reform. Would infrastructure rebuilding solve our complex economic problems? Not entirely—but it would be a down payment on once again financing the American Dream.

THE NEW COLLABORATION: LINCOLNOMICS IS A CULTURE OF INNOVATION

A task of the new collaboration would be to create a broadly based culture of innovation and public-private improvements. This culture already exists in the Bay Area, New York City, and other bastions of higher education and wealth. But it doesn't necessarily thrive in the heartland, where innovation could unknot rail traffic or replace factories lost to automation or globalization.

What would this new culture look like? Walk into most any major public library and ask for the "maker space." There, you'll find free software, 3-D printers, and laser cutters for making thousands of things from scratch. Some of these mini tech-hubs include sewing machines and recording studios. Even community colleges have them. These publicly accessible maker spaces democratize the invention and building of just about anything. Sure, many objects—from plastic chess pieces to mini-robots—are made from kits or preexisting programs. But there is still great power in making things—especially for an entire generation that will be saddled with building or rebuilding bridges, rail connections, freight terminals, and water plants. Lincoln the inventor would be grinning ear to ear at such a prospect.

State and local governments, not surprisingly, have stepped up to create a new culture of collaboration. In 2019, state ballot initiatives raised nearly $8 billion for transportation projects; as Americans drive more than 3 trillion miles a year, in total, that falls far short of the estimated $836 billion in necessary national highway improvements. But it shows that regional and state governments are engaged in the unquestionable demand for public funding: Americans spent about 7 *billion* hours in traffic delays, costing an estimated $616 annually per motorist.

In the quest to create a new culture of innovation based on inclusiveness and holistic thinking (that can tackle such issues as climate change and economic inequality), what would Lincolnomics embrace? The philosophy would certainly promote cooperation, and the making—and remaking—of complex systems. It'd have to reject the myth that a lone inventor suddenly comes up with an idea *all by himself*, changing the world and making him an instant billionaire. Steve Jobs, Bill Gates, and Elon Musk had thousands behind them. They were supported by large teams that brought their products into the world. And Lincolnomics would want to know why they were doing it. What would be the point, if they failed to improve human life and labor?

"Brilliant individuals who could *not* collaborate tended to fail," observes Walter Isaacson in *The Innovators*. "Human creativity involves values, intentions, aesthetic judgements, emotions, personal consciousness and a moral sense." Bookmark those last two attributes: Without personal consciousness and a moral sense, every economic rationale in the world falls flat. We build things because it helps other humans, because what we do matters.

Returning to Lincoln on the matter of personal consciousness being necessary to bring about positive social change: It was the internal sense that he lacked something in education or standing that fueled his pragmatic view on infrastructure. Lincoln knew he, and millions like him emerging from the wilderness and prairies, would be forgotten and abused by a lack of social and economic progress. His plans for himself (and later America and beyond) rejected "a harsh social narrative that vilified those left behind—a worldview that workers often internalized," opines Nicholas Kristof in *The New York Times*, writing about today's labor crisis that has "moved from an inclusive capitalism in the postwar era to a rigged system that hobbles unions, underinvests in children and then punishes those left behind." This neglect of Americans exiled from decent, living-wage labor results in despairing, epidemic realities: drug and alcohol abuse, and early death.

Just as Lincoln knew he was not morally deficient for lacking a proper education in his youth in the back woods of Kentucky, Illinois, and Indiana, he would not believe that Americans displaced by globalization, automation, and corporate downsizing have character defects. He was all-in on the bootstraps mentality of the American ethos—himself, the ideal model of a self-made man—but he did not buy into the toxic view that coming from somewhere else, speaking some language other than English, or having skin that is not white means you should not have access to opportunities of upward mobility offered to white, English-speaking Americans.

As we've witnessed recently (and throughout history), this regressive attitude not only fails to promote long-term social and economic progress—it leaves innovation and collaboration behind. It's an issue that needs to be addressed globally, particularly in the context of workplace automation, climate change, population growth, diminishing resources, and a rising tide of nationalism. A more inclusive, worldwide perspective is needed to expand Lincoln's vision of internal improvements for a growing human population.

A STOP ON THE LINCOLN HIGHWAY

When most of us think of Lincoln, we think of his monuments. They are everywhere across the US, particularly in Illinois—the state where he matured into a president. There is one that once stood a few feet from the corner of the Lincoln and Dixie Highways.

Entitled "A. Lincoln: On the Road to Greatness," the statue was erected by the Mayor of Chicago Heights with the help of private donations. Historians can't be sure that Abe ever came through this part of Illinois, although his friend Gurdon Hubbard did—it was a stop on the "Chicago Road," also known as "Hubbard's Trail."

In recent decades, Chicago Heights has become more known for its faded industry and past organized crime activity. In its heyday, the city was highly industrious, hosting a Ford stamping plant (which, at the time of this writing, has laid off hundreds of workers) and smaller metalworking businesses. It once had a bustling downtown that sported a fancy little hotel designed by Louis Sullivan, and a "Lincoln-Dixie" movie theater. Street cars linked it to Chicago and smaller cities like Joliet. Its Bloom Township high school is an art deco gem. At one time, there were enough jobs for nearly everyone; workers could raise their kids in prosperity and send them to college.

Now, Chicago Heights' Lincoln statue stands mostly as an aspirational reminder. Like many industrial heartland hubs, the city struggles mightily with poverty, crime, and economic development. Its once-thriving downtown is a deteriorating shell. The dynamic Polish, Italian, Greek, and Slovak immigrant neighborhoods are hurting. Chicago Heights is a living symbol of what needs to be done to revive thousands of places once embraced by economic progress.

The Lincoln Highway itself was a lifeline, like all major roads and expressways, that grew into something more expansive. Although it does not connect Chicago Heights directly to Chicago—it was deliberately routed around the city—the route created a corridor of growth that would later be bisected by several interstate highways. Trucks traveling long distances would no longer have to wait for stoplights and rail traffic. People driving coast to coast could take in the immense beauty of the country while enjoying roadside camping—and later, tens of thousands of motels, rest stops, and specialized restaurants and services. It conferred upon towns where few would normally visit a palpable economic vitality. Lincoln would have appreciated that and want us to keep working on a global approach to fostering economic opportunity and equality.

CHAPTER XI

LINCOLNOMICS

Global Building
for Today and the Future

"Out of the smoke and stench, out of the music and violet dreams of the war, Lincoln stood perhaps taller than any other of the many great heroes. This was in the mind of many. None threw a longer shadow than he. And to him, the great hero was The People. He could not say too often that he was merely their instrument."

—Carl Sandburg

I wake abruptly in a small, cramped, odd-smelling hotel room in Lisbon, Portugal. I'm supposed to be on a relaxing family vacation, but it's as if a boisterous cricket lodged itself in my mind.

Maybe it's the sleepless night on the plane, an entire day of frustration in the Chicago passport office, or my body clock six hours behind Portuguese time—I just can't stop unspooling the thread between Lincoln's time and the present. It's the spider-like web that many people visualize before a migraine, only this visual skyrocket is a nonstop flare of ideas.

My brain is ablaze. Lincoln would have relished the fact that we could fly across the Atlantic, hop on a bus, cross a massive bridge above a river wider than the Mississippi, much less cross an ocean that once took months to navigate by ship in mere hours. All this and Spain's superb AVE high-speed rail system, too. Bridges and railroads connecting entire countries! How Lincoln is that? As we cross the wishbone cable-suspension Vasco da Gama Bridge that links the north and south of Portugal across the Tagus River, I experience a child-like awe. At eleven miles long, the man-made structure is one of the longest spans in Europe, named after the sixteenth-century explorer who first reached India by sea. I sense that through the public funding of infrastructure (by the Portuguese and other European governments, in this case), Lincoln's DNA is embedded in this bridge.

When he defended the Rock Island Railroad in his corporate lawyering days, Lincoln established a legal precedent: infrastructure is key to a country's social and economic capital. He rejected the old premise that steamboats owned the great river and had the right to destroy a railroad bridge should it obstruct their way. Lincoln argued that ordinary people can and should use a *public amenity* to cross rivers and bring goods to market, and save time and money doing so. Countries with deep-sea access, fleets, and ports—and later, with railroads, container ships, and air flights—could transport spices from the East to preserve foods in the West. The Chinese, Arabs, Portuguese, Spanish, French, English, and Americans built transportation infrastructure over centuries; global trade benefitted the creation of a merchant and later a middle class, but this was not an idea they originally championed. Kings, queens, and corporations like the East India Company largely controlled the flow of wealth. Not until the time of Lincoln did the idea that commonplace people could more equitably benefit from infrastructure begin to be realized.

Conversely, technological innovations like gunpowder from China, celestial navigation from the Arabs, and English longitudinal instruments and ships paved the way for even greater exploitation, colonization, and expansion of the slave trade. Lincoln wasn't a historian, but he had a profound awareness that the triumphs of his age—from better steam engines to public education—would help to lift *all* boats, even if built by those born to poverty in a log cabin.

And by stressing that labor was greater than capital, Lincoln shifted the onus of acquiring capital for infrastructure endeavors from states to the federal government. How could a farmer in Illinois better sell his grain, swine, and produce in New Orleans or New York? Lincoln saw the difficulties as a river boatman and sought to improve opportunities for the men manning the rudder or shoveling coal into engine boilers. To Lincoln, the creation of a robust infrastructure was nothing less than employing labor to *create* capital and reach markets previously out of reach to the average producer of goods. Better yet, Lincoln's early belief in *intellectual* capital (after all, he is America's only patent-holding/inventor president) would be the mortar that built a colossus. How to make agriculture more productive? Educate more agricultural scientists by giving states free land for colleges. How to build a better transportation system? Give railroads land to expand their networks.

All of this led to a robust, national system for elevating people beyond their hometowns, enabling them to learn, create, build, and invent with the government's full support. It became the American *Innovation* System, built on the strong bones of Henry Clay's American System. In Lincoln's time, no longer would capital—of the social and intellectual variety, particularly—be exclusively controlled by royals, elites, or mercantilist corporations. Consequently, the Second Industrial Revolution emerged in America based on the premise of the independent inventor: the Edisons, Westinghouses, and Teslas of the world. Lincoln didn't live to see those fruits of his labor, but his son Robert did, and even had a part in financing it.

As I rose before dawn in Lisbon, my mind turned over the question: How did Lincoln see innovation, and why is it important today? While he did not use the word in the context that we use it, to him, innovation was an economic lever. In Lincoln's America, one could file a patent and eventually benefit from one's intellectual capital—as did Morse and countless others who enriched themselves by innovating products and selling them in global markets. Innovation is useless to the individual, however, if someone else can steal or acquire their intellectual capital without compensation—a significant problem in the global internet era.

The global explosion of logistics in the nineteenth century was fuel for Lincoln's dream. The Illinois Central, one of the largest railroads in the world when he took office, would expand to the South and New Orleans after his death. The rail lines from the East, which mostly ended in Iowa in 1860, would cross the continent; the Transcontinental Railroad's final spike was driven in 1869, thanks to thousands of Chinese and Irish laborers, hundreds of whom perished during the construction of the line. The Homestead Act enabled European-American settlement in the West, at horrific cost to Native Americans. Then the petroleum age would come along, creating our current dilemma: toxic skies, soiled landscapes, and global warming.

LINCOLN AND GLOBAL INFRASTRUCTURE

Much of *Lincolnomics* focuses on the built infrastructure that was inspired and propelled by Lincoln's American vision, but there is tremendous work yet to be done on worldwide political infrastructure, which is still evolving. The Thirteenth and Fourteenth Amendments were not fully realized until the mid-twentieth century by the Voting

Rights Act and other Civil Rights legislation. Women's suffrage was not ratified until 1920, and not extended to *all* women until more than forty years later. The twenty-first century has seen a spate of new protections for child labor and LBGTQ rights, along with other forms of social progress, but government globally is largely deficient in addressing climate change, water shortages, human migration, and political unrest. At the time of this writing, in the United States, there is no meaningful regulation of the internet or social media, and no data privacy, national health insurance, or plan to protect and retrain workers who have lost jobs. Lincoln would be excited and daunted by the array of work to do to improve our modern infrastructure. Today, we still struggle mightily with health care, human rights, incarceration, policing, and human rights in the US and across the globe.

The US boasts an enormous list of needed infrastructure projects. Bridges, tunnels, dams, levees, railroad networks, roadways, and public works facilities are in desperate need of repairs and upgrades. The Chicago El system, run by the Chicago Transit, is rusting away—more than 100 years old, in some parts. For that matter, public transit and public works systems in *every* city need billions in capital. While some cities are able to fund expansion of their systems, most make do with "spit and bailing wire," the steelmaker term for a dying steel mill's repair. New York's subway system, for example, is using switches from the early twentieth century. A railroad bridge down the street from my home in Illinois nearly washed out during a rain event.

According to the American Society for Civil Engineers (ASCE), which issues a periodic "Infrastructure Report Card," the amount of work to be done is estimated at more than $2 trillion. What kind of work? Here's a short list, according to the ASCE's Infrastructure Report Card:

CUMULATIVE INFRASTRUCTURE NEEDS BY SYSTEM BASED ON CURRENT TRENDS, EXTENDED TO 2025

ALL VALUES IN BILLIONS OF CONSTANT 2015 DOLLARS
2016–2021 (10 YEARS)

Infrastructure Systems	Total Needs	Estimated Funding	Funding Gap
Surface Transportation	$2,042	$941	$1,101
Water/Wastewater Infrastructure	$150	$45	$105
Electricity	$934	$757	$177
Airports	$157	$115	$42
Inland Waterways & Marine Ports	$37	$22	$15
Dams	$45	$5.6	$39.4
Hazardous & Solid Waste	$7	$4	$3
Levees	$80	$10	$70
Public Parks & Recreation	$114.4	$12.1	$102.3
Rail	$154.1	$124.7	$29.4
Schools	$870	$490	$380
TOTALS	$4,950	$2,526	$2,064

It's essential for policymakers to see the direct link between economic activity and infrastructure the way Lincoln did. Without the public infrastructure to efficiently move people, goods, and traffic, everyone's ability to make money and prosper is impaired. As of its 2016 study, the ASCE estimated that the failure to update infrastructure will cost:

- $7 trillion in lost business sales by 2025
- $3.9 trillion in losses to the US GDP by 2025
- 2.5 million American jobs lost by 2025

On top of those costs, American families will lose upwards of $3,400 in disposable income each year—about nine dollars each day.

Infrastructure's profound impact upon any economy is felt in other areas. Clean water means fewer waterborne illnesses. Clean air means less respiratory disease. Well-maintained roads, bridges, and tunnels mean fewer accidents and fatalities. In sum, infrastructure adds up to lower overall health-care costs and fewer lost work hours, which impact all of society. Public investment—and the policy to sustain it—is a keystone for economic stability and progress.

UPGRADING THE TROUBLED
EDUCATION INFRASTRUCTURE

Education has a vital role in extending our lifespans and improving our economic well-being. Public colleges and private institutions funded by federal and state grant dollars made quantum leaps in our knowledge of everything from basic biology to public water systems. Many of our great inventors and industrialists didn't have the robust college educations available today, but the land-grant university created vast networks of research and development that led to advances in agriculture, engineering, biological science, and our information age.

It's easy to romanticize John Deere's steel plow created out of a rusty sawblade, or Cyrus McCormick's invention of a reaper that could harvest the vast prairies, but these revolutionary innovations could not have happened without a culture of imagination and the ability to profit from invention. Meatpacking, food processing, plastics, and electric cars were spurred in part by the ability to exploit opportunity. Although it's been gamed over the years in ways large and small, the modern patent law system certainly helped. But the innovation culture had its start somewhere. When Lincoln signed the Morrill Act, he set into motion one of the greatest systems of knowledge innovation the world had ever seen. One could argue that land-grant colleges are responsible for more societal and economic advancement than any other institutions; yet they are not enough in an information age increasingly dominated by artificial intelligence, robotics, and automated supply chains.

The great institutions of European learning—Oxford, Cambridge, the Sorbonne—had been off limits to the majority of the population for centuries. Land-grant colleges assaulted the elitist model of high education. Sons and daughters of farmers and tanners became engineers and agronomists, learning how to develop antibiotics and design better factories; such intellectual infrastructure begat America's colossal public infrastructure. I sincerely believe this was an integral part of Lincoln's vision. The education he desired his entire life would not be denied to others. Everyone deserved a chance at economic ascension. But he would frown at the state of our intellectual infrastructure, as state and federal governments make public college unaffordable without loans that force students into debt—the shackle that prevents people from buying cars, appliances, homes, and from retiring. It's an economic stun gun that halts the economic progress Lincoln revered.

Rising college costs have a fairly straightforward explanation: Governments dramatically reduced their subsidies of public education, so the institutions raised their tuition—up sixty-three percent between 2008 to 2020.

In the year 2020, college loan debt was a $1.7 trillion burden and climbing every day. From private trade schools to big state universities, the price tag is so high that the total student loan tab is larger than the combined amount owed on credit cards and auto loans in the US At an average of more than $41,000 annually, college tuition is unaffordable out of pocket for most American families; grants that pay for most of these bills are scarce. Still, colleges need to fill classrooms, pay professors, add research buildings, and attract alumni. Without a national or state program to offset these costs, colleges pass along their expenses to those who can least afford to pay. Worse yet: Student loan debt can't be discharged in bankruptcy, even if you're ill or unemployed, due to lobbying by banks and intermediaries. You just owe more over time as interest accumulates.

Numerous policies have been proposed by progressive politicians to remedy the student loan problem. Nevertheless, if we're to honor and sustain Lincoln's legacy, our society needs to drastically reduce the cost of college and vocational education. The mushrooming debt alone stifles economic advancement on a tragic scale.

AUTOMATION AND ITS MASSIVE ELIMINATION OF LABOR

On my last research field trip, I am only a handful of blocks away from the site of Lincoln's nomination for president, Gurdon Hubbard's "Wigwam" on the Chicago River. There's no evidence of the structure save for a plaque on a skyscraper. During Lincoln's day, I would have been only a hundred feet from docks on the nation's most bustling inland waterway, one that he helped create. Sail east on the river and end up in Lake Michigan on the way to Eastern ports and the Erie Canal. From Lake Michigan, sailing scarcely a mile west and turning left on the South Fork of the river, riverboatmen would find their way to the Illinois & Michigan Canal—the prized short-cut to the Illinois River, and the Mississippi and gulf ports such as New Orleans. During the Civil War, a year after his election, Lincoln and the Union would fight to open this river route to Union forces, a series of battles not won until the summer of 1863.

Vicksburg was not on my mind that night as I spoke before the Chicago Cigar Society on the subject of labor and capital. But Lincoln's focus on free labor was in my thoughts—in today's context of the age of automation, where there is not enough free labor. Machines and software are replacing millions of jobs, a potentially catastrophic labor issue for future generations. The era of corporate paternalism died decades ago. No longer can one rely upon a decent factory job, much less a white-collar career at a major corporation. Automation has eliminated opportunity from retail sales jobs to insurance adjusters. And it was only just begun as artificial intelligence became implemented in every office.

Lincoln's concerns about labor take on a new importance in the twenty-first century. The theme for today focuses on providing enough *quality* labor for future generations of workers. A simple definition of "quality" means living wages sufficient enough to afford a middle-class lifestyle anywhere in the country.

The massive shift replacing human and animal labor with machines, begun when Lincoln first wandered out of the woods of Indiana and Kentucky, continues exponentially. About 4 million jobs have already been lost in manufacturing. Due to advances in artificial intelligence, machine learning, and robotics, millions of white-collar jobs are targeted for elimination. All told, some 73 million jobs could disappear by 2030, reports the McKinsey Institute. (This figure could be a conservative estimate, given the dark impact of the COVID-19 pandemic.)

While little attention is paid to this powerful trend, nearly every large company embraces it, particularly tech giants and the Chinese government. This ongoing trend is exacerbated by the coronavirus crisis. (Countless jobs continue to be eliminated as employers downsize their workforces as I write this.)

As found by three highly respected studies, up to half of the workforce will be automated within the next thirty years. According to McKinsey, "in about 60 percent of occupations, at least one-third of the constituent activities could be automated, implying substantial workplace transformations and changes for all workers."

The most labor-intensive industries will be most impacted: Trucking and taxiing will be hurt by self-driving vehicles; warehousing, retail, and logistics will be impacted by automated supply chains. Ravaged by largely automated online shopping, the retail sector led all industries for job losses in 2018–2019; more than 150,000 positions were eliminated (according to the outplacement firm Challenger, Gray & Christmas). Steel mills that employed tens of thousands of workers now employ only hundreds. In media, machines write more than one billion press releases annually. Many "digital" news sites do no reporting at all, and simply run press releases.

White-collar jobs are most threatened, now. Any task involving forms and basic back-office services can be automated. In health care, machines can read, store, and interpret data from facial images and documents to x-rays; they also do robotic surgery. Virtually anything on paper that can be scanned, stored, sorted, and analyzed is part of this new wave of artificially intelligent processing.

What can we do to offset the rise of automation? I imagine Lincoln would have loved to answer this quandary: Concentrate our educational system on promoting purely human skills that are unlikely or difficult to automate—emotional intelligence, communication, collaboration, and "big picture" skeptical thinking. Education, particularly public schools, is the key.

Lincoln knew he came up short on formal education, so he worked hard on his analytical and people skills. He studied judges, juries, and defense arguments. Logic was his guide, along with pure factual presentations; law was a way of understanding the world—and navigating it. Few were as good on their feet as Lincoln, playing to country juries the way an operatic vocalist sings an aria. These skills weren't learned in law school or college, neither of which he attended.

Who fares best in the hyper-automation age? Those who think about systems, ethics, and labor. In short, people like Lincoln. There is still a profound need for uniquely complex human skills: diplomats, elected officials, teachers, mental health professionals, and caregivers are essential to every society. The world population is aging, too, which presents a whole set of demands. There's a need for an expanded workforce, as well: With some 10,000 baby boomers turning sixty-five every day, we will need more gerontologists, nurses, home-care assistants—a whole infrastructure geared to those who want to "age in place" or need twenty-four-hour care.

Granted, the growth in automated labor will also *create* new jobs. We'll need to build and fix robots and automation systems. Companies that design factories, workplaces, and supply-chain networks will thrive.

Yet we can't ignore the unending, growing conflict between labor and capital: Employers are always looking to cut their head counts and labor expenses. Robots and software don't ask for fringe benefits or overtime—at least, not now.

We need a policy plan that helps people become lifelong learners who have a mastery of the four infrastructure "I"s: innovation, integration, insight, and improvisation. Today's world requires novel insights to fix global problems like climate change; to increase reliable food and water supplies; end needless wars; and address massive human migration.

More than ever, we'll need to communicate and collaborate—to be more like Lincoln. He was not formally educated to become a lawyer, legislator, policymaker, and commander-in-chief. Sure, he read a few books, but most of what he built was achieved by acting on his feet while making a few dollars as a postmaster, surveyor, and state assemblyman. Lincoln was a master of the four "I"s, to his core. Little details and the big picture were perspectives he acquired over time, his facile mind providing the tools to accomplish great things. Winning or losing court cases and political battles made him stronger, more confident. And through the tumultuous nature of his marriage and his relentless grief over his lost children and the war's toll, Mary provided him comfort and stability at home. With a confidence absent from many others, she believed in him.

LINCOLN, EDUCATION, AND PROSPERITY WORK HAND IN HAND

Prosperity is a strange mixture of hope, promise, and action. Lincoln would appreciate that great policy ideas like land-grant colleges did indeed create a more enlightened, flexible labor force. But are they still up to this herculean task when four-year college bills are unaffordable for many middle-class families and college loan debt tops $1.7 trillion? What about a broad safety net that allows for retraining, integrated education, and transitional assistance? No such plan has emerged.

Fortunately, we have a minor jumpstart on developing engines of creativity. Most major business schools house affiliate "incubator" and "accelerator" startup labs that drive innovative enterprise. The "maker" movement encourages hands-on invention with digital tools from public libraries to research and development labs. Modern manufacturing integrates human life with new processes.

Unfortunately, neither government nor our modern educational system is prepared for extensive automation. We still relentlessly drill students through standardized tests, which do not measure what one needs to succeed in a highly automated workplace. A much nimbler and more comprehensive policy program is needed if the bulk of our workforce is to survive and prosper in the coming decades.

CLIMATE CHANGE AND ITS IMPACT ON GLOBAL INTERNAL IMPROVEMENTS

Lincoln, raised in the coal and steam age, likely heralded the smokestacks of steamboats, factories, and railroad locomotives as symbols of progress. Burning wood (and later coal and petroleum) was the fuel of the machine age, speeding products to market and moving people across a vast continent. What would Lincoln think about the fossil fuel era, global warming, and climate change? All signs point to him embracing the need to update, revise, and improve infrastructure; there are dire economics and human services components to this global crisis. Any habitations along coastal zones will need to be lifted, removed, or reinforced as sea levels rise. Bridges, culverts, roads, and tunnels must be modified for increased rainfalls. New water systems must be implemented where water is scarce or polluted. We are clearly unprepared for violent cyclones, rainstorms, wildfires, and floods. There is a mammoth list of improvements for every country; we will need a new vision and plan to adjust our infrastructure for this new reality.

And it's not just that climate change is a driver of infrastructure improvements: This subject has been sorely neglected for decades. Some areas haven't seen improvements at all, particularly in rural areas where money has been too scarce for even basic repairs. Nineteen percent of the US population lives in ex-urban counties, which account for a disproportionate 68 percent of the country's total lane and road miles, reports the US Department of Transportation. As superhighways and urban projects receive top priority for federal, state, and local dollars, country roads get the short shrift. Flooding and heavier rain events further exacerbate the deteriorating conditions of these byways.

The direct link between infrastructure improvement and environmental risk management is undeniable and its future impacts draconian. Climate change will likely push some 120 million people into poverty, per the UN. Farmers are losing fertile, tillable land to desertification. Rivers flood out once productive fields. Rising sea levels are infiltrating freshwater aquifers and sinking entire islands in the Pacific region. But combatting these environmental catastrophes with sound policy and public spending will produce major benefits: An $1.8 trillion investment in climate mitigation measures could produce more than $7 trillion in social and environmental benefits, according to the Global Commission on Adaptation.

Unchecked, the climate catastrophe will wreak havoc on significant systems from the transportation network to the energy grid. Government and industry need to collaborate not only to measure the overall risk, but to prepare for and mitigate it. Would Lincoln care about modern sustainability? His Whig philosophy pushed economic development at all costs, but it's safe to say he would be concerned with infrastructure's intersection with social progress. Jobs seeded by commerce and industry created a tide that raised all boats. But a society's infrastructure needs change over time.

A study by the McKinsey Global Institute claims that the specific impacts of rising temperatures should be viewed holistically by policymakers and individuals alike:

> Climate science tells us that further warming and risk increase can only be stopped by achieving zero net greenhouse gas emissions . . . Managing that risk will thus require not moving to a "new normal" but preparing for a world of constant change. Financial

markets, companies, governments, or individuals have mostly not had to address being in an environment of constant change before, and decision making based on experience may no longer be reliable. For example, engineering parameters for infrastructure design in certain locations will need to be re-thought, and homeowners may need to adjust assumptions about taking on long-term mortgages in certain geographies.

The McKinsey report narrowed down climate change impacts to these areas:

- Livability/Workability
- Food Systems (agriculture and distribution)
- Physical Assets (buildings, infrastructure)
- Infrastructure Services (energy distribution, grids, alternative energy)
- Natural Capital (rivers, lakes, glaciers)

McKinsey puts climate change in economic terms. What if global breadbaskets produced less food for a growing world population? How will tropical areas survive during massive heat waves and a paucity of air conditioning, fresh water, and electricity? Who will put up the trillions in damages caused by typhoons, hurricanes, wildfires, and other climate disasters? When the most populous regions run short of water due to evaporated glaciers, how will that finite resource be replenished? These questions are speculative, yet they pose real, titanic challenges for world leaders and governments. Here are some of the dire scenarios we face, according to the report:

Increase in average temperatures. Global average temperatures are expected to increase over the next three decades, resulting in a 2.3-degree Celsius average increase relative to the preindustrial period by 2050. This means we can expect an average local temperature increase of between 1.5 and 5.0 degrees Celsius relative to today. The Arctic is expected to warm more rapidly than elsewhere—as it already has been, to drastic effect in our oceans and tides.

Extreme precipitation. In parts of the world, extreme precipitation events—defined here as a once in a fifty-year event (that is, with a 2 percent annual likelihood) in the 1950–81 period—are expected to become more common. The likelihood of extreme precipitation events will grow more than fourfold in some regions, including parts of China, Central Africa, and the East Coast of North America.

Hurricanes. The likelihood of severe hurricane precipitation—that is, an event with a 1 percent likelihood annually in the 1981–2000 period—is expected to double in some parts of the southeastern United States, and triple in some parts of Southeast Asia, by 2040. Both areas are densely populated with large, globally connected economic activity.

Drought. As Earth warms, the spatial extent and the share of time spent in drought is projected to increase. By 2050, up to eight years in a decade will be spent in drought conditions in some parts of the world, notably the Mediterranean, Southern Africa, and Central and South America.

Will a Lincoln-like focus on infrastructure adequately address all of these—and more—dire situations? Not without concerted public policy and reform shifts by our most powerful institutions, particularly the banking and corporate sectors.

Institutions have been slow to acknowledge the worldwide economic threat of climate change. The World Bank, for example, announced only in 2019 a $50 billion "Action Plan for Climate Change Adaptation and Resilience."

"Our new plan will put climate resilience on an equal footing with our investment in a low carbon future for the first time. We do this because, simply put, the climate is changing so we must mitigate and adapt at the same time," World Bank Chief Executive Officer

Kristalina Georgieva announced in a press release. "We will ramp up our funding to help people build a more resilient future, especially the poorest and most vulnerable who are most affected."

There's no question that banks, Wall Street, insurance companies, investors, and global institutions have recognized the threat of climate change and are responding to it (albeit largely inadequately, when it comes to for-profit institutions). The bigger question is of government action and direct infrastructure funding and policy. Is it too little, too late for a Green New Deal?

"Climate change poses unprecedented challenges to human societies, and our community of central banks and supervisors cannot consider itself immune to the risks ahead of us," says François Villeroy de Galhau, governor of the Banque de France, in a report from the Bank of International Settlements. His observations have been echoed by the European Central Bank and rejected by the Trump administration at the time of this writing in 2020.

GLOBAL DEVELOPMENT AS FREEDOM: INFRASTRUCTURE'S ROLE

When I saw Nobel-Prize winning economist Amartya Sen speak years ago, climate change was not on my mind. His talk was held in the wake of the 2008 financial crisis; hardly any global leader aside from Al Gore was talking about the environment. But Sen's classic *Development as Freedom* had a profound impact on global thinkers. It isn't enough, Sen argues, that we promote economic growth in gross domestic product as an end in and of itself. He sees human progress and capabilities as a cornucopia of freedom:

> Development requires the removal of major sources of unfreedom: Poverty as well as tyranny, poor economic opportunities as well as

systematic social deprivation, neglect of public facilities as well as intolerance or activity of repressive states.

Sen references the needs of people stuck in poverty due to repressive and corrupt regimes, and the lack of opportunity in these crushing environments. In a sense, Sen's argument is akin to Lincoln's before the Civil War, equating economic progress with advances in political and social infrastructure. Economic ascension first requires extending basic liberties to all while addressing fundamental human needs and rights—a worldwide crisis from Myanmar to Syria, Western China to Central America.

While the infrastructure updates are slowly addressed by governments from Brussels to Beijing, policymaking may be too sluggish to keep up with the rapid advance of climate change impacts. Certain low-lying areas are immediately imperiled from Ho Chi Minh City to New York City's boroughs. Massive global infrastructure programs designed largely for commercial, geo-political leverage—like China's Belt and Road Initiative (one of history's largest such projects)— address development while ignoring the human rights quotient that Sen advocates.

Take China's Belt and Road Initiative, for example. The ingenious combination of old Silk Road overland routes with established shipping lanes promises to link China with Africa, Europe, and the rest of Asia—seventy-one countries in all. Some $1 to $8 trillion will be spent building ports, harbors, rail lines, and other commercially oriented infrastructure. It will saddle countries from Djibouti to Sri Lanka with debt. The massive debt incurred for these projects may impair "host" countries' ability to provide other forms of infrastructure, such as clean water and sanitation systems. *The Guardian* wrote in a special report: "Governments from Malaysia to Pakistan are starting to rethink the costs of these projects. Sri Lanka, where the government leased a port to a Chinese company for ninety-nine years after struggling to make repayments, is a cautionary tale." Will these countries be able to repay their massive loans to China?

Critics of the plan are concerned that the People's Republic is advancing its totalitarian, human rights–repressive political model as it develops the ports and transportation connections its Belt and Road Initiative is creating. It even may have specific military aims. Such intentions should not be ignored by the world's democracies; all infrastructure policy implicates human rights. The need for clean water should not be subverted to political hegemonies.

COMPASSIONATE CAPITALISM: LINCOLNOMICS' ULTIMATE AIM

Lincoln's view of progress as an egalitarian ideal—indeed, that he wanted to increase access to it for all—argues for a renewed, global look at his life and politics. Although voting rights would not be conferred to those who were not white men until after his death, Lincoln's spirit lives in the idea of a more perfect union.

Lincolnomics means compassion in politics and capitalism, a spiritual economics. Although he paid supreme deference to labor, the sixteenth president was no Marxist or socialist. He prospered as a lawyer representing common people as well as corporate interests—though it's impossible to know how Lincoln would have fared in the Gilded Age of robber barons, when his party deemed *laissez-faire* capitalism to be the best course for America until the Progressive Era. He may have seen worker exploitation by the reigning monopolies and trusts as antithetical to his worldview, in which workers had a chance to ascend the economic ladder.

In order to form a more perfect union between labor and capitalism, our America needs a new narrative, one that is compassionate for workers of every age and educational level in an increasingly automated economy that is downsizing unskilled labor. This delicate, fractured relationship should renew itself with a revised definition of the American Dream, first articulated by James Truslow Adams in 1931, around when Keynes wrote about the "economic problem." Nobel Prize-winning Economist Robert Shiller points out that Adams's concept went viral in a "long slow, epidemic" since he first coined the phrase. The dream itself was not of unbridled consumerism and a systematic ravaging of the planet. At the beginning of the Great Depression, it sounded more like the Human Potential movement of the 1960s and 1970s:

> It is not a dream of motor cars and high wages merely, but a dream of a social order in which each man and woman shall be able to attain to the fullest stature of which they are innately capable, and recognized by others for what they are, regardless of the fortuitous circumstances of birth or position.

This "capabilities" approach echoes Lincoln. What if, instead of focusing on GDP, productivity, consumer goods, and profits, the global economy looked to developing a sustainable society and meaningful work bolstered by a *right* to a broadly inclusive social safety net? Humanity's well-being would displace net worth as a measure of social success.

Lincoln is not remembered in our world of total cyber information as a president who enabled society to prioritize human capital—that is, developing people's innate abilities and capabilities. Nor do most associate him with infrastructure, education, or economic equality. Shiller found the strongest connection between the words "honesty" and "Lincoln" when he did a Google Ngram word analysis. Indeed, "Honest Abe" was incredibly forthright about what economic progress meant to him in his lifetime. It behooves us to revisit his narrative—especially on how to improve the human condition.

PRAGMATIC PROGRESS

Many of the railroads born during the building of the Transcontinental Railroad still dominate East-West corridors, and have ballooned and consolidated through mergers and the dissolution of short-haul lines. More than a century of growth created some festering logistical issues. And it will take billions to fully address the problem, which has only gotten worse in the twenty-first century as freight railroads act as intermodal systems, shipping all manner of goods from the West, from Chinese containers to shale oil to Eastern refineries. When it comes to public and private transportation, everyone expects the trains to run on time, to avoid traffic jams and flight delays. We demand it. This is part of our pragmatic nature.

It's vexing to be delayed, but the vast majority of us fail to think of the sweeping cause: systemic infrastructure failures. On one trip back to Chicago on the Amtrak's Zephyr, my family was delayed for hours on the western side of Denver as we waited for freight trains to come through the Rockies to Chicago. Today, one can fly across the continent in about four hours. A transcontinental train ride, assuming no delays for freight trains and mechanical issues, takes the better part of four *days*. Such timing assumes your connection in Chicago is a relatively seamless one and that you're not sitting on sidings waiting for freight haulers, who have mostly owned the tracks since the advent of the railroad and land-grant age.

Air travel can be even more frustrating. Despite vast advances in global transportation infrastructure, weather and crowded air traffic corridors still delay flights. A straightforward journey from Chicago to New York, or Los Angeles to Tokyo, can get complicated. Much technology and infrastructure need to be updated. While airport construction is relatively well funded, the rest of the transportation infrastructure is not. Roads, bridges, tunnels, and public transportation are funded through periodic and massive transportation packages, which used to be simply identified as "highway" bills. As was the case in the nineteenth and twentieth centuries, funding from state and local sources is not up to the task of maintaining and modernizing the vast network.

Part of the larger issue is that congressmen and presidents always contend with regional interests, which were most pronounced in the nineteenth century. Those tensions never truly abated, even after two world wars, the heady post–World War II era, and into our modern age. City growth, which pitted metropolitan interests against largely agricultural states, created an even more stringent political divide. Farming, increasingly dominated by corporations, wanted their "fair share"—which translated into billions of dollars in subsidies. And when capital flowed to areas where technology development flourished, such as Silicon Valley, Seattle, Boston, New York City, and Washington, DC, it created even deeper socioeconomic rifts.

The political meta-narrative—in Lincoln's time and now—was not development itself, but rather how to ensure that the means of funding development was not punitive to states, sub-regions, and the middle class. Fair funding continues to be a challenge, although some important discussions and short-term solutions were explored during the height of the Civil War.

LINCOLN AS A GUIDE

For some, it is easy to relate emotionally to Lincoln and how his thinking evolved: He was afraid that if he did not become educated or elevate his station, he'd be splitting rails and working fields the rest of his life. Worry probably dominated his self-improvement ethos more than any other emotion. In this pandemic age, we experience immense anxiety and grief compounded by fear of climate change, automation, globalization. Those immersed in labor fear the loss of their jobs. Those in areas hardest hit by unemployment and climate change face the loss of their homes. Indeed, fear motivates politics in a Janus-like fashion: We often look backward for answers that are not there instead of looking forward without fear.

"Especially common in our highly competitive society," wrote Dr. Martin Luther King, Jr., in his "Antidotes for Fear" sermon, "are economic fears, from which . . . come most of the psychological problems of our age . . . Employees are plagued by the prospect of unemployment and the consequences of an ever-increasing automation." Dr. King called upon his Atlanta congregation to address their fears through faith and love, elevating the dignity of work.

Lincoln, whose faith was complex, believed in the free individual using creative and just means to achieve social progress. It's only speculative to presuppose Lincoln's views of intricate global dilemmas like climate change, corporate governance, and worker rights, but his words and writings demonstrate that he saw the power of unfettered human rights as the best platform to address universal needs. The best we can do today is embrace Lincoln's regard for economic advancement as something fundamental to democracy, and reject efforts to hurl us further into the toxic politics of racism and nativism, two destructive sentiments of his era.

I'd like to believe that in the face of mass unemployment, pandemic, economic decline, climate change, and the absence of rights for global workers, Lincoln would argue for a solid connection between appropriate infrastructure and civil systems jointly able to serve commerce, national interests, and human needs. Lincoln believed that somehow, the "better angels of our nature" would unite us in pursuing these ends. His platform and deeds formed one of the most enduring planks of American policy, influencing every president from Grant to both Roosevelts, Eisenhower, and Barack Obama. Each saw the value of Lincolnomics in rebuilding America, creating decent jobs and a more equitable society. Now, in these times of profound despair and political discord, we need Lincoln more than ever. His ideas prevail in building a just, healthier society and planet.

In our ever-fluid, grief-riven present—haunted each second by hyperactive social media, political discord, disease, mass communication, climate change, and a technocracy that challenges our mortality—I am still comforted by Lincoln's words and the sheer power and utility of his ideas. Unlike those cold marble monuments of him, these living kernels of humanity are warm and growing. They are viable organisms. We need to sow and fertilize Lincolnomics if we're to survive and prosper on this planet.

Lincolnomics' Impact on Social Infrastructure— A View from the Pandemic

Lincoln lives on, his ideals and words informing us during a pandemic, civil rights revolution, and environmental crises. There's much work to be done as the impact of COVID-19 shined a glaring light on the inequities in our health-care system.

The Fourteenth Amendment, mandating that equal protection be granted and enforced by the states and federal government, was the policing mechanism (inspired by Lincoln) in the Reconstruction and post-Reconstruction eras. Today, it goes much further: The Fourteenth Amendment "forces a state to govern impartially—not draw distinctions between individuals solely on differences that are irrelevant to a legitimate governmental objective. Thus, the equal protection clause is crucial to the protection of civil rights," according to the Cornell Legal Information Institute:

> In terms of public services, it's not an unreasonable stretch to say
> that the amendment means equal protection in the event of a health

crisis or against environmental injustice. We see how that can be applied in a health crisis. Several troubling statistics emerged at the height of the COVID-19 crisis that firmly suggested that African Americans were not receiving equal protection from environmental and viral threats.

As I finished writing this book, evidence emerged across the country of how the virus was adversely impacting communities of color. In April 2020, the *New York Times* reported: "African Americans are getting infected and dying from COVID-19 at disproportionately high rates. And counties with higher levels of pollution are seeing greater numbers of coronavirus deaths than cleaner ones," citing public health data. In Louisiana, some 70 percent of those who died from the virus were Black; in Illinois, 43 percent; in Michigan, 40 percent. In these Midwestern states, it should be noted, African Americans made up no more than 15 percent of the population at the time. The same pattern was observed in North and South Carolina, Connecticut, and Las Vegas, Nevada. Of those states reporting infections by race, Milwaukee County was the worst (initially), where 73 percent of coronavirus mortalities were African American.

The racial disparity factor is due to pronounced inequities in the fractured US health-care system and institutional and cultural racism against African Americans and people of color. They are less likely to be insured, more likely to have chronic conditions like diabetes and hypertension, and often have poor access to community health care. In short, Black Americans do not receive equal protection or treatment from the American health-care system, a racist inequality older than Lincoln.

Dr. Georges Benjamin, executive director of the American Public Health Association, cited disparities, ranging from lack of insurance to inequal treatment within the system:

I think the biggest challenge is the fact that people of color, African Americans, start out with health outcomes that are disproportionately poor when compared to white Americans. The highest risk, if you get this disease, is to someone 60 or older with chronic disease. With African Americans, you start with a population that is disproportionately sicker, and if it gets exposed, it will have a higher death rate. The reasons for the health inequities include access to health care, and differences in the quality of care African Americans receive. A lot of what makes you healthy happens outside the doctor's office, so all the social determinants—including racism and discrimination, housing, access to transportation and education—are a factor.

In addition to unequal treatment in the health care system, Black Americans and other people of color in America are disproportionately harmed by pollution. Their neighborhoods tend to be areas with significant air and water pollution, the presence of which has been linked to "serious health problems, including cardiovascular and pulmonary disease. Those chronic health conditions, scientists say, increase vulnerability to the coronavirus," the *New York Times* reported. During the pandemic's spread, Latinx communities were also hit harder than white ones.

Under Lincolnomics, which internal improvement addresses this entrenched inequality? Universal health care is certainly a start, bolstered by a network of community health centers. The American health-care infrastructure is a broken jigsaw puzzle of Medicare, Medicaid, Veteran's Administration, private/employer-offered policies, Children's Health Insurance, the Affordable Care Act, and federal and state plans. It's a fragmented nightmare, particularly if you happen to live in an area underserved by hospitals, general practitioners, and quality long-term care—or simply don't have decent health insurance, or any health insurance at all.

DEATHS OF DESPAIR

The public health side of the internal improvements debate undeniably demands our attention: The widening abyss between the well-served and underserved crosses ethnic, geographic, and racial lines. Neglected populations—from urban enclaves to rural America—suffer from what academia calls "deaths of despair." I knew many of these suffering Americans when I covered the dramatic decline of the steel industry as a journalist in the late 1970s and early 1980s. Men and women, suddenly unemployed and lacking decent pensions or health care, lost their homes, began abusing substances, and died well before their time. Life expectancy for unemployed, middle-aged, white males has dropped precipitously. Structural unemployment touches nearly every industry. Without a safety net beyond short-term jobless insurance, many Americans become impoverished. It isn't that the economically dislocated are doomed by any moral flaws; the punishing lack of living-wage work is emotionally devastating and economically deadly.

Social scientists will tell you that people who have suffered economic violence—mostly by unemployment—face a higher risk of chronic disease and early death. Recent landmark research by Princeton economists Anne Case and Angus Deaton found a number of factors that contribute to deaths of despair. Decent-paying jobs, often with union-negotiated benefits, have evaporated over the past two generations. Those living-wage jobs "that once supported the blue-collar aristocracy" were not replaced, even in a relatively robust overall economy from 2010 to 2020. Low-paying, nonunion hourly service jobs dominated employment growth in recent years. This trend mostly impacted the white working class. They discovered:

> Our story of deaths of despair; of pain; of addiction, alcoholism and suicide; of worse jobs with lower wages; of declining marriage;

and of declining religion is mostly a story of non-Hispanic white Americans without a four-year degree.

With the persistent disappearance of high-paying factory jobs came another startling development in the US employment market: "Many occupations that did not require a bachelor's degree, now do." And the wage disparity between high school and college graduates is dramatic. Case and Deaton found that the earnings premium between those with only a high school diploma and those with a bachelor's degree was 80 percent. As many deeply indebted college graduates discover, a degree does not guarantee gainful employment. Many companies are downsizing or automating white-collar positions.

Other than creating a truly universal health-care system offering comprehensive treatment for addiction and mental illness, the Princeton economists favor bolstering the national minimum wage for hourly workers. Other economists, such as Thomas Piketty, call for a "Universal Basic Income"—a flat monthly payment to every worker. Yet such a program does not address the need to have meaningful employment paying living wages. We need a viable program to bolster workers who are transitioning and training for new jobs.

The federal government, Case and Deaton conclude, overall "need[s] to strengthen the safety net to minimize the harm" of rapacious corporate practices, job loss, and political inaction to rein in corporate capitalism.

WHERE INFRASTRUCTURE FUNDING WILL COME FROM

Ultimately, a greater portion of infrastructure funding needs to come from federal and corporate sources. States, counties, and cities cannot shoulder the lion's share of the burden—especially when it comes to interstate (and Interglobal) transportation modes like airports, highways, and rail corridors. Of course, "federal funding" can mean many things, although there are multiple alternatives.

Congress has the power to regulate—and tax—interstate commerce; it can raise the federal fuel tax. Everyone derives value from the use of public infrastructure, and therefore all benefit from it. This includes multinational companies, which use interstates and international airports, and hire graduates from land-grant colleges. Why should they remain "free riders" when it comes to infrastructure? The responsibility for funding broad-based infrastructure should be shared by government—local, regional, state, and national—and corporate institutions. A modern Lincolnomics program would foster a new era of public-private partnerships. Instead of building canals and railroads, we'd rebuild roads, bridges, schools, and community centers. Inner cities would house business incubators instead of elite colleges. Economic opportunity would migrate from wealth centers like Silicon Valley and Manhattan to neglected, underserved areas.

BLACK LIVES MATTER

There cannot be increased economic opportunity under a Lincolnomics template without equity, culturally and institutionally, being afforded to people of color and to every underserved community. After more than 2,000 US protests, which spread globally in late May and throughout the summer of 2020, millions are demanding reforms. The May 25 murder of George Floyd by police in Minneapolis renewed a raft of long-term grievances and lethal inequities.

Not only does American policing need to be reformed to focus on community protection, the entire justice system needs a thorough examination and restructuring. African Americans are incarcerated at a rate five times higher than white Americans in US state prisons, according to the Sentencing Project. In five states (Louisiana, Oklahoma, Mississippi, Arizona, and Arkansas), that disparity is more than ten to one. African Americans are twice as likely to be killed by police than white people, research shows, even though Black Americans account for only 13 percent of the US population, as *The Washington Post* found. From 2015 through June 2020, the *Post* recorded more than 5,000 fatal police shootings. With only two exceptions—Arizona and Oklahoma—eight of the ten states with the highest incarceration rates were members of the Confederacy or border states that permitted slaveholding.

In addition to the devastating emotional impact police shootings and incarceration have on the families and children of those killed and imprisoned, the economic impact on families is just as devastating. "A criminal record can reduce the likelihood of a callback or job offer by nearly 50 percent," a study by the NAACP found. "The negative impact of a criminal record is twice as large for African American applicants." Money spent on the prison system—which could be spent on community services and education in underserved communities— totals more than $80 billion annually. Spending on jails and prisons has tripled relative to the funding of pre-K to grade-12 public education over the past thirty years.

Attacks of institutional discrimination across the board would be well-served by a broad-based, socioeconomic focus. Restrictive public policy has impeded economic aspirations: The American Dream has been routinely denied to people of color. Atlanta Federal Reserve President Raphael Bostic noted in the wake of 2020 anti-racism protests:

> Over the course of American history, the examples of such institutionalized racism are many, and include slavery, federal law (consider the Three-Fifths Compromise our founding fathers established to determine federal representation), sanctioned intimidation during

Reconstruction, Jim Crow laws in southern states, redlining by bankers and brokers, segregation, voter suppression, and racial profiling in policing. These institutions hurt not only the African Americans they've targeted, but the systemic racism they've codified also hurt, and continues to hurt, America and its economy. By limiting economic and educational opportunities for a large number of Americans, institutionalized racism constrains this country's economic potential. The economic contributions of these Americans, in the form of work product and innovation, will be less than they otherwise could have been. Systemic racism is a yoke that drags on the American economy. This country has both a moral and economic imperative to end these unjust and destructive practices.

There is a direct, glaring relationship between racist violence, discrimination, and economic activity. Both overt and covert bias and violence aimed at communities of color depressed the innovation and prosperity that would otherwise follow the mainstream American path.

In research focused on the period when Reconstruction ended in the 1870s and into the twentieth century, Lisa Cook of Michigan State University found a troubling suppression of innovative economic activity in Black communities:

The shock of an increase in the scope and intensity of hate-related violence in the late [nineteenth] and early [twentieth] centuries depressed economic activity, as measured by patent activity, by 1 percent per year, or the equivalent of a year's worth of total U.S. patent activity, among African Americans. This violence would have implied a fall of 40 percent and greater volatility in output among most U.S. inventors during that period.

AFTERWORD

If Washington, the financial-industrial system, and state legislators commit to deeply examining Lincoln's principles of internal improvements, criminal justice institutions should be a system worth reforming. Inequality is a pernicious, extant disease, from the streets to the vast network of American prisons. Money spent disproportionately jailing people of color is better spent on education, job creation, and robust economic opportunities—where they are needed most. Instead of building prisons, we could repair roads, create a high-speed rail network, add and improve rural and urban internet connections, make our schools world class, and render higher education debt-free. And that's just a short list. Many more improvements are needed in every community.

HOW WOULD THE PARTY OF LINCOLN EMBRACE LINCOLNOMICS?

Referring to the "Party of Lincoln" does not denote, in my humble opinion, the current iteration of the Republican Party (or any contemporary party for that matter). It refers to a party that embraced the proto-Whig values of protecting domestic manufacturing, a cohesive national banking system, building all forms of infrastructure, and supporting individual economic progress. This emerging entity would be an amalgam of FDR's New Deal programs (without racist housing laws and practices), Teddy Roosevelt's Progressive Era "Square Deal," and even a heavy dose of packages by big builder presidents like Eisenhower and Hoover (who greenlighted the dam named for him). A modern "Party of Lincoln" would embrace personal economic opportunity and eschew crony capitalism and monopolistic control of entire swaths of the economy. Indeed, what would the platform of this fictional political entity look like?

A New Emphasis on Living Wages. A national program would seek to employ as many people as possible in living-wage jobs. This means raising the minimum wage to local cost-of-living indexes that enable workers to afford much more than rent. It means supporting the right to universal health care, and benefits like paid child and elder care—and organizing to gain these benefits without corporation suppression. The safety net for working people would be expanded with working parent stipends and paid medical leave. Immigration reform streamlining status and citizenship requests would be essential.

A Comprehensive Program of Internal Improvements. An ongoing, sustainable component of annual spending is needed to fix transportation and utility systems on every level; to provide brick-and-mortar maintenance funding for public schools, hospitals, and municipal facilities; and a robust health infrastructure that can handle everyday, natural, and biological disasters (such as pandemic events). The federal government would provide the prime funding, which could be doled out to states, counties, and local government, perhaps by a sovereign wealth investment fund similar to those in countries like Singapore and Norway. Public-private partnerships would issue "infrastructure" bonds to finance public amenities.

A Fair Taxation System. To provide capital for these projects, government would lower taxes on labor and property (which is currently overtaxed) and impose levies on capital and passive investments. A sovereign wealth fund would act as a bulwark supporting infrastructure initiatives from a comprehensive health system to ongoing physical improvements, such as roads and bridges. How can capital be taxed? First by creating a robust, progressive income tax that eliminates loophole deductions for corporations and individuals who bring in above $500,000 annually. A financial transaction tax on trading securities could be considered. With these implementations, working people's income taxes could be lowered. Trillions of dollars offshored by US-based corporations and individuals could be repatriated and invested in the sovereign fund. Social Security could also be bolstered and expanded.

Aggressively Funded Public Education. Land grants worked fine in the nineteenth century, but education has never been entirely free in the modern era. At the least, bachelor's degrees at public and community colleges should be free. More federal brick-and-mortar money should go to public schools in general. Grant interest-free loans would be eliminated; ideally, student debt on a whole would be forgiven. Higher education should be the entrée to economic advancement and lifelong learning, not a decades-long albatross of arrears.

Institutional Reform on Voting Accessibility, Policing, Incarceration, and Economic Opportunity. This extensive list includes instituting universal mail-in balloting; eliminating all voting restrictions; making driver's license voter registration automatic; enacting policing and incarceration reforms; and creating more economic opportunity in communities of color. Entire books have and will be dedicated to each of these subjects, but the difficult, meaningful work of reforming institutional policy is ahead of us. Each of these initiatives promote progress toward societal equality.

If much of this sounds like the platform of a modern progressive candidate, that's no coincidence. Yet the spirit of these ideas has been around since the days of Lincoln and his many successors. They must be revisited, revived, and updated for twenty-first-century societal needs; as witnessed in the coronavirus pandemic, these Whig ideals have never been more relevant. Even some enlightened conservatives see the need for robust public education, reduced incarceration, and aspirational economic policies. If the American Dream is to be preserved, we have to reimagine Lincoln's ideas and policies.

I know that many will argue that expanding the federal government's reach and scope is the road to serfdom or tyranny. This fear has been a trope since the founding of the Republic; I respect that caution to a point. But as the US economy has grown over time, millions are left in the dust. No matter how much they drudged, workers fell further behind, unable to fully benefit from the fruits of their labor. In contrast, smaller countries have raised their taxes to provide universal health care, education, and childcare and improve standards of living. If there's no other lesson we can learn from Lincolnomics, it's that we can improve well-being for a greater number of people. For the living proof, just drive on an interstate highway—or any highway, for that matter; take a local or cross-country train ride; tour a homesteaded farm; gaze upon an airport traffic control tower; or visit a land-grant public university.

More pointedly, one of the main reasons Americans don't enjoy a comprehensive social safety net is a long-entrenched fallacy that people of color, immigrants, and poor folks are somehow morally inferior to those who lifted themselves up by their bootstraps. "Racism explains why the country lacks the safety net its citizens deserve," observed Eduardo Porter, economics correspondent for the *New York Times*.

Slavery is hardly a bygone afterthought. If we're to rectify the national sins of the past, billions should be poured into impoverished communities of color to create living-wage jobs, solid educational futures, quality health care, and social and economic prosperity. Any new plan to enhance infrastructure should be inclusive, targeting areas neglected due to racial and socioeconomic disparities. We can transact progress through the aspirational lens of economic equality, which Lincoln championed, but which still hasn't been remotely achieved in our time. From the Poor People's Campaign to the Black Lives Matter movement, we have a lot of work to do. One approach might be implementing Universal Basic Income and a universal pension not tied to employment. No matter what we do, a strong social safety net is needed for all.

While Lincoln elevated his own standing and reunited the Union, he never lost sight of the fact that everyone needs help along the way. His programs implore us to do the right thing for the greatest number of people. It's more than a set of aspirational ideals. Will racism, economic disparity, and class hatred ever be abolished with a proclamation, Constitutional amendment, or by a Congress free of corporate influence? Likely not. But we can do a dramatically better job of practicing "with malice toward none."

APPENDIX I

Lincoln's Patent Application Letter

Among his many attributes, Lincoln was a problem solver who could think like an engineer. He was fascinated with better ways of doing things. He loved the idea that technology could make life easier and aid commerce. During his brief career as a river flatboat pilot, he had to deal with unreliable modes of transit—the Sangamon River, for one—before railroads dominated the landscape. Lincoln thought he had a solution and invented a boat that could raise itself through buoyant air chambers when there wasn't enough water to move the craft along. While he made a model of it—and filed a patent—during his one term in the US House, it's not known if anyone built or used it. By the time he was back home in Springfield and immersed in his law practice, railroads made the humble Sangamon an obsolete transportation option. Yet this patent shows Lincoln's knack for innovation, a sentiment he would carry with him into the White House.

March 10, 1849

To all whom it may concern:

Be it known that I, Abraham Lincoln, of Springfield, in the county of Sangamon, in the state of Illinois, have invented a new and improved manner of combining adjustable buoyant air chambers with a steam boat or other vessel for the purpose of enabling their draught of water to be readily lessened to enable them to pass over bars, or through shallow water, without discharging their cargoes; and I do hereby declare the following to be a full, clear, and exact description thereof, reference being had to the accompanying drawings making a part of this specification. Similar letters indicate like parts in all the figures.

The buoyant chambers A. A. which I employ, are constructed in such a manner that they can be expanded so as to hold a large volume of air when required for use, and can be contracted, into a very small space and safely secured as soon as their services can be dispensed with . . .

. . . I wish it to be distinctly understood, that I do not intend to limit myself to any particular mechanical arrangement, in combining expansible buoyant chambers with a vessel, but shall vary the same as I may deem expedient, whilst I attain the same end by substantially the same means. What I claim as my invention and desire to secure by letters patent, is the combination of expansible buoyant chambers placed at the sides of a vessel, with the main shaft or shafts C, by means of the sliding spars, or shafts D, which pass down through the buoyant chambers and are made fast to their bottoms, and the series of ropes and pullies, or their equivalents, in such a manner that by turning the main shaft or shafts in one direction, the buoyant chambers will be forced downwards into the water and at the same time expanded and filled with air for buoying up the vessel by the displacement of water; and by turning the shaft in an opposite direction, the buoyant chambers will be contracted into a small space and secured against injury.
Witness

Z. C. ROBBINS

A. LINCOLN

H. H. SYLVESTER

APPENDIX II

Lincoln's Major Speeches and Other Writings on Infrastructure

Public Lands in Illinois
(Report to Illinois Legislature), January 17, 1839

In one of his first major reports on the use of public lands for internal improvements, Lincoln lays out the case in the Illinois General Assembly for why the state (and later federal) government should buy land for infrastructure such as canals and railroads. See these sources for the full text and annotations:

"Report of Committee on Finance regarding the Purchase of Unsold Federal Lands, [17 January 1839]." *Papers of Abraham Lincoln.* papersofabrahamlincoln.org/documents/D200154

"Public Lands in Illinois." *Illinois Library Digital Collections.* January 17, 1839.digital.library.illinois.edu/items /f336eaa0-0d92-0135-23f6-0050569601ca-7#?c=0&m=0&s=0 &cv=0&r=0&xywh=-221%2C33%2C840%2C410

Speech before the Chicago River and
Harbor Convention, July 6, 1847 (Chicago, Illinois)

This is believed to be Lincoln's first speech before a national audience. Prior to the late 1850s, Lincoln was an obscure, one-term congressman from "the West" who was in the minority Whig party (the Republican Party hadn't been formed yet). The convention, however, was one of the largest and most highly organized events demonstrating to the rest of the country—and President Polk's Democrat Party allies—that states from New York to Illinois favored a massive federal infrastructure plan. Although Lincoln clearly took a back seat to the event's organizers (which included stellar national voices like newspaperman Horace Greeley), his remarks are mostly political and conciliatory. He makes some glancing blows on the "constitutionality" of the plan, although he avoids making a solid legal argument. Nevertheless, he added his voice to a chorus of boosters who are advancing the cause of internal improvements on a broad scale. The organizers demanded action on improvements that would benefit East Coast and Midwestern states.

Mr. Lincoln, member of Congress from Illinois, being called upon, addressed the Convention, in substance, as follows:

GENTLEMEN: I had supposed that it was not proper for me, residing in Illinois, to occupy the time of the Convention in making a speech. I will, however, avail myself of the few minutes allowed me until the return of the committee on resolutions, as no one else, perhaps, is desirous to do so.

I desire, for the sake of harmony, to make a few remarks—not of division and discord, but of harmony. We meet here to promote and advance the cause of internal improvement. Parties have differed on that subject, but we meet here to break down that difference—to unite, like a band of brothers, for the welfare of the common country. In harmony and good feeling, let us transact the business for which we have assembled and let no firebrands be cast amongst us to produce discord and dissensions, but let us meet each other in the spirit of conciliation and good feeling. The gentleman from New York made such a speech as he believed to be right. He expressed the sentiments he believed to be correct, and however much others may differ from him in those views, he has a right to be heard, and should not be interrupted.

If it was the object of this Convention to get up a grand hurrah, a few of its members are pursuing the proper course to effect that object. But such was not the purpose of this Convention. In the course of debate, it is impossible to speak without alluding, in some manner, to constitutional questions. In all speeches, on every occasion, there are remarks to the point and collateral remarks. Let us avoid collateral remarks in this Convention, as far as possible. Democrats do not wish to do any thing in this Convention that will conflict with their past course, and if questions should come up which they do not approve, they should be permitted to protest against them. I hope there will be no more interruption—no hisses—no jibes. I pledge myself that the delegates from Illinois will keep quiet.

The argument of the gentleman from New York upon the constitutionality of the power to make appropriations should be examined. I do not feel that I can do it—time will not permit—but some one more able, more competent to do the subject justice, will reply. All agree that something in the way of internal improvement must be done. The difficulty is to discriminate, when to begin and where to stop. There is great danger in going too far. Members of Congress will be influenced by sectional interests and sectional feelings. I have not taken the pains to write out my opinions upon the construction to be put upon the constitution. Any construction, that there is something to be done for the general good and no power to do it, would be wrong. I do not go for sectional improvements though all are more or less sectional. Is there any way to make improvements, except some persons are benefitted more than others? No improvement can be made that will benefit all alike. A pertinent question was asked the gentleman from New York, to which he did not reply: Who is to decide differences of opinion on constitutional questions? What tribunal? How shall we make it out? The gentleman from Pennsylvania, the Hon. Andrew Stewart, says Congress must decide. If Congress has not the power, who has? Is it not, at least, for Congress to remedy the objection, and settle this great question? If there is any other tribunal, where is it to be found? My friend from Pennsylvania, Mr. Benton and myself, are much alike on that subject.

I come now, to the subject of abstractions. The gentleman from New York (Mr. David Dudley Field) made a slight mistake, when he said that the Revolutionary War was caused by abstractions. They denied Parliament the right to tax them without representation. This is not a parallel case, but totally different. The abstractions of the present day are not the abstractions of the Revolution.

I have the highest respect for the gentleman from New York. In his speech, he made a beautiful appeal in behalf of the Constitution. He implores us, by all considerations, to foster and protect it. He loves the Constitution. I hope I may love it as well as he does, but in a different way. He looks upon it as a new work, which may be sifted the seeds of discord and dissension. I look upon it as a complete protection to the Union. He loves it in his way; I, in mine. There are many here who entertain the same views which I do, who will, I doubt not, sustain me, and with these remarks I beg leave to close.

"Abraham Lincoln, Speech to Northwestern River and Harbor Convention, Chicago, Illinois, July 6, 1847." House Divided: The

Civil War Research Engine at Dickinson College. hd.housedivided.
dickinson.edu/node/40440

"Internal Improvements" Speech in the House of Representatives, June 20, 1848 (during Lincoln's sole term in Congress)

This is a long speech in which Congressman Lincoln again assails President's Polk's stance opposing internal improvements legislation. For the full text, see the Schiller Institute:

"June 19-25, 1848: Congressman Abraham Lincoln Assails President Polk's Veto of Internal Improvements." archive.schillerinstitute.com/educ/hist/eiw_this_week/v2n25_jun19_1848.html

And these original documents in the Library of Congress, fifteen pages of manuscript images:

"Abraham Lincoln papers: Series 1. General Correspondence. 1833-1916: Abraham Lincoln, Tuesday, June 20, 1848 (Speech on Internal Improvements)." *Library of Congress.* loc.gov/resource/mal.0012600/?st=gallery

Jonathan Baldwin's Turner's proposal for an "Industrial University" in 1851 (Illinois), University of Illinois manuscript collection

This seminal document by Jonathan Baldwin Turner, whom Lincoln said was one of his influences in signing the land-grant college act championed by Senator Justin Morrill, laid out the framework for what would become the University of Illinois (Champaign-Urbana). Turner, an abolitionist and Yale graduate, taught at nearby Illinois College in Jacksonville.

This plan was presented more than a decade before the Morrill Act, while Lincoln was a lawyer in Springfield and had not reemerged on the political scene. As far as I can tell, Lincoln had no direct involvement in this effort, although it likely influenced his thinking on public education.

"A Plan for an Industrial University for the State of Illinois." *Illinois Library Digital Collections*. 1851. libsysdigi.library.illinois.edu/oca/Books2007-10/planforindustria00turn/planforindustria00turn.pdf

Discoveries and Inventions Lectures, 1858-59

After the Lincoln-Douglas debates, Lincoln lost the Senate election to his rival, Stephen Douglas (whose Democrat allies controlled the Illinois legislature), but gained a national following. His creativity was at full throttle; he gave lectures on subjects that weren't explicitly political nor touching upon the evils of slavery. This little-known speech on invention was given in various venues at the end of the decade—the first oration was in Bloomington, Illinois—before he would become president. It provides some key insights into Lincoln's cornucopia of interests. Widely regarded as a failure by most historians—it is, of course, eclipsed by the Gettysburg Address, inaugural speeches, and Cooper Union addresses—the Discoveries and Inventions lecture is the most prosaic examination of his mindset, loaded with biblical quotations as historical references.

While this speech clearly lacks the elegant brevity and power he displayed at Gettysburg, it's pure Lincoln: His mind leaps logically from idea to idea. He argues for progress, telling his audience how the Bible and history informed us. It's not known how his audiences reacted to this long-winded and pedantic speech, but nonetheless it's important for the kernels of insight he shares on why innovation and invention is important to him. For the full text, see this source:

"Lecture on Discoveries and Inventions." *Abraham Lincoln Online.*
1858–9. abrahamlincolnonline.org/lincoln/speeches/discoveries.htm

Wisconsin Agricultural Fair Speech, September 30, 1859 (Milwaukee, Wisconsin)

In 1859, the Wisconsin Fair convened on property now owned by Marquette University in downtown Milwaukee. Lincoln shared his thoughts on "agricultural discovery," his parlance for making farming more productive through focused education, research, and development. Like his "Discoveries" speeches, it was more of an academic lecture, not imbued with the elegantly concise prose Lincoln would use in coming years as president. Nevertheless, these ideas would later surface and translate into his support for the Morrill Act, establishing land-grant colleges across the country, and the creation of the Department of Agriculture.

Note Lincoln's emphasis on improving agricultural productivity. This is still an essential theme, with increasing farm automation and environmental management, as we struggle to feed our expanding global population in an era of climate change. Read down for an exposition of his "labor and capital" argument, which would resurface in future presidential speeches. Here's an excerpt:

The successful application of *steam power,* to farm work is a *desideratum*—especially a Steam Plow. It is not enough, that a machine operated by steam, will really plow. To be successful, it must, all things considered, plow *better* than can be done with animal power. It must do all the work as well, and *cheaper*; or more *rapidly,* so as to get through more perfectly *in season*; or in some way afford an advantage over plowing with animals, else it is no success. I have never seen a machine intended for a Steam Plow. Much praise, and admiration, are bestowed upon some of them; and they may be, for aught I know, already successful; but I have not perceived the demonstration of it.

For the full text, see this source:

"Address before the Wisconsin State Agricultural Society." *Abraham Lincoln Online*. September 30, 1859. abrahamlincolnonline. org/lincoln/speeches/fair.htm

Illinois Constitutional Convention Letter (Resolution to Lincoln on Expanding the I&M Canal), March 17, 1862

When the Illinois & Michigan Canal was completed in 1848, Lincoln saw it as a marvelous achievement, yet could see its limitations. Traveling down a section of it on his way back from Chicago with his family, he saw it needed to be made bigger to accommodate larger boats and steamships. His fellow Illinoisians felt the same way, so they drew up a resolution calling for its expansion. At the time, railroads were definitely prime competition, yet the narrow canal was still moving cargo and people. Better yet, it was profitable. Tolls and land sales put it in the black. Other than the commercial purpose, his home state legislators saw an urgent need to "allow steamboats and vessels of war to pass from the Illinois River to Lake Michigan."

Concluding that the project was of "national importance in a time of war," the message resounded with Lincoln, who would mention it in his third message to Congress.

"Abraham Lincoln papers: Series 1. General Correspondence. 1833-1916: Illinois Constitutional Convention, Monday, March 17, 1862 (Resolution recommending enlargement of Illinois and Michigan Canal)." Library of Congress. March 17, 1862. loc.gov/ resource/mal.1512100/?sp=2&r=-0.134,0.114,1.487,0.524,0

Third Annual Message, December 8, 1863

At the height of the Civil War, Lincoln was not only focused on winning and reuniting the Union, he was looking to the future. His speech, condensed here, makes several references to foreign relations with countries such as Spain and Japan, indicating that he was beginning to think of the restored Union as a global power.

After addressing some matters of foreign diplomacy, Lincoln gets down to the business of how to expand America's technological reach. A transatlantic telegraph cable is the initial proposal. Then, he turns to the need for immigrant labor, necessary to exploit the vast natural resources in the Western territories. Although he doesn't mention it here, immigrant labor would also build the Transcontinental Railroad.

After discussing the state of the Treasury—tax receipts and expenditures—Lincoln slips in a brief thought on the country's natural resources, fundamental to building a robust national infrastructure. His reference is in the context of building a superior naval force during the war, but Lincoln was also likely looking forward to when such resources could be used in peacetime.

In the middle of the speech, Lincoln again gazes West, evaluating the progress of homesteading and land grants. He expresses concerns about the Indian policy needing to be "remodel[ed]," noting, "it is hoped that the effect of these treaties will result in the establishment of permanent friendly relations with such of these tribes as have been brought into frequent and bloody collision with our outlying settlements and emigrants." Suggesting "immediate legislative action" on Indian affairs, he turns back to one of his favorite subjects: transportation infrastructure.

In one short section, Lincoln suggests better water routes between the East and West and references progress on the "Pacific" (Transcontinental) Railroad, another piece of legislation he signed. The remainder of his Third Annual Message fleshes out details of the Emancipation Proclamation. Here are some key excerpts:

On a transcontinental, underseas telegraph cable . . .

Satisfactory arrangements have been made with the Emperor of Russia, which, it is believed, will result in effecting a continuous line of telegraph through that Empire from our Pacific coast.

I recommend to your favorable consideration the subject of an international telegraph across the Atlantic Ocean, and also of a telegraph between this capital and the national forts along the Atlantic seaboard and the Gulf of Mexico. Such communications, established with any reasonable outlay, would be economical as well as effective aids to the diplomatic, military, and naval service.

On immigration . . .

I again submit to your consideration the expediency of establishing a system for the encouragement of immigration. Although this source of national wealth and strength is again flowing with greater freedom than for several years before the insurrection occurred, there is still a great deficiency of laborers in every field of industry, especially in agriculture and in our mines, as well of iron and coal as of the precious metals. While the demand for labor is much increased here, tens of thousands of persons, destitute of remunerative occupation, are thronging our foreign consulates and offering to emigrate to the United States if essential, but very cheap, assistance can be afforded them. It is easy to see that under the sharp discipline of civil war the nation is beginning a new life. This noble effort demands the aid and ought to receive the attention and support of the Government.

APPENDIX II

On natural resources development . . .

Our country has advantages superior to any other nation in our resources of iron and timber, with inexhaustible quantities of fuel in the immediate vicinity of both, and all available and in close proximity to navigable waters. Without the advantage of public works, the resources of the nation have been developed and its power displayed in the construction of a Navy of such magnitude, which has at the very period of its creation rendered signal service to the Union.

On homesteading and land grants . . .

It has long been a cherished opinion of some of our wisest statesmen that the people of the United States had a higher and more enduring interest in the early settlement and substantial cultivation of the public lands than in the amount of direct revenue to be derived from the sale of them. This opinion has had a controlling influence in shaping legislation upon the subject of our national domain. I may cite as evidence of this the liberal measures adopted in reference to actual settlers; the grant to the States of the overflowed lands within their limits, in order to their being reclaimed and rendered fit for cultivation; the grants to railway companies of alternate sections of land upon the contemplated issues of their roads, which when completed will so largely multiply the facilities for reaching our distant possessions.

This policy has received its most signal and beneficent illustration in the recent enactment granting homesteads to actual settlers. Since the 1st day of January last the before-mentioned quantity of 1,456,514 acres of land have been taken up under its provisions. This fact and the amount of sales furnish gratifying evidence of increasing settlement upon the public lands, notwithstanding the great struggle in which the energies of the nation have been engaged, and which has required so large a withdrawal of our citizens from their accustomed pursuits.

On better transportation infrastructure . . .
The attention of Congress during the last session was engaged to some extent with a proposition for enlarging the water communication between the Mississippi River and the northeastern seaboard, which proposition, however, failed for the time. Since then, upon a call of the greatest respectability, a convention has been held at Chicago upon the same subject, a summary of whose views is contained in a memorial addressed to the President and Congress, and which I now have the honor to lay before you. That this interest is one which ere long will force its own way I do not entertain a doubt, while it is submitted entirely to your wisdom as to what can be done now. Augmented interest is given to this subject by the actual commencement of work upon the Pacific Railroad, under auspices so favorable to rapid progress and completion. The enlarged navigation becomes a palpable need to the great road.

"December 8, 1863: Third Annual Message." University of Virginia's Miller Center. December 8, 1863. millercenter.org/the-presidency/presidential-speeches/december-8-1863-third-annual-message

"Abraham Lincoln papers: Series 1. General Correspondence. 1833-1916: Abraham Lincoln to Congress, Tuesday, December 08, 1863 (Annual Message)." Library of Congress. December 8, 1863. loc.gov/item/mal2849800/

APPENDIX III

A Note on Sources—
Visiting Lincoln's America

Commuter trains slow and pull into the Prairie Crossing/Libertyville train station serving my community as I wait my turn to say a few words to dedicate a new station shelter for Metra, Chicagoland's commuter rail system. Although the station is one of 242, it's exquisitely detailed with arts and crafts touches like wooden beams and Cherokee-red trim. It's a handsome building that echoes the aesthetics of my own community just across a busy highway. At the moment, I am thinking of trains, but also of Lincoln.

"This is a significant year, since we're recognizing the 150th anniversary of the completion of the Transcontinental Railroad, which no less than Abraham Lincoln signed into law," I stated in my brief dedication in 2019 with other local dignitaries, including my colleague Libertyville Commissioner Jennifer Clark, and Norm Carlson, the chairman of Metra Commuter Rail.

Metra's system provides commuter service throughout the Chicago metropolitan area, although some of the lines are owned by long-distance giants like the Union Pacific and Burlington Northern. There's a "Heritage" line that connects Chicago to Lockport, only a few feet from "Lincoln's Landing" and one of the remaining sections of the Illinois & Michigan Canal. Surprisingly, one can reach all of these places from my little commuter stop, in addition to accessing the Amtrak transcontinental routes. Many of the suburban trains (including my community's routes) have their terminus at Chicago's Union Station, where you can ride the rail to the East, West, and Gulf Coasts in fabled trains like the "Southwest Chief," to Los Angeles; the "Lakeshore Limited," to New York's Penn Station; the "California Zephyr," to San Francisco; and the legendary "City of New Orleans." All of these trains start in Union Station, where you only have to walk a few feet from the commuter platforms to the Amtrak departure gates.

I adore train travel and can relate to Lincoln on this transportation pleasure: I have taken these trains on various family vacations, which have been some of our best adventures, across the Rockies, through the Appalachians, to Washington, DC; New York City; Williamsburg, Virginia; and New Orleans. I've also traveled on the "Empire Builder" from Chicago to Seattle—and back—writing my first travel piece for *The Chicago Heights Star* more than forty years ago. What do all of these treks have in common? Each began at my little commuter rail station, where we transferred to other trains in Union Station. More importantly, they evolved from Lincoln's powerful, lifelong advocacy of railroads—including the Pacific Railroad Act, signed during the Civil War, which greenlit the last link of the Transcontinental Railroad from the Mississippi/Missouri River towns to San Francisco. It was one of the greatest engineering feats of the age.

Since I've traveled throughout the country and Illinois on a train system Lincoln and his contemporaries seeded, I offer this geographic bibliography. Consider this yet another note on sources, since I conducted research at all of these locales. Better yet, see them for yourself: In looking for Lincoln, there are still plenty of places you can still visit where Lincoln left his mark. Many of them are still accessible by train. They include:

- *Chicago.* Lincoln was nominated for president in 1860 in the Windy City, in a structure long since demolished—the Wigwam—at the corner of Wacker Drive and Lake Street, where the Chicago River forks east (there's a plaque on a skyscraper on that corner; you have to look carefully to find it). The city that he saw mostly went up flames during the Great Chicago Fire of 1871, which destroyed nearly all of the central city. Nevertheless, you can see Lincoln monuments everywhere, from his majestic statues in Lincoln and Grant Parks to a trove of history in the archives of the Chicago History Museum (at the southern end of Lincoln Park, one of Chicago's most dynamic neighborhoods). **chicagohistory.org/**

- *Civil War Museum.* This unique museum, about one hour north of Chicago in Kenosha, Wisconsin, is a real find. Focusing on the experience of soldiers from the Midwest, it has excellent exhibits, presentations, and a research center. **museums.kenosha.org/civilwar/**

- *Illinois Central Railroad Landmarks.* From Galena to New Orleans, the ICRR was one of the nation's first long-distance railroads. The Chicago terminus of the commuter line of the ICRR (now Metra) is below the street in the eclectic Millennium Station at Randolph and Michigan. If you go upstairs to the Randolph Street entrance, you can walk into the stunning Chicago Cultural Center. Upstairs is the dramatic Grand Army of the Republic Memorial room and Tiffany dome, beau arts masterpieces that memorialize the Civil War. Entrance to the Center is free. I've traveled the length of the old ICRR route (ironically, the railroad is now owned by the Canadian National Railroad). You can still take the famed Amtrak "City of New Orleans" from Union Station in Chicago to New Orleans, as well as trains to the Atlantic and Pacific Coasts (as of this writing). **amtrak.com/city -of-new-orleans-train; thechicagoloop.org/a.cult.garm .00000.html**

- *Kaskaskia and Vandalia.* The state capitals before moving to Springfield, these small towns were pivotal to Lincoln's view on merging politics with economic development. While Kaskaskia, the first capital, has long since succumbed to the ravages of the Mississippi just south of St. Louis, you can still visit the *second* state capital at Vandalia (where Lincoln served in the legislature), a state historic site and a link in the "National Road" and stop along the original ICRR line. **vandaliaillinois.com/for-visitors/explore-vandalia/old-state-capitol/**

- *The Illinois & Michigan Canal.* Although long abandoned in favor of wider, deeper channels and railroad lines, Lincoln was an early champion of this essential link between the Great Lakes/St. Lawrence watershed and New Orleans. The I&M National Canal Heritage Area is a corridor that stretches 100 miles from Chicago to LaSalle, Illinois. Nearly every town along the old canal has some interesting stops. One of particular interest is the drive along Archer Avenue into Chicago, which parallels the old canal, best seen in Lockport and Lemont. Further north, the canal route runs along the larger Sanitary and Ship Canal, then disappears under the Stevenson Expressway (I-55). The best museums are in Lockport in the "Lincoln's Landing" area. There are also sites of interest in Pullman and Bridgeport (Chicago), Summit (the Chicago Portage Historic Site on Harlem Avenue), Joliet, Morris, Ottawa, Utica, and LaSalle. Along the southern (and mostly east-west) portion of the canal, there's a lovely trail created out of the towpath. Lincoln came down the canal in 1848 with his family, and was a canal commissioner. **iandmcanal.org/stateparks.com/chicago_portage.html**

APPENDIX III

- *Springfield.* His home for twenty years, Lincoln is
everywhere in this present-day state capital. The home
site and historic district (run by the National Park
Service) has a visitor center, where you can sign up for
guided tours. Also see the superb presidential museum
and national library, a few blocks from his home, law
office, and the old state capitol. Lincoln's tomb is on the
north side of town. There are *two* buildings in
Springfield that were and are state capitols: the "old"
red-domed building, where Lincoln gave his "House
Divided" speech, and the "new" silver-domed capitol
(originally built in the 1880s), where the current state
government resides. The "Lincoln and Herndon" law
office is across the street from the old capitol. The
present state capitol was built some twenty years after
Lincoln's assassination. All of these buildings are within
a few blocks of each other and within short walking
distance of the Amtrak station. The New Salem
historical village (a state park) is a short drive north of
town, and well worth the visit. If you want to do research
through the Lincoln Presidential Library, you can do
most of your work online, although the adjoining
museum is always worth visiting. **nps.gov/liho
/planyourvisit/lincoln-home-tour.htm;
lincolnlibraryandmuseum.com/**

- *Lincoln National Heritage Area.* While not a national park
with defined boundaries, the Lincoln Heritage Area is
nominally run by the National Park Service. Covering
several key sites where Lincoln worked, visited, and lived,
it's a good place to start to sample Lincoln when on the
road. Also check out related homestead sites in Indiana

and Kentucky. **nps.gov/places/abraham-lincoln -national-heritage-area.htm**

- *Lincoln's Highways.* National roads and the interstates succeeding them were Lincoln's dream. US Route 30 is most of the main leg of the original Lincoln Highway, which stretches from New York City to San Francisco (but was jogged south to avoid going directly through Chicago). Before train travel, Lincoln would've gone by stagecoach or horse on his judicial circuit throughout the state. Stagecoach routes typically followed trails originally used by Native Americans. The Lincoln Highway Association is a good source for the first transcontinental highway. Although most of the main route wasn't much of a road in Lincoln's time, Route 66 still holds some allure. Many sections of the "Mother Road" are still richly celebrated in Illinois and have some tangential connection to Lincoln's travels, particularly in the section between Springfield and Chicago.

- *Other Lincoln Sites.* If you want to go full tilt on Lincoln, I suggest making a trip to Kentucky and Indiana to see where he briefly lived as a boy. The Lincoln Birthplace, near Hodgenville, Kentucky, features a "symbolic" birthplace cabin and some other attractions. The Lincoln Boyhood Home is a National Memorial near Little Pigeon Creek in Lincoln City, Indiana. Both are run by the National Park Service, but well off the beaten track. **nps.gov/abli/index.htm; nps.gov/ libo/learn/historyculture/little-pigeon-creek.htm; lincolnhighwayassoc.org/; historic66.com/**

US Infrastructure Rebuilding Proposals

At the time of this writing in 2020, Congress was considering several ways to rebuild US infrastructure. Here's a general summary:

- A framework to address climate change incorporating ways to tackle global warming with proposals such as: increasing the availability of charging stations and other fueling options for electric and zero-emissions vehicles; making roads safer for pedestrians and bicyclists; and investing in zero-emission buses for public transit to reduce traffic congestion.
- $1.5 trillion in infrastructure improvements, with an emphasis on "green infrastructure" that will reduce carbon emissions to zero by 2050.
- Sharply increase spending on roads and transit, water projects, affordable housing, broadband, and schools.
- Upgrade hospitals and US Postal Service trucks.

My Stake in Lincolnomics— A Full Disclosure

My interest in infrastructure goes back decades; I care deeply about infrastructure revival in part because I am a public servant as I write this—an elected, part-time county commissioner. I've lobbied for public improvements in Lake County, Illinois, the third-largest county in the Prairie State with a population slightly less than that of Washington, DC. There are no conflicts of interest, here. (Other than enjoying the fruits of public amenities like everyone else, none of it directly profits me.) I want to see public infrastructure improved as a way of addressing climate change, road upgrades, public health issues, and more. My community is hardly alone in the struggle of infrastructure improvement; it's a widespread problem across the US

Since I've always been concerned for the most vulnerable among us, *Lincolnomics* became, in part, a way of seriously questioning what we need to do going forward. So many roads, literal and figurative, lead back to our sixteenth president—with much new construction and rebuilding sorely needed. More importantly, the *idea* of Abraham Lincoln and his struggles never wanes in the American cultural landscape, nor should it. Millions around the world need to hear his message on infrastructure in an era of climate change, social upheaval, and global health emergencies. Lincoln's eloquence and ideas have never been more relevant.

An Additional Note on Sources

Most of my research was conducted with original sources, namely Lincoln's speeches and correspondence, also contained in the multi-volume *Collected Works*. Much of this material is in the Library of Congress collection, which was donated by his son Robert and originally collated by his friend Judge David Davis (and today, contains more than 40,000 documents). Fortunately, color digitized versions of Lincoln's writings became available just as I began my research. Essential biographies include those by William Herndon, Michael Burlingame, Sidney Blumenthal, and David Herbert Donald.

Most of Lincoln's speeches and correspondence are digitized, except for his legal papers, which is a work in progress at the Lincoln Presidential Library. Since the originals are difficult to read online, even in color PDF files, I relied upon other repositories such as the Dickinson College Civil War Research Engine, University of Virginia's Miller Center, and The Schiller Institute.

I was greatly aided by the Lincoln Presidential Library and Museum in Springfield, Illinois; the Chicago History Museum; the Newberry Library in Chicago; and other archives throughout the country. The University of Illinois-Champaign Library and Illinois College also provided assistance. As did the many saintly librarians who assisted me in this journey, who plumbed the amazing Illinois Interlibrary System for ancient books and documents from colleges across the Prairie State.

I encourage readers to explore the many Lincoln databases across the country and in his *Collected Works* for more details.

BIBLIOGRAPHY

"Abraham Lincoln and Internal Improvements." May 22, 2014. abrahamlincoln.org/

"Abraham Lincoln's Patent Model." Smithsonian: National Museum of American History, Behring Center. americanhistory.si.edu/collections/search/object/nmah _213141

Adelmann, Gerald. "Lockport, Illinois: A collective heritage." Bank of Lockport, 1980.

"Agricultural Systems: Improving food systems around the world." February 2020. landgrantimpacts.org/wp-content/uploads/sites/3/2020/03/Ag-Summary2-Global.pdf

Ahtone, Tristan. "Land-Grab Universities." *High Country News*. March 20, 2020 pulitzercenter.org/reporting/land-grab-universities

Ambrose, Stephen. *Nothing Like it in the World*. Touchstone, 2000.

"America's Original Wire: The Telegraph at 150." Associated Press. CBSnews.com. October 24, 2011. cbsnews.com/news/americas-original-wire-the-telegraph-at-150/

Andes, Scott. "Five Reasons Why 'Downtown Universities' Matter for Economic Growth." *The Brookings Institution*. October 11, 2017. brookings.edu/blog/metropolitan -revolution/2017/10/11/five-reasons-why-downtown-universities-matter-for -economic-growth/

Andreas, A.T. "Illinois & Michigan Canal." *History of Cook County, Illinois* (1884). Will County Historical Society, 1986.

Ausik, Paul. "Job Losses in 2019 Highest in 4 Years as Manufacturing and Auto Industries Falter." October 3, 2019. 24/7WallSt.com.

Baker, Jean H. *Mary Todd Lincoln: A Biography*. Norton, 2008.

Baldwin, Robert. "A map of Virginia, North and South Carolina, Georgia, Maryland with part of New Jersey." Library of Congress. 1755. loc.gov/resource/g3860 .ar138100/?r=-0.129,0.053,1.15,0.405,0

Balesi, Charles. "Joliet and LaSalle's Canal Plans." *Encyclopedia of Chicago*. Chicago History Museum, Newberry Library, 2004. encyclopedia.chicagohistory.org /pages/1437.html

BIBLIOGRAPHY

Baptist, Edward. *The Half Has Never Been Told: Slavery and the Making of American Capitalism.* Basic Books, 2014.

Basler, Roy. (ed.) *The Collected Works of Abraham Lincoln.* 8 vol. Rutgers University Press/Abraham Lincoln Association, 1955.

Blackburn, Robin. "Lincoln and Marx." *Jacobin.* August 28, 2012. jacobinmag.com /2012/08/lincoln-and-marx/

Blumenthal, Sidney. *The Political Life of Abraham Lincoln: A Self-Made Man 1809-1849.* Simon & Schuster, 2016.

Borritt, Gabor S. *Lincoln and the Economics of the American Dream.* University of Illinois Press, 1994.

Bostic, Raphael. "A Moral and Economic Imperative to End Racism." Federal Reserve Bank of Atlanta. June 12, 2020. frbatlanta.org/about/feature/2020/06/12 /bostic-a-moral-and-economic-imperative-to-end-racism

Brooks, David. "The Future of American Politics." *The New York Times.* January 31, 2020. nytimes.com/2020/01/30/opinion/us-politics.html?searchResultPosition=1

Brown, Arthur L, R. J Onstott, and Franks & Sons. New Salem, home of Abraham Lincoln to 1837. Mason City, Illinois, 1837. Map. Library of Congress. loc.gov /item/75693219/

Burlingame, Michael. *Abraham Lincoln: A Life.* Johns Hopkins Press, 2008. 2 vol.

Burlingame, Michael. *The Inner World of Abraham Lincoln.* University of Illinois Press, 1994.

"The Cabinet: Edwin M. Stanton (1814-1869)." mrlincolnandfriends.org/the -cabinet/edwin-stanton/

"The Cabinet: William H. Seward (1801-1872)." Mr. Lincoln & Friends. mrlincolnandfriends.org/the-cabinet/william-seward/

Candeloro, Dominic and Barbara Paul. *Chicago Heights At The Crossroads of the Nation.* Arcadia, 2004.

Carriel, Mary Turner. *The Life of Jonathan Baldwin Turner.* University of Illinois Press, 1961.

Case, Anne and Angus Deaton. *Deaths of Despair and the Future of Capitalism.* Princeton University Press, 2020.

Catton, Bruce. *The Civil War.* Houghton Mifflin, 2004.

"The Chase Manhattan Corporation." Britannica. britannica.com/topic/The-Chase -Manhattan-Corporation

Chernow, Ron. *Grant.* Penguin, 2017.

"Civil Rights." *The Legal Information Institute.* Cornell Law School. law.cornell.edu /wex/civil_rights

"Civil War Timeline." National Park Service. nps.gov/gett/learn/historyculture /civil-war-timeline.htm

Coe, Alexis. "What We Still Don't Get About Washington." *The New York Times.* February 17, 2020.

BIBLIOGRAPHY

Cohen, Patricia. "The Struggle to Mend America's Rural Roads." *The New York Times.* February 18, 2020. nytimes.com/2020/02/18/business/wisconsin-roads.html

collegedebt.com/

"The Constitution of the United States," Amendment 13.

"The Constitution of the United States," Amendment 14.

"The Constitution of the United States," Amendment 15.

Conzen, Michael P. *The Illinois & Michigan Historical Heritage Corridor.* Northern Illinois University Press, 1988.

Cook, Lisa. "Violence and Economic Activity: Evidence from African-American Patents, 1870 to 1940." Michigan State University. March 2011. msu.edu/~lisacook /pats_paper14_0411_final.pdf

Cornelius, James. "Lincoln as a Self-Made Man." *Abraham Lincoln: Self-made in America.* Abraham Lincoln Presidential Library and Museum. May 2012.

Cothran, Boyd and Ari Kelman. "How the Civil War Became the Indian Wars." *The New York Times.* May 25, 2015. opinionator.blogs.nytimes.com/2015/05/25/how -the-civil-war-became-the-indian-wars/

Cox, Anna-Lisa. "Black Pioneers Not Wanted Here." *The New York Times.* September 22, 2019.

"Criminal Justice Fact Sheet." September 2020. naacp.org/criminal-justice -fact-sheet/

Cronon, William. *Nature's Metropolis: Chicago and the Great West.* Norton, 1991.

Cross II, Coy. *Justin Smith Morrill: Father of the Land-Grant Colleges.* Michigan State University Press, 1999.

Currey, J. Seymour. "Mr. Lincoln's Visit to Waukegan." *Journal of the Illinois State Historical Society* 4, no. 2. July 1911). 178-83.

Davidson, Alexander and Bernard Stuve. *The History of Illinois.* H.W. Rokker, 1874.

De Tocqueville, Alexis and Richard D. Heffner, ed. *Democracy in America.* Penguin Books, 1984.

de Borchgrave, Alexandra Villard and John Cullen. *Villard: The Life and Times of an American Titan.* Doubleday, 2001.

"Deep Waterway from Lake Michigan to the Mississippi River." Will County Historical Society. February 1983.

Desmond, Matthew. "In Order to Understand the Brutality of American Capitalism, You Have to Start on the Plantation." The 1619 Project. *The New York Times Magazine.* August 14, 2019.

Devine, Shauna. "The Civil War and the Army Medical Museum." National Museum of Civil War Medicine. February 15, 2017. civilwarmed.org/army-medical-museum/

Dividing the National Map. Photograph. Library of Congress. 1860. loc.gov/ item/2008661606/

"Dixie Highway and Gurdon Hubbard." WTTW Chicago Time Machine. interactive .wttw.com/timemachine/dixie-highway-and-gurdon-hubbard

Donald, David Herbert. *Lincoln.* Touchstone, 1995.

Dotson, Michael E. "In Search of the Golden Fleece: A Study of the Fur Trade in Will County 1673-1825." *Quarterly Will County Historical Society.* Spring 1986.

Dowd, Katie. "150 years since Chinese workers were brought in to build the transcontinental railroad." *SFGate.* May 26, 2015. seattlepi.com/national/article/150-years-since-Chinese-workers-were-brought-in-6286513.php

dpi.uillinois.edu/

Dretske, Diana. *Lake County, Illinois, An Illustrated History.* Lake County Discovery Museum, 2007.

Duster, Alfreda. *Crusade for Justice: The Autobiography of Ida B. Wells.* University of Chicago Press, 1991.

Duster, Alfreda. "Ida B. Wells: African Americans at the World's Columbian Exposition." *The Encyclopedia of Chicago.* encyclopedia.chicagohistory.org/pages/1495.html

El Issa, Erin. "2019 American Household Credit Card Debt Study." NerdWallet. December 2, 2019. nerdwallet.com/blog/average-credit-card-debt-household/

Emerson, Jason. *Robert Todd Lincoln: A Giant in the Shadows.* Southern Illinois Press, 2012.

Ewing, Jack. "Climate Change Could Blow up the Economy: Banks Aren't Ready." *The New York Times.* January 23, 2020. nytimes.com/2020/01/23/business/climate-change-central-banks.html

"First Debate: Ottawa, Illinois (August 21, 1858)." National Park Service. nps.gov/liho/learn/historyculture/debate1.htm

Foner, Eric. *Free Soil, Free Labor, Free Men: The Ideology of the Republican Party Before the Civil War.* Oxford University Press, 1995.

Foner, Eric. *The Second Founding: How the Civil War and Reconstruction Remade the Constitution.* Norton, 2019.

"The Fourteenth Amendment." *The Legal Information Institute.* Cornell Law School. law.cornell.edu/constitution/amendmentxiv

Friedman, Lisa. "A Troubling Story for Communities of Color." *The New York Times.* April 9, 2020.

Friefeld, Jacob. "This Week in History: Lincoln Signs the Homestead Act." Abraham Lincoln Presidential Library and Museum. illinois.gov/alplm/museum/blog/Pages/blog43.aspx

Gallagher, Winifred. *How the Post Office Created America.* Penguin, 2016.

Gardner, Andrew. "How Did Washington Make His Millions?" *Colonial Williamsburg.* slaveryandremembrance.org/Foundation/journal/winter13.washintgon.cfm

"General Survey Act of 1824." *American Historama.* american-historama.org/1801-1828-evolution/general-survey-act-1824.htm

"Geology of the Chicago Wilderness Region." *An Atlas of Biodiversity.* Chicago Wilderness project. cdn.ymaws.com/www.chicagowilderness.org/resource/resmgr/Publications/2_Atlas_of_Biodiversity_Geol.pdf

BIBLIOGRAPHY

"Georgetown University: Slavery, Memory, and Reconciliation." slavery.georgetown .edu/

"Glaciers Smooth the Surface." Illinois State Geological Survey. Prairie Research Institute, 2020.

Greenburg, Joel. *A Natural History of the Chicago Region*. University of Chicago Press, 2002.

"Grenville Dodge." National Park Service. nps.gov/people/grenville-dodge.htm

Grossman, Ron. "That Terrible Scourge of Camp Life." *The Chicago Tribune*. March 8, 2020.

Guelzo, Allen. *Abraham Lincoln: Redeemer President*. Eerdmans Publishing, 1999.

Hagemann, Frances L. *A History of American Indians of the Chicago Metropolitan Region and Western Great Lakes*. Floating Feather Press, 2004.

Hankey, John P. "Illinois Central Railroad." *Encyclopedia of Chicago*. Chicago History Museum, Newberry Library, 2004. encyclopedia.chicagohistory.org/pages/627.html

Hannah-Jones, Nikole. "What is Owed." *The New York Times Magazine*. June 30, 2020.

Hansel, Ardith K. "Glaciation." *The Encyclopedia of Chicago*. Chicago History Museum and Newberry Library, 2014.

Haupt, Herman. *Moving the Union Army*. Big Byte, 2014.

Herndon, William. *Herndon's Life of Lincoln*. Da Capo, 1983.

Herscher, Andrew, Ana Maria León, et al. "Decolonizing the Chicago Cultural Center." Settler Colonial City Project. September 16, 2019. issuu.com /settlercolonialcityproject/docs/20190910_sccp_dccc

Herscher, Andrew, Ana Maria León, et al. "Mapping the Chicagou/Chicago: A Living Atlas." Settler Colonial City Project. September 16, 2019. issuu.com /settlercolonialcityproject/docs/20190910_sccp_mcc

"History of the U.S. Capitol Building." *Architect of the Capital*. aoc.gov/history-us -capitol-building

"History of Waukegan." City of Waukegan, Illinois. waukeganil.gov/181/History -of-Waukegan

Holzer, Harold. *Lincoln at Cooper Union: The Speech that Made Abraham Lincoln President*. Simon & Schuster, 2004.

Holzer, Harold and Norton Garfinkle. *A Just and Generous Nation: Abraham Lincoln and the Fight for American Opportunity*. Basic Books, 2015.

Hormats, Robert. "Abraham Lincoln and the Global Economy." *Harvard Business Review*. August 2003.

Hubbard, Gurdon. *The Autobiography of Gurdon Saltonstall Hubbard*. Lakeside Press, 1911.

Hudson, John C. "Railroads." *Encyclopedia of Chicago*. Chicago History Museum, Newberry Library, 2004. encyclopedia.chicagohistory.org/pages/1039.html

Humphrey, Grace. *Illinois: The Story of the Prairie State*. Bobbs-Merrill/Forgotten Books, 2018.

"The I&M Canal Shapes History." Canal Corridor Association. 2004. csu.edu/cerc /researchreports/documents/IMCanalShapesHistory2004.pdf

Ihejirika, Maudlyne. "The Only Thing She Really Had Was the Truth." *Chicago Sun-Times*. May 5, 2020.

"Ike, Gettysburg, and the Cold War." National Park Service. nps.gov/eise/index.htm

Immerwahr, Daniel. *How to Hide an Empire: A History of the Greater United States.* Farrar, Straus and Giroux, 2019.

Inskeep, Steve. *Imperfect Union: How John and Jessie Fremont Mapped the West.* Penguin Press, 2020.

"To Irishman." Letter to *Joliet Courier*. April 6, 1840. Archives of Will County Historical Museum and Research Center.

Isaacson, Walter. *The Innovators: How a Group of Hackers, Geniuses and Geeks Created the Digital Revolution.* Simon & Schuster, 2014.

Jackson, Rex. *James B. Eads: The Civil War Ironclads.* Heritage Books, 2004.

James, Edmund. "The Origin of the Land-Grant Act of 1862." *University of Illinois Bulletin.* November 7, 1910.

"Jane Addams: A Foe of War and Need." *The New York Times.* May 22, 1935. archive .nytimes.com/www.nytimes.com/learning/general/onthisday/bday/0906.html

Kassa, Melat and Zane Mokhibar. "Working Economics Blog: Income & Poverty 2018." *Economic Policy Institute.* September 10, 2019. epi.org/blog/ by-the-numbers-income-and-poverty-2018/

Kearns Goodwin, Doris. *Leadership in Turbulent Times.* Simon & Schuster, 2018.

Kearns Goodwin, Doris. *Team of Rivals: The Political Genius of Abraham Lincoln.* Simon & Schuster, 2005.

Keating, Ann. *The World of Juliette Kinzie: Chicago Before the Fire.* University of Chicago Press, 2019.

Keating, Ann and Theodore Karaminski. "Camp Douglas." *Encyclopedia of Chicago.* Chicago Historical Society, 2005. encyclopedia.chicagohistory.org/pages/207.html

Keating, Ann and Theodore Karaminski. "Stephen A. Douglas." *Encyclopedia of Chicago.* Chicago Historical Society, 2005. encyclopedia.chicagohistory.org/ pages/207.html

Kent, David. *Lincoln: The Man Who Saved America.* Fall River Press, 2017.

Keynes, John Maynard. "Economic Possibilities for Our Grandchildren." *Essays in Persuasion.* Norton, 1963.

King, Dr. Martin Luther, Jr. "Antidotes to Fear." *Strength to Love.* Fortress Press, 2010.

King, Dr. Martin Luther, Jr. *Strength to Love.* Fortress Press, 2010.

"Kinzie, John H." *Papers of Abraham Lincoln.* papersofabrahamlincoln.org/persons /KI36592

Kinzie, Juliette Magill. *Wau-bun, The Early Days in the Northwest.* Philadelphia, J. B. Lippincott & Co., 1873.

Klein, Christopher. "The Epic Road Trip That Inspired the Interstate Highway System." History.com. May 27, 2020.

Klitzman, Zach. "A Universal Right for All—Lincoln and Education." *President Lincoln's Cottage.* September 4, 2019. lincolncottage.org/a-universal-right-for -all-lincoln-and-education/

Kolata, Gina. *Flu: The Story of the Great Influenza Pandemic of 1918 and the Search for the Virus that Caused It.* Atria, 1999.

Kristof, Nicholas. "Are My Friends Deaths Their Fault or Ours?" *The New York Times.* January 18, 2020. nytimes.com/2020/01/18/opinion/sunday/deaths-despair-personal -responsibility.html?searchResultPosition=6

Kuo, Lily and Niko Kommenda. "What is China's Belt and Road Initiative?" *The Guardian.* July 30, 2018.

Lamb, John. "Illinois and Michigan Canal." *Encyclopedia of Chicago.* Chicago History Museum, Newberry Library, 2004. encyclopedia.chicagohistory.org/pages/626.html

Laris, Michael. "House passes $1.6 trillion infrastructure bill, but McConnell calls it 'pointless political theater.'" *The Washington Post.* July 1, 2020.

Leu, Jon. "Historians uncover details of Abe Lincoln's ties to Council Bluffs." *The Daily Nonpareil.* April 29, 2020. nonpareilonline.com/news/local/historians-uncover-details-of -abe-lincoln-s-ties-to-council/article_124cb2cb-9d32-5fd7-ae9a-3b22b7922ea3.html

Lewis, Patricia. "Jonathan Baldwin Turner—Evangelist of the Land-Grant University Movement." *Agricultural Researches.* September 14, 2018.

"The Life of Gurdon Saltonstall Hubbard." *The Chicago Portage.* drupal.library.cmu .edu/chicago/node/44

Lincoln, Abraham. "Abraham Lincoln, Application for Patent on an Improved Method of Lifting Vessels over Shoals, March 10, 1849." House Divided: The Civil War Research Engine at Dickinson College. July 5, 2013. hd.housedivided.dickinson. edu/node/40503

Lincoln, Abraham. "Buoying vessels over shoals." patents.google.com/patent /US6469A/en

Lincoln, Abraham. "Survey of Huron, Illinois, 21 May 1836." Abraham Lincoln Presidential Library and Museum. papersofabrahamlincoln.org/documents/D208375

Low, John N. *Imprints: The Pokagon Band of Potawatomi Indians and the City of Chicago.* Michigan State University Press, 2016.

Lueckenhoff, Sandra. "Abraham Lincoln." *Missouri Law Review* 61: 2. 1996.

Madison, James. "Federalist No. 10: The Union as a Safeguard Against Domestic Faction and Insurrection." *The Federalist Papers.* Signet Classic/Penguin Group, 2003.

Madson, John. *Tallgrass Prairie: A Nature Conservancy Book.* Falcon Press, 1993.

Martin, Jim. "The Homestead Act of 1862." *Library of Congress.* May 20, 2019. blogs .loc.gov/law/2019/05/the-homestead-act-of-1862/

Marvel, William. *The Great Task Remaining: The Third Year of Lincoln's War.* Houghton Mifflin, 2010.

BIBLIOGRAPHY

McClelland, Edward. "The Man Who Made Illinois Politics Shady." *Chicago Magazine*. January 19, 2020.

McCloskey, Dierdre Nansen. *Bourgeois Equality: How Ideas, Not Capital or Institutions, Enriched the World*. University of Chicago Press, 2016.

"McCormick v. Manny." *Public Resource*. January 16, 1856. law.resource.org/pub/us /case/reporter/F.Cas/0015.f.cas/0015.f.cas.1314.3.pdf

McGinty, Brian. *Lincoln's Greatest Case: The River, The Bridge and the Making of America*. Liveright, 2015.

McMurtry, Gerald. "A. Lincoln, A Manner of Buoying Vessels." *Abraham Lincoln Online*. Civil War Museum in Kenosha, Wisconsin. abrahamlincolnonline.org /lincoln/education/patent.htm

McWhirter, Christian. "Artifact Spotlight: Huron Map." Abraham Lincoln Presidential Library and Museum. illinois.gov/alplm/museum/blog/Pages/blog52.aspx

Minucci, Stephen. "Internal Improvements and the Union: 1790-1860." *Studies in American Political Development*. Fall 2004.

Montgomery, Scott L. "What Really Kept Alexander Hamilton on the $10 Bill." *Fortune*. April 24, 2016. fortune.com/2016/04/24/alexander-hamilton-harriet-tubman/

Moran, Dan. "IDOT rolling out Lake County's Rebuild Illinois transportation improvements for 2020." *Chicago Tribune*. January 3, 2020.

"Morrill, Justin S. (Justin Smith), 1810-1898." Civil War photograph album, ca. 1861-65. Photonegative. Library of Congress. memory.loc.gov/cgi-bin/query /r?ammem/mcccartes:@field(DOCID+@lit(mcccartes/021063f))::

Morrill, Justin Smith. "Speech of Hon. Justin S. Morrill, of Vermont, on the bill granting lands for agricultural colleges." 1858. archive.org/details/speechofhonjusti01morr/page /n2/mode/2up

Morris, Charles. *The Dawn of Innovation: The First American Industrial Revolution*. Public Affairs, 2012.

Morris, Jan. *Lincoln: A Foreigner's Quest*. Simon & Schuster, 2000.

Mufson, Steven and Dino Grandoni. "House Democrats unveil ambitious climate package, steering toward a net-zero economy by 2050." *The Washington Post*. June 30, 2020.

Mumford, Lewis. *The Story of Utopias*. Viking, 1922.

National Museum of American History. "$1 Legal Tender Note from the Series 1862-1863 greenback issue." Public Domain. commons.wikimedia.org/w/index. php?curid=33422091

Neely, Mark. *The Last Hope on Earth: Abraham Lincoln and the Promise of America*. Harvard University Press, 1997.

Nellis, Ashley. "The Color of Justice: Racial and Ethnic Disparity in State Prison." *The Sentencing Project*. June 14, 2016. sentencingproject.org/publications/color-of -justice-racial-and-ethnic-disparity-in-state-prisons/

BIBLIOGRAPHY

O'Connor, Matthew. "Grossi Convicted in Kickback Scam." *The Chicago Tribune.* April 23, 1996. chicagotribune.com/news/ct-xpm-1996-04-23-9604230211-story .html

Ogorek, Cynthia L. *The Lincoln Highway Around Chicago.* Arcadia Publishing, 2008.

O'Neil, Lonnae. "Public Health Expert Says African Americans are at Greater Risk from Coronavirus." *TheUndefeated.com.* March 13, 2020. theundefeated.com/features /public-health-expert-says-african-americans-are-at-greater-risk-of-death-from -coronavirus/

Onion, Rebecca and Claudio Saunt. "Interactive Time-Lapse Map Shows How the U.S. Took 1.5 Billion Acres from Native Americans." *Slate.* June 17, 2014. slate.com /blogs/the_vault/2014/06/17/interactive_map_loss_of_indian_land.html

"Oscar Micheaux (1884-1951)." imdb.com/name/nm0584778/

Parkman, Francis. *France and England in North America.* Vol. 1. Library of America, 1983.

Pfeiffer, David A. "Bridging the Mississippi: The Railroads and Steamboats Clash at the Rock Island Bridge." Prologue Magazine 36, no. 2. Summer 2004.

Piketty, Thomas. *Capital in the 21st Century.* Belknap/Harvard Press, 2014.

Pohlad, Mark. "Harriet Monroe's Abraham Lincoln." *Journal of the Abraham Lincoln Association* 37: 2. 2016.

Porter, Eduardo. "Why America Will Never Get Medicare for All." *The New York Times.* March 15, 2020.

Powell, Farran and Emma Kerr. "What You Need to Know About College Tuition Costs." U.S. News. September 17, 2020. usnews.com/education/best-colleges /paying-for-college/articles/what-you-need-to-know-about-college-tuition-costs

Preston, Benjamin. "As States Add Money to Fix Roads, U.S. is Urged to Ante Up." *The New York Times.* January 23, 2020. nytimes.com/2020/01/23/business/us-road -infrastructure.html?searchResultPosition=1

Preston, Daniel. "James Monroe: Domestic Affairs." University of Virginia's Miller Center. millercenter.org/president/monroe/domestic-affairs

Purtle, Helen R. "Lincoln Memorability in the Medical Museum of the AFIP." *Bulletin of the History of Medicine.* Jan.-Feb. 1958. 68-74. jstor.org/stable/44444039?seq=1

Rabin, Roni Caryn. "Coronavirus Threatens Americans With Underlying Conditions." *The New York Times.* March 14, 2020.

"Rainfall Impacts in Lake County." lakecountyil.gov/4185/Rainfall-Impacts-in-Lake -County

Rauber, Paul. "Up to Speed, Two Months, One Page." *Sierra.* Jan.-Feb. 2020. sierraclub.org/sierra/up-to-speed

Redd, Jim. *The Illinois & Michigan Canal: A Contemporary Perspective in Essays and Photographs.* Southern Illinois University Press, 1993.

Rediker, Marcus. *The Slave Ship, A Human History.* Penguin, 2007.

Richardson, Robert, Jr. *Emerson: The Mind on Fire.* University of California Press, 1995.

Robert Lincoln, son of President Abraham Lincoln, half-length portrait, seated. Washington, D.C.: Brady's National Photographic Portrait Galleries. Photograph. Library of Congress. loc.gov/item/2008680396/

Rose, William E. "The Chicago Portage and Laughton Trading Post Area: 'The Waterway West.'" June 1975. *The Chicago Portage*. drupal.library.cmu.edu/Chicago /node/132

Rosenberg, Jennifer. "The Assassination of William McKinley." ThoughtCo. January 15, 2020.

thoughtco.com/u-s-president-william-mckinley-assassinated-1779188

Rutkow, Eric. *American Canopy*. Simon & Schuster, 2012.

Safi, Michael and Amantha Perera. "'The biggest game changer in 100 years': Chinese money gushes into Sri Lanka." *The Guardian*. March 16, 2020.

"Salmon P. Chase." National Park Service. nps.gov/people/salmon-p-chase.htm

Sandburg, Carl. *Abraham Lincoln: The Prairie Years and the War Years*. Galahad Books, 1954.

Saunders, George. *Lincoln in the Bardo*. Random House, 2017.

Saunt, Claudio. *West of the Revolution: An Uncommon History of 1776*. Norton, 2014.

Secrest, Meryle. *Frank Lloyd Wright: A Biography*. Knopf, 1992.

Sen, Amartya. *Development As Freedom*. Anchor Books, 1999.

Sharf, Albert. "Indian Trails, Villages of Chicago, Dupage and Will Counties, Illinois." Map. Newberry Library. 1900.

Sheaff, J. A. Map of the projected railway from Harrisburg to Pittsburg [sic] with proposed extensions to Cleveland, Cincinnati and St. Louis, in connexion [sic] with the public works of Pennsylvania, Ohio, Indiana and Illinois. Philadelphia, 1840. Map. Library of Congress. loc.gov/item/98688348/

Shepherd, Nicholas H, photographer. Abraham Lincoln, Congressman-elect from Illinois. Three-quarter length portrait, seated, facing front. Springfield, Ill., 1847. Photograph. Library of Congress. loc.gov/item/2004664400/

Shiller, Robert J. *Narrative Economics: How Stories Go Viral and Drive Major Economic Events*. Princeton University Press, 2019.

Simon, Paul. *Lincoln's Preparation for Greatness: The Illinois Legislative Years*. University of Illinois Press, 1971.

"Slave Labor Commemorative Marker." *Architect of the Capital*. aoc.gov/art /commemorative-displays/slave-labor-commemorative-marker

"The Slave Trade in Portugal History Essay." *UK Essays*. May 12, 2016.

Southern Pacific Company. "A List of Government And Railroad Lands in California, Open to Preemption or Homestead or to Purchase." Pamphlet. Digital Public Library of America. dp.la/item/7986e0d9726310d6108b9970404261c1

Spearle, Steve. "Lincoln's legacy offers lessons in statesmanship." *Springfield Journal Register*. February 8, 2020.

Stiglitz, Joseph. *The Roaring Nineties*. Norton, 2003.

BIBLIOGRAPHY

Sullivan, Louis H. *The Autobiography of an Idea*. Dover, 1956.

Survey of Huron, Illinois. [1836-05-21.] papersofabrahamlincoln.org/documents /D208375. Papers of Abraham Lincoln Digital Library.

Swift, Earl. *The Big Roads: The Untold Stories of the Engineers, Visionaries and Trailblazers who Built American Superhighways*. Houghton-Mifflin-Harcourt, 2011.

Tate, Julie, Jennifer Kenkins, and Steven Rich. "Fatal Force: Police Shootings Database." *The Washington Post*. June 16, 2020. washingtonpost.com/graphics/ investigations/police-shootings-database/

Temple, Wayne. *Lincoln's Connections with the I&M Canal, His Return from Congress in '48 and His Invention*. Illinois Bell, 1986.

Thebault, Reis, Andrew Ba Tran and Vanessa Williams. "The Coronavirus is Killing African-Americans at an Alarmingly High Rate." *The Washington Post*. April 7, 2020.

Tracey, Jonathan. "The Utility of the Wounded: Circular #2 and Medical Dissection." *The Gettysburg College Journal of the Civil War Era*. May 2019. cupola.gettysburg.edu/ cgi/viewcontent.cgi?article=1105&context=gcjcwe

Trex, Ethan. "5 Things You Didn't Know About Salmon Chase." *Mental Floss*. May 21, 2010. mentalfloss.com/article/24750/5-things-you-d idnt-know-about-salmon-chase

Tucker, Dan. (ed.) *Lincoln's Notebooks*. Black Dog and Leventhal, 2017.

Turner, Jonathan Baldwin. "A Plan for the Industrial University in the State of Illinois." Turner papers collection. University of Illinois-Champaign Urbana Library, 1851.

Twain, Mark. *Life on the Mississippi*. Bantam, 1988.

Umolu, Yesomi, Sepake Angiama, and Paulo Tavares. *. . . and Other Such Stories*. Columbia University Press. October 2019.

"The U.S. Army Corps of Engineers: A Brief History." *US Army Corps of Engineers*. usace.army.mil/About/History/Brief-History-of-the-Corps/

"Value of 1891 $1 Silver Certificate—Martha." Antique Money. antiquemoney.com/ value-of-1891-1-silver-certificate-martha-washington/

vandaliaillinois.com/

"Vandalia State House." Historic Reservation Division. illinois.gov/dnrhistoric/ Experience/Sites/Southwest/Pages/Vandalia-StateHouse.aspx

Vasile, Ronald S. "Mule Drivers and Ditch Diggers: Family Stories and the Illinois & Michigan Canal." Paper presented at the Illinois History Symposium, Springfield, IL. December 1998.

Villard, Henry. *Memoirs*. 2 vol. Houghton-Mifflin, 1904.

"The Visit of Abraham Lincoln to Council Bluffs." *The Annals of Iowa* 4:6. 1900. ir.uiowa.edu/cgi/viewcontent.cgi?article=2587&context=annals-of-iowa

Wasik, John F. *Keynes's Way to Wealth: Timeless Lessons from the Great Economist*. McGraw-Hill, 2014.

Wasik, John F. *Lightning Strikes: Timeless Lessons of Creativity from the Life and Work of Nikola Tesla*. Sterling, 2016.

Wasik, John F. *The Merchant of Power: Sam Insull, Thomas Edison and the Creation of the Modern Metropolis*. St. Martin's, 2008.

Wasik, John F. *Winning in the Robotic Workplace: How to Prosper in the Automation Age*. Praeger, 2019.

Watson, Gaylord. City of Chicago. 1871. Map. Library of Congress. loc.gov/item /2011593046/

Weingroff, Richard F. "The Lincoln Highway." *Federal Highway Association*. fhwa.dot .gov/infrastructure/lincoln.cfm

Welk, Jesse and Michael Burlingame (ed). "Abraham Lincoln and Internal Improvements." *The Real Lincoln: A Portrait*. Houghton Mifflin, 2003.

Whitehead, Colson. *The Underground Railroad*. Doubleday, 2016.

Whitman, Walt. *Leaves of Grass*. Doubleday Duran, 1940.

Willcockson, Tom. *Passage to Chicago: A Journey on the Illinois & Michigan Canal in the Year 1860*. Canal Corridor Association, 2016.

"William Jennings Bryan." Britannica. britannica.com/biography/William-Jennings -Bryan

Williams, Mentor S. "The Chicago River and Harbor Convention, 1847." Oxford University Press. March 1949. jstor.org/stable/1892668?seq=1

Wills, Garry. *Lincoln at Gettysburg: The Words that Remade America*. Touchstone, 1992.

Woetzel, Jonathan, Dickon Pinner, et al. "Climate Risk and Response: Physical Hazards and Socioeconomic Impacts." McKinsey Global Institute. January 2020. mckinsey.com/business-functions/sustainability/our-insights/climate-risk-and -response-physical-hazards-and-socioeconomic-impacts

"World Bank Group Announces $50 Billion Over Five Years for Climate Adaptation and Resilience." Press release. January 19, 2019.

worldbank.org/en/news/press-release/2019/01/15/world-bank-group-announces -50-billion-over-five-years-for-climate-adaptation-and-resilience

"World's Tallest Lincoln Statue." *Altas Obscura*. atlasobscura.com/places/worlds -tallest-lincoln-statue

Wright, Frank Lloyd and Bruce Books Pfeiffer, ed. *Frank Lloyd Wright Collected Writings*. Vol. 1. Rizzoli, 1992.

wrightinmilwaukee.com/

1619 Project, The. *The New York Times Magazine*. August 14, 2019.

"2018 Illinois Infrastructure Report Card." American Society of Civil Engineers. infrastructurereportcard.org/state-item/illinois/

INDEX

INDEX

INDEX

"Good Roads Movement," 195
Gooding, William B., 45
Google Ngram, 231
Gore, Al, 228
Gould, Jay, 151
Grant, Ulysses S., 92, 103
Great Chicago Fire, 181, 185, 267
"Great Debates," 37
Great Depression, 189, 202, 231
"Great Enrichment," xviii
"great enterprise," 136
Great Railway Strike (1877),167
"Great River," 5
Great War, 191, 195
Greeks, 175
Greeley, Horace, 73, 75, 204, 254
Green New Deal, 228
greenbacks, 156, 156–57, 160–63
Grinton, William, 42
gross domestic product. See GDP
Guardian, The, 229
Guelzo, Allen, 159
Guggenheim Museum, 181
Gulf of Mexico, 44, 48, 54, 68, 105, 262

habitations, 224
Hagemann, Frances, 5
Hamilton, Alexander, 138, 156, 162
Hammond, Alexander, 118–20
Hampton Roads, Virginia, 105
Hanks, John, 19, 56
Hardin County, Kentucky, 14
Harrison, William Henry, 25
Harvard Business Review, 122, 151
Haupt, Herman, 109–10
Hawthorne, Nathaniel, 143
Hemingway, Ernest, 176, 179
Herndon, William "Billy," 62, 269, 274
High Plains, 48
High Sierras, 143
"highway" bill, 233
Ho Chi Minh City, 229
Ho-Chunk Nation, 5
"hog butcher to the world," 140
Holzer, Harold, 124–25, 158–59
Homestead Act, 132–33, 141, 144–45, 214
Homesteader, The (film), 146
Hooker, Joseph, 108
Hormats, Robert, 122, 151–52
"horseless" carriages, 140, 194
House of Representatives, 34, 63, 74, 85, 116, 257
housework, 171
Hubbard Trail, 9
Hubbard, Gurdon, 9–10, 25, 45, 208, 219
Hull Settlement House, 174, 177–80
Hull, J. W., 90,
human capital, 231
Hurd, Jacob, 66–67
Huron (town), 52–54
hurricanes, 2, 226–27
hydraulic cement, 48

hyper-automation, 222

I&M Canal, 41–42, 44, 47, 50–51, 58, 72, 74, 80, 84, 101, 138, 185, 197, 260
Ida B. Wells Drive, 184
Illinois & Michigan Canal. *See* I&M Canal
Illinois Bar, 60
Illinois Central Railroad v. County of McLean, 71
Illinois Central, xi, 25,37–38, 60, 70–71, 79, 87, 97, 100, 102, 133–34, 186, 196, 214
Illinois River, 6, 9, 16, 21–22, 24, 34, 36–37, 44, 46, 49, 52, 54–56, 58, 78, 80, 220, 260
Immerwahr, Daniel, 38
immigrant neighborhoods, 208
"In God We Trust," 160
income tax, 31, 154, 159, 203, 246
   creation of, 157–58
"Indian Country," 23
Indian Removal Act (1830), 3–4, 43
"Indian" boundaries, 23
Indianapolis Speedway, 194
Industrial Revolution, xv, 54, 86, 138, 166. *See also* Second Industrial Revolution
"industrial" universities, 115
Infrastructure Report Card, 215
infrastructure
   education infrastructure, 127
   education infrastructure, upgrading, 217–19
   four infrastructure "I"s, 222
   funding, source of, 241–42
   global development, role in, 228–30
   global infrastructure, 214–17
   infrastructure needs, 216
   public infrastructure, 60, 196, 199, 203, 217, 218, 242, 273
   transportation infrastructure, 10, 198, 212, 232–33, 261, 264
inland waterways, infrastructure needs, 216
innovation, aiding, 120–22
Insull, Samuel, 149, 187–88
"internal improvements," x, 53, 58, 257
International Harvester, 188
International Workingmen's Association, 166
interstate commerce, 28, 32, 55, 57, 242
Interstate Era, 194, 199
Interstate System, 197–99
invention royalties, 153
Irish, 29, 45–46, 50–51, 132, 137, 214
Isaacson, Walter, 206
Isham, Lincoln and Beale, 186
Italians, 175

J.P. Morgan, 149, 152, 188
Jackson, Andrew, 3, 32–33, 157, 160
Jackson, Mississippi, 104
Jackson, Stonewall, 105
Jacksonville, Illinois, 37 111, 113, 176
Japanese architecture, 180
Japanese Empire, 192
Jefferson, Thomas, 6

INDEX

INDEX

INDEX

═══ ACKNOWLEDGMENTS ═══

I'd like to profoundly thank my initial editor, Melanie Madden, and my agent, Marilyn Allen, for finding a home for this book during a tough time in world history and the publishing business in particular. I had worked with Melanie and Marilyn on my Tesla book. We were a great team. The project was shepherded by Horizon editors Keith Wallman, who has a passionate love of history, and Emily Hillebrand, who took great care in editing this book.

Jerry Adelmann, Openlands' executive director, was beyond generous in opening my eyes to the creation and history of the I&M Canal. His customized tour of the Lockport "Lincoln Landing" area showed me multiple resources.

James Cornelius, former curator at the Lincoln Presidential Library and Museum, and owner of the Prairie Archives Bookstore (next to Lincoln's law office in Springfield, Illinois), was instrumental in introducing me to several Lincoln-themed books that I wouldn't have found on my own. His careful reading and notations were invaluable. Thanks to my friend and fellow journalist Jim Nowlan for connecting me with James.

Sidney Blumenthal, whom I met through my friend and fellow author Thomas Geoghegan, was kind enough to talk to me when I was first starting out my research on this book. Blumenthal's multivolume series on Lincoln's political life was highly influential in understanding the president. Warmest thanks to Tom for introducing me to Sidney and Tom's wonderful writing and friendship throughout the years.

Diana Dretske, of the Lake County Forest Preserves Dunn Museum, pointed out some materials within the museum's archives. Everyone at the museum was helpful in placing Lincoln in Lake County. The Dunn Museum, in Libertyville, Illinois, has some items that opened my eyes to local soldiers and their experiences. Thanks to all of my fellow Forest Preserve commissioners and staff for enduring my many references to my research and Lincoln.

The Civil War Museum in Kenosha, Wisconsin, was a treasure trove of information on Lincoln and the war. Thanks to Gina Radandt, collections manager, and the entire staff.

John Lustig at the Illinois State Museum in Lockport introduced me to a great bibliography of materials on the I&M Canal. Thanks also to Pamela Owens, director, and Arselysis Loveday of Lockport's Gaylord Building.

Another Lockport institution is the Will County Historical Museum and Research Center. Many thanks to Sandy Vasko and Brian Conroy. Another resource on the I&M Canal is the Irish American Heritage Center on the North Side of Chicago. Not only does the center have an excellent library, they have an excellent pub that serves fine Irish beers. Thanks to Kathy O'Neill and their many helpful librarians.

When ordering numerous obscure papers, documents, and books through the great Illinois Interlibrary Loan system, I mainly employed the services of the Grayslake Area Public Library, my home library. Thanks to all of the incredible adult reference librarians in my hometown (such as John and Jill), and director Sara Brown. Working with great librarians was a part of research that I relished. I also located some unique documents and maps at the Newberry Library in Chicago, a private library open to the public. Thanks to Becky Lowery, Matthew Rutherford, and Will Hansen.

ACKNOWLEDGMENTS

The Waukegan Historical Society and Waukegan History Museum was a wonderful resource for Lincoln's one visit to the town. Thanks to all of the volunteers who keep history alive, and Director Josh Bill. Another Lake County Institution is the History Center of Lake Forest/Lake Bluff. Laurie Stein, curator, and Carol Summerfield, director, guided me to some important local materials. Thanks to Hon. S. Mike Rummel, who sent me in that direction.

I also owe thanks to my many Lake County government colleagues, including Board Chair Sandy Hart; Recorder of Deeds Mary Ellen Vanderventer; Treasurer Holly Kim; Finance & Administrative Committee Chair Paul Frank; and all of my fellow board members, particularly Jessica Clark and Jessica Vealitzek. And to all of my constituents: This was my day job (really) during some dark times!

I'm also indebted to the army of librarians at the College of Lake County in Grayslake, Illinois (reference librarians Erika Behling and Anne Chernaik, and college President Dr. Laurie Suddick); US Library of Congress; the University of Illinois-Champaign/Urbana Library and Archives; the Illinois Lincoln Presidential Library and Museum in Springfield, Illinois; Lincoln College Library; Illinois College Library; and the Chicago History Museum. Much thanks due to my many reviewers, including Jim Nowlan, Jacob Freifeld, Don Rose, Ann Durkin Keating, James Cornelius, Gina Radandt, and Rick Perlstein.

Most importantly, thanks and endless love to my wife, Kathleen Rose, and daughters, Sarah Virginia and Julia Theresa, who indulged Dad on one more book while sheltering in place. Authors still vainly hope the world will be somehow better if they can just get their precious words on paper. We'll need a lot more than that for global healing, but I humbly hope I did my part.

John F. Wasik is the author of nineteen books and has spoken all across North America. As a journalist, he's written for the *New York Times, Forbes, The Wall Street Journal,* AARP, *Barron's, Fortune.com, Money, Reader's Digest,* and *Washington Monthly,* and was a columnist for Bloomberg News, Reuters, and other national publications.

As a contributor to *The New York Times,* he's written widely on business, investment, and other social issues. In 2018, Wasik was named an Illinois Road Scholar by The Illinois Humanities Council and has done presentations on innovation and creativity over the past two decades.

His book *Lightning Strikes: Timeless Lessons in Creativity from the Life and Work of Nikola Tesla* explores the creative legacy of the inventor of alternating current/motors, radio, and robotics. His writing is being read all over the world: Wasik's *Keynes's Way to Wealth* was translated into Chinese, German, and Japanese.